WITH

A STRATEGY FOR RENEWING OUR DEMOCRACY

WITH

A STRATEGY FOR RENEWING OUR DEMOCRACY

DAVID MATHEWS

KETTERING FOUNDATION PRESS

KETTERING
FOUNDATION
PRESS

With: A Strategy for Renewing Our Democracy is published by the Kettering Foundation Press. The interpretations and conclusions contained in the book represent the views of the author. They do not necessarily reflect the views of the Charles F. Kettering Foundation, its directors, or its officers.

EDITORS: Laura Carlson and Kristin Cruset
COPY EDITORS: Lisa Boone-Berry and Ellen Dawson-Witt
RESEARCH AND FACT-CHECKING: Sherri Goudy
DESIGN AND PRODUCTION: Alligator Tree Graphics

Sawing figures cover graphic by Laura Halsey Design based
on an icon made by Gan Khoon Lay from www.freeicons.io.

This book is printed on acid-free paper.
First edition, 2022
Manufactured in the United State of America

ISBNs
Print: 978-1-945577-64-2
PDF: 978-1-945577-65-9
EBook: 978-1-945577-66-6
Library of Congress Control Number: 2022930778

CONTENTS

ACKNOWLEDGMENTS

This book began to take shape decades ago. What is in it is based on the contributions of legions of people:

The faculty members at the University of Alabama in the 1970s who encouraged students to be producers of their own education.

The professionals in the Department of Health, Education, and Welfare who experimented with changing established ways of formulating regulations to make government rulemaking more open to rank-and-file citizens, not just well-financed special interests.

My colleagues at the Kettering Foundation, who have brought their own experiences and values to launch research that can strengthen democracy at a time when it is threatened by multiple crises around the world.

The people in the National Issues Forums network, who have demonstrated that citizens, even though sometimes written off as hopeless amateurs or worse, are grossly underestimated. These participants in 40 years of deliberative decision-making on complex and contentious issues, both local and national, have shown, more times than not, how citizens can move from divisive and hasty reactions to the more shared and reflective judgments that are needed for them to do their part in collaborating with governing institutions.

I gratefully acknowledge these and all the many other debts like them.

PREFACE

WHO WANTS ME TO KNOW?

Before you begin reading this book, you may want to know who is behind all this information. Once, when I was making a presentation of research, someone asked, "Who wants me to know this?" I thought that was a reasonable question, and I will try to answer it now.

THE KETTERING FOUNDATION

Part of the answer to the question is the Kettering Foundation, where I work. Kettering is a nonpartisan, nongovernmental research institute, not a grant-maker. I wrote this book with a great deal of help from my colleagues there, and I drew heavily on the foundation's decades of research on how democracy can work as it should.

I should also explain that Kettering's research isn't the kind done in academic institutions. The foundation was created by inventors, and the way they went about their research has stayed with us. (Charles Kettering invented, among other things, the self-starter for automobiles.) When I joined the foundation's board in 1972, some of the trustees had actually known Orville and

Wilbur Wright, the airplane inventors from Dayton, Ohio, where Kettering has one of its offices. (The other is in Washington, DC.) Although interested in practical solutions, the inventors looked for the problems behind the problems or the sources of the difficulties they were trying to overcome. Then, they observed experiments to find answers. We have drawn on that research legacy in our study of democracy.

Today, the foundation looks for experiments that might counter the problems behind the problems keeping our democracy from working properly. These aren't just problems *in* or *within* a democratic country; they are the malfunctions *of* democracy itself.

At Kettering, we watch three areas for experiments that promise to deal with these malfunctions. In one area, we look at how people take on the responsibilities of citizenship, such as making sound decisions together to guide the work they must do together. To understand this decision-making, we have observed, among other groups, those using the National Issues Forums (NIF) issue books, which are based on the foundation's research on deliberative decision-making.[1]

Another area of Kettering research has to do with how citizens in communities come together to combat the problems that affect everyone. That includes how people decide what should be done about their problems. (All the areas of research are interrelated.) The work of democracy is just that— real work. We try to understand how it is done so that people can make the difference they want to make.

The third area of research focuses on the major institutions involved in various ways in governing our country. That includes governments, civic organizations, philanthropies, schools and colleges, religious congregations, the media, businesses, scientific institutes, and others. We try to understand how these institutions relate to a democratic citizenry. And we hope to learn whether citizens are effective in engaging the institutions. The only country we study is the United States, but our research is enriched by what organizations in other countries share with us. Because not all the institutions concerned with democracy think of it the way we do, we make it clear that our type of democracy requires self-responsibility, which can't be exported or imported.

All the foundation's research is done collaboratively. We don't do studies *on* others; we do studies *with* them. We are learning from what they are learning. And Kettering tries to go about its work in a way that is compatible with the kind of democracy we study, a democracy that depends on shared learning to make long-lasting, constructive change.

Research done with other organizations and institutions in the US may imply a partnership, as in the joint ownership of a single business. Few of these other groups, however, are research institutes like Kettering. So, there is usually no one "business" owned in common. The other groups are more like allies or "fellow travelers" than partners. Kettering exchanges what its research shows for accounts of what its allies are learning from their experiments to find better ways to deal with their problems.

THE AUTHOR AND HIS COLLEAGUES

This book has my name on it, but it's actually a joint enterprise with my colleagues at Kettering. The foundation's research is done by a small group of program officers, an army of associates, a cadre of independent scholars, and generations of research assistants. In addition, much of what is on these pages came directly from citizens who told us about their efforts to make democracy work well and the obstacles they encountered. I have also incorporated insights from Kettering's editors, along with comments from a host of outside reviewers. When I say "we," I am talking about this company; there are scores of fingerprints on every page.

Influences

Of course, who I am and what my experiences have been have influenced what is in this book. I grew up in the rural South. My undergraduate education was in history at the University of Alabama (U of A). Later, I got a PhD from Columbia University's Graduate School of Arts and Sciences. I also served in the Army (Infantry) Reserves and married my childhood sweetheart, Mary

Chapman. We have two daughters, Lee Ann and Lucy, six grandchildren, and a growing generation of wonderful great-grandchildren.

I returned to the U of A and planned to teach history, which I did for a decade while also serving as president of the institution during the turbulent 1970s. When Gerald Ford became President, he appointed me Secretary of the United States Department of Health, Education, and Welfare (HEW). My next job was at the Kettering Foundation, where I have been a trustee and president. Throughout my career, I've also been a bit of a farmer; that's my heritage, having come from a family of farmers and teachers.

Life and Education in Grove Hill, Alabama

I have been deeply influenced by my family and the Alabama town, Grove Hill, where I grew up and still have a home (*Figure 1*). I was a member of the local Baptist church and benefited enormously from the ministry of Brother Charles Granade. Grove Hill's closest claim to fame is that we are across the river from Monroeville, better known as Maycomb in Nelle Harper Lee's *To Kill a Mockingbird*. Mary and I visited with Nelle often; we shared her attachment to small towns.

I got my love of history from my grandfather, David Chapman (D.C.) Mathews (*Figure 2*).[2] He and my father, Forrest Lee Mathews, were elected superintendents of our county school. They had a great influence on the mind-set I brought to Washington. One of my most vivid memories is a story my grandfather told about raising funds as a superintendent to end the disparities between rural areas whose schools were open for only five months and those in towns that had nine-month terms. He called the difference "un-American, undemocratic, and not Christian," and he "swore a mighty oath to change the system." The whole county was poor, but the voters increased their taxes to pay for schools that would all be open to all children for nine months. The experience justified my grandfather's faith in citizens. He inspired that faith in me.[3]

The members of my family were foot soldiers in a robust, sweaty, self-reliant form of democracy. What party do I belong to? I've never been

FIGURE 1. *Street scene in Grove Hill, Alabama, circa 1976. (From David Mathews' photo collection at the Kettering Foundation.)*

FIGURE 2. *The author's grandfather, David Chapman Mathews. (From David Mathews' personal photo collection.)*

attracted to partisan politics. I had met only a few Republicans before I went to Washington, where I identified myself as an independent, which I am. I explained that to President Ford before he selected me to be in the cabinet.

The University of Alabama

In the 1970s, the University was facing the challenge of integration after the collapse of segregation—notably marked by Governor George Wallace's failed "Stand in the Schoolhouse Door" speech in 1963. I learned firsthand how much of a burden segregation was and how liberating yet challenging it was to be free of it. I also came to appreciate the difference between removing restrictive segregation laws and the equally difficult task of bringing people together who hadn't much experience working freely with one another as equals. The University that had served only some Alabamians could now serve the state as a whole. I welcomed that challenge. The end of segregation freed up energy on the Alabama campus, which produced a host of new academic and outreach programs in the 1970s. Board minutes for March 30, 1979, show that 42 of the then 56 academic programs (dating back to 1894) were established in the 15 years after desegregation—31 of them in the 1970s.

The 1970s was turbulent for colleges and universities—protests against the war in Vietnam were occurring on most campuses. Some students died and buildings were burned. Yet, this was an environment open to change.

One of several new divisions created at the University was the College of Community Health Sciences (CCHS).[4] The state was losing doctors, and new ways of providing health care weren't reaching people. Alabama needed to change its health-care system, as well as increase its medical workforce. That situation informed the mission of CCHS, which was to be part of a comprehensive, university-wide initiative involving business and law, social work, education, psychology, and a new school of nursing. The College is an example of what I meant by serving Alabama as a whole. The state was to be the University's campus.

Two other University programs—one dealing with mental illness and the other with disabilities—also gave me a useful background for dealing with policies at HEW. The major state institution serving people with a mental illness, Bryce Hospital, was located adjacent to the University campus. Overburdened and underfinanced, the hospital couldn't provide the best quality of care. In 1971, in *Wyatt v. Stickney*, Judge Frank Johnson, who was a good friend, affirmed a citizen's right to due process and competent care in a landmark federal ruling. Because of the University's involvement with Bryce, I learned a good deal about treating people struggling with mental illness, particularly the importance of keeping their ties with friends and relatives.[5]

Broadening the University's outreach to all Alabamians also meant paying greater attention to some of the state's most vulnerable citizens—children with disabilities. The institution began several programs to serve these young-sters and then expanded the programs throughout the 1970s.[6] These programs also reached children whose disabilities were not severe enough to warrant institutional care yet precluded attending regular school. With the assistance of Governor Albert Brewer and concerned parents like Ralph Porch, we opened the Brewer-Porch Children's Center in 1970 to serve these students. This experience helped me at HEW when the Department was writing regu-lations that would affect people with disabilities. I became more aware of the importance of collaboration involving the affected children, their families, and those assisting them.

While at the University, I participated in the New South Movement, which helped change the region's century-old political system. That gave me an opportunity to work with a new generation of political leaders like Georgia's governor, Jimmy Carter. My grandfather and great grandfather had served in the Alabama legislature, and I became very familiar with the legislative system when seeking funding for the University. Congress is different in some ways, but that experience served me well in Washington.

WHAT'S NEXT?

Chapter I begins an analysis of the very serious problems now confronting democracy in our country and around the world. These problems are frightening, and there is no certainty about what will counter them. The foun-dation's researchers and editors who produced this book want to use it to find out how Americans from all walks of life are affected by these problems. That research is already underway.

What we have now about renewing democracy is just a small snapshot of a very large scene. We haven't found everything that is happening, and what is available currently will surely change. Kettering is reorganizing its outreach to listen better. We are quite serious about trying to understand what it takes for democracy to work as it should.

NOTES

1. The National Issues Forums is a loose network made up of nonpartisan organizations spread across the country. They convene forums to encourage responsible public deliberation wherever public decisions are made, whether in school boards or Congress. The convenors range from libraries, schools, and colleges to faith-based institutions and civic organizations. Even prisons have used these forums. And forums are now online at Common Ground for Action (https://www.nifi.org/en/cga-online-forums).

    While the network is independent from the Kettering Foundation and not funded by it, Kettering research on public concerns is used in preparing some of the study material on issues selected by the convenors in the network. The issues have varied from foreign policy to domestic concerns like the solvency of the Social Security system. The research identifies at least three options for action and lays out the pros and cons of each. Giving each option a "fair trial" is a cardinal principle of NIF deliberations. Local forum sponsors also create their own issue books on topics close to home. I have been involved with NIF in various capacities from its inception, which was before Kettering played a role.

2. I can imagine that D. C. Mathews' political values came from his Celtic ancestors who settled in Alabama as yeoman farmers. My family, like many in the area, was of Welsh, Scottish, and Irish stock, which has a long history of independence and dissent.

3. David Mathews, *Why Public Schools? Whose Public Schools? What Early Communities Have to Tell Us* (Montgomery, AL: NewSouth Books, 2003), 122-123.

4. David Mathews, "The Community Health Initiative at the University of Alabama and the College of Community Health Sciences, 1969 to 1980" (unpublished, 2002). Another innovation was the New College, where students were responsible for educating themselves through internships and by creating new majors with faculty supervision. See David Mathews, "Free to Change: A Decade of Engagement" (unpublished, 2011).

5. To better serve those suffering from mental illness, the University strengthened long-standing relationships with Bryce and Partlow Hospitals. Ray Fowler, chair of the psychology department, was deeply involved in projects with both hospitals, as were many other members of the department. Ray also joined with law school professor Jay Murphy and his wife, Alberta, in supporting the landmark *Wyatt v. Stickney* ruling in 1971, a decision that established the constitutional right to adequate treatment for people with mental illness in Alabama's state facilities. Tinsley E. Yarbrough, *Judge Frank Johnson and Human Rights in Alabama* (Tuscaloosa: University of Alabama Press, 1981), 151-181.

6. The faculty secured an HEW grant in 1974 (before I was at the Department) for a

demonstration program known as the Rural Infant Stimulation Environment, or RISE, project. When federal funding for RISE ended in 1977, the University not only picked up the cost but also broadened the program. Nathan Ballard, a student with cerebral palsy, captured the spirit of RISE in his book (written with Michael Rogers), *Nathan: He Would Be Somebody ... It Was Just a Matter of Time* (Elk Grove, CA: RBC Publishing, 2000).

CHAPTER I

WHAT AMERICAN DEMOCRACY FACES

Our democracy's current troubles aren't new. They have been growing for some time. Democracy's underpinnings have been deteriorating for decades. We saw the effects in Washington on January 6, 2021.[1] Americans were shocked. It couldn't happen here! But it did. Emotions had been raw before then—grief, anger, resentment, pent-up frustration. Yes, and fear. People have felt whipsawed between crushing despair and fragile hope. Did one election cause all our problems? Is another likely to solve all of them?

So much happened so fast in 2020 and 2021 that I had to write and rewrite these opening paragraphs more times than I could count. Not skilled with a computer, I used a ballpoint pen and paper. Office supply stores must have seen a jump in sales. No sooner had I described one crisis than another burst on the scene. The same turmoil has affected our language and ability to talk with one another. Words I once used that had a commonly accepted meaning took on an offensive cast. I was constantly checking a dictionary for synonyms.

I know people on different sides of the country's many divisions. I want this book to speak to all of them about what we can do to strengthen our democracy. I don't have any model or formula for what we should do. That will require a burst of the kind of institutional and civic inventiveness that has served this country well in the past. But whatever we want to do, it will have to be done together if it is to last.

What was happening in crisis after crisis was so blatant that we may not have been inclined to look behind the gripping dramas. Yet we absolutely must if we are to understand what our democracy is facing.[2] Its erosion has cut deep and is widespread, and it isn't confined to the United States. Other democracies have been affected. That is sobering. Modern democracy seems to have fundamental problems in the way it works. Still, there are counter-measures we can take. This book talks about some of them.

The United States of America many thought of as a bright city on a hill seemed to be pulled down as they had watched in outrage. For many others, the values the country has prized were being denied in the harsh realities of everyday life. Not plenty, but poverty. Not justice, but injustice. The US itself appeared to be divided into a jumble of disconnected pieces. Pundits said we were having a national identity crisis; we didn't seem to know who we were as Americans.

How could the powerful governing institutions of the US let this happen? They have long been losing the confidence of citizens. This loss of trust is mutual, as many institutions have lost confidence in the people. As early as 1964, the confidence people had that the government would do the right thing began to decline (*Figure 3*). This was the first sign of what would become an avalanche that would reach other governing institutions.

What Are "Governing" Institutions?

I think of "governing," at its most basic, as the organization of collective efforts for collective well-being. The institutions that do the governing have authority that is granted by citizens and legally conferred or based on their expertise. The governing system is made up of institutions that range from the local to the national level. They are the legislative, executive, and judicial branches of government. These also include nongovernmental bodies like schools, colleges and universities, foundations, civic organizations, and the media.

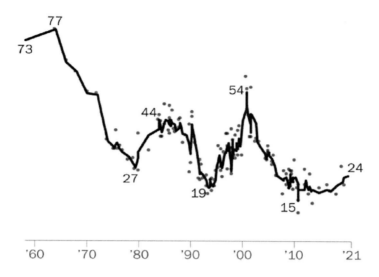

FIGURE 3. *Trust in government has been declining since the mid-1960s. This graph shows the percentage of the public who "trust the federal government to do what is right always/most of the time." ("Americans See Broad Responsibilities for Government; Little Change Since 2019," Pew Research Center, Washington, DC, May 2021.)*

On the people's side of the relationship, different Americans, for different reasons, have felt that they aren't recognized, understood, or treated fairly by the governing institutions. Their criticisms are more than the usual complaints about poor service and bureaucratic red tape. The institutions don't seem to think citizens are competent to choose for themselves. And people feel that control over their own lives has been slowly slipping out of their hands.[3] So, they clutch what control is left even more tightly. Yet many Americans also doubt that they have the power to make a difference in what is happening to them.

The power of institutions is another matter; they have obvious resources to use: money, statutory authority, professional expertise. However, many institutions aren't sure that the citizenry has resources to contribute to governing the country. Even if people did, they appear too divided to be effective. This book looks at the doubts about the citizenry and the valid reasons for them.

That recognized, several chapters report on things that only citizens can provide and the kind of powers they can draw on, which are different from institutional powers. The book also offers evidence that Americans are less divided than is usually reported. That is particularly so at the community level, although local institutions aren't immune from the divisiveness so evident nationally. Even churches, for example, report being affected by polarization among their congregations. On the other hand, the news has been filled with stories of people crossing all kinds of dividing lines to join forces for the benefit of both neighbors and strangers.

THE PROBLEMS BEHIND DEMOCRACY'S PROBLEMS

Democracies have never been trouble free, yet they are resilient. Their most serious difficulties are fundamental ones of democracy itself, which keep it from functioning as it should. The mechanisms for self-rule malfunction because of deep-seated problems *behind* the obvious problems. I've cited two of the major ones: people's distrust of institutions and institutions' distrust of citizens. These kinds of problems are compounded by structural dysfunctions in areas like racial, ethnic, and gender relationships. Adding to these difficulties, although democracy is valued by a majority, there are those who no longer believe in it.[4] Alarmingly, this is the case with some young people.

Declining Confidence

Falling confidence in governing institutions, particularly at the federal level, was spotted by Robert Teeter in 1976. His report showed "tremendously increasing rates" of public alienation from, and cynicism about, government.[5] Teeter traced this change in attitudes back to the late 1960s. These findings were confirmed in a 2015 Pew report, which found that "the share [of Americans] saying they could trust the federal government to do the right thing nearly always or most of the time reached an all-time high of 77 percent in 1964. Within a decade . . . trust had fallen by more than half, to 36 percent. By the end of the 1970s, only about a quarter of Americans felt that they could trust the government at least most of the time."[6] This decline would grow even more as we entered the 21st century.[7]

The decline hasn't happened because citizens have lost their sense of civic responsibility or duty. In 2020, civic duty was very visible in the massive voter turnout for the presidential election. Instead, the problem is the lack of day-to-day impact. The usual way people try to exercise political influence is through appeals to officials in charge of governing institutions. Yet often they don't trust these officials. And they may not recognize their own power to act, which isn't always dependent on what institutions do or don't do.[8]

Because it has been growing for decades, I believe that the public's dissatisfaction with its governing institutions isn't likely to end quickly. And the tone has changed in alarming ways. Frustration and anger have turned into sharp bitterness as the political environment has become supercharged with hyper-partisanship, which has spread onto our Main Streets. The governing institutions' lack of confidence in the public has made matters even worse.[9]

This book deals not with the size of the government, but with the way the major governing institutions, the governments themselves, function and relate to the citizenry. This relationship has been an issue since before the 1970s when both Republicans and Democrats, who have different views on the scope of government, have been leading the institutions in Washington.

A House Divided

Loss of confidence in institutions has been compounded by a tidal wave of divisiveness in the country that has pitted people against one another, not as opponents but as enemies. This divisiveness takes many forms and is highly contagious. Are we entering what Thomas Hobbes called the worst of all worlds, where there is a war of everyone against everyone?[10] Remember Abraham Lincoln's warning: "A house divided against itself cannot stand."[11] About the only thing everybody agrees on now is that there is too much divisiveness.[12]

Despite the rancor, there is research that finds more agreement on many issues than is usually recognized.[13] Though TikTok is not traditional research, its users were challenged to share the qualities they admired in people of the opposing political party. Republicans said they admired Democrats for their concern for the environment, their commitment to equality, and their passion for their beliefs. Democrats saw merit in Republicans' emphasis on hard work, respect for veterans, and belief in free speech for all.[14] Day to day, most Americans aren't swept up in ideological warfare. And there have been a number of initiatives set up to create more common ground.[15] These efforts draw on people's survival instincts, which put a premium on cooperation.[16]

Where Are the Checks and Balances?

Why else has trust declined so much? Today, many Americans feel unable to influence, or even communicate with, not just governments but many other large governing institutions, which are becoming even larger and more distant, like the voices on recorded messages.[17] People sense that power over them is more centralized and inescapable. For some time, citizens have felt relegated to the sidelines, where they sit uncertain about their ability to make an impact in their own democracy.[18] Sitting on the sidelines while watching power grow elsewhere frustrates people, and they become very angry.

To guard against concentrated power, democracy's safeguard has been a system of checks and balances that gives the three separate branches of government offsetting authority. Yet, for many reasons, some as benign as greater efficiency, that separation has been shrinking. Most people may not be familiar with the finer points of constitutional law on the separation of powers.[19] Nonetheless, they still may be less inclined to trust our political system when they don't see that separation.

I know that there are valid reasons for centralization in some situations. In the federal government, large departments often exercise all three constitutional powers. They legislate (through rules and regulations), execute, and adjudicate because it is more efficient. A consolidation of power, however, is particularly problematic if people see power being concentrated in an unelected bureaucracy.[20] Some scholars think that the public's negative feelings don't have as much to do with bureaucracies themselves as with what

I mentioned earlier, people's perception that control of their lives has been slipping out of their hands for years.[21] They have little confidence in the institutions they believe have allowed this to happen.

Challenging Economic Conditions

Democracies are challenged, too, by structural conditions in society that endanger everyone. I noted these earlier as problems-behind-the-problems of democracy. These include conditions in the economic system that prevent the benefits from labor going equitably to all who do the labor. When such conditions exist, democracies must work especially hard to remedy them. Both the citizenry and the governing institutions have to be involved—collaboratively.

PUBLIC ENGAGEMENT WITHOUT A PUBLIC?

Aware of the lack of trust, some of those leading the governing institutions have attempted to counter the growing public alienation. How effective have they been? Initiatives to improve the relationship with the citizenry have had a variety of names: public participation, public engagement, civic engagement, consultation, public accountability. The *National Civic Review* has featured stories about some of these. In one city, council members held coffee chats with constituents.[22] Other councils had their attorney attend their meetings so they could change ordinances in real time with community members watching.[23] Still others used visioning processes that invited citizens to imagine what they would like their community to be in the future.[24] And a number of cities have tried participatory budgeting to put some control in the hands of citizens.[25] The efforts are commendable. There are federal versions, such as public hearings on new policies. Whatever the intent of these efforts, how do people feel about them?

Regrettably, declining public confidence hasn't been arrested by the decades of participation and civic engagement efforts. Even more alarming, according to scholars like Brian Cook, some of these participatory practices may have been counterproductive, unintentionally widening the divide that they were intended to close.[26] Whether or not this is the case, the loss of public confidence has increased even as engagement efforts have grown.

I don't mean to dismiss the usual remedies for countering the loss of public confidence. When I worked in the federal government, I encouraged using them. They have value. Yet I have come to the conclusion that what I did didn't go far enough, especially when it didn't engage people in doing the things only citizens can do.

WHAT'S NEXT?

The next chapter responds to challenges posed in this one. If a good many citizens have little confidence that governing institutions will do what they believe they should do and if citizens feel pushed to the sidelines, unable to make a constructive difference, these are serious problems in a country that thinks of itself as a democracy. And if the leaders of the governing institutions have a similar lack of confidence in the citizenry, the relationship is in even more trouble. Those who believe the government should do less will still be unhappy with the amount of government they do have. And those who want the government to do more won't necessarily like their relationship with the institutions upon which they are more dependent.

If what institutions are currently doing to engage citizens and build support isn't sufficient, what else might be needed? Would better engagement practices be enough? Or would a fundamental realignment in the relationship between the citizenry and the institutions be required? If so, what would that look like?

NOTES

1. Reports on what was happening in the country from 2016 to 2020 can be found in sources from across the political and ideological spectrum. Here are just a few: Gerald F. Seib, "How the U.S. Became a Nation Divided: Political, Cultural and Economic Gaps Have Hardened Amid Anxiety Born of the Financial Crisis and a Fundamental Argument over American Values," *Wall Street Journal*, December 17, 2019, https://

www.wsj.com/articles/how-the-u-s-became-a-nation-divided-11576630802; "What Trump Showed Us About America," *Politico* November 19, 2020, https://www.politico.com/news/magazine/2020/11/19/roundup-what-trump-showed-us-about-america-435762; Alia E. Dastagir, "A Close Presidential Election Deepens the Nation's Divide. How Do We Live Together Now?" USA TODAY, November 6, 2020, https://www.usatoday.com/story/news/nation/2020/11/06/2020-election-american-divided-polarized-and-unsure-how-cope/6179404002/. Other regularly viewed sources include *Fox News*, the *New York Times*, the *Washington Post*, and the Clarke County, Alabama, *Democrat*.

2. This analysis is based on various sources, including Katherine J. Cramer, *The Politics of Resentment: Rural Consciousness in Wisconsin and the Rise of Scott Walker* (Chicago: University of Chicago Press, 2016); Arlie Russell Hochschild, *Strangers in Their Own Land: Anger and Mourning on the American Right* (New York: New Press, 2016); Michael J. Sandel, *The Tyranny of Merit: What's Become of the Common Good?* (New York: Farrar, Straus and Giroux, 2020); Yuval Levin, *The Fractured Republic: Renewing America's Social Contract in the Age of Individualism* (New York: Basic Books, 2016).

3. In 1977, survey researcher Daniel Yankelovich said, "All of our surveys over the last decade show that every year, more and more people are coming to believe that the part of their lives that they are able to control is diminishing." Richard D. Lyons, "Refusal of Many to Heed Government Health Advice Is Linked to Growing Distrust of Authority," *New York Times*, June 12, 1977.

4. Richard Wike et al., "Globally, Broad Support for Representative and Direct Democracy," Pew Research Center, October 16, 2017, https://www.pewresearch.org/global/2017/10/16/globally-broad-support-for-representative-and-direct-democracy/; and Roberto Stefan Foa and Yascha Mounk, "The Democratic Disconnect," *Journal of Democracy* 27, no. 3 (July 2016): 5-17.

5. Robert Teeter, "The Present National Political Attitude as Determined by Pre-election Polls," November 1976, Box 62, Folder "Post-Election Analysis—Speeches and Reports (2)," Robert Teeter Papers, Gerald R. Ford Presidential Library, Ann Arbor, MI. Another study we have found useful in tracing declining confidence in government is by Seymour Martin Lipset and William Schneider, *The Confidence Gap: Business, Labor, and Government in the Public Mind* (New York: The Free Press, 1983).

6. Pew Research Center, *Beyond Distrust: How Americans View Their Government* (Pew Research Center, November 2015), 18.

7. This lack of confidence or trust in the government to do what people think it should do poses a different question from one about how active the government should be. Do we want more government or less? The response to that question fluctuates with

people's need for the government to play a stronger role because of a crisis like the attacks on September 11, 2001, or the 2020 pandemic.

8. For a summary of research on this topic, see Nick Felts, John Doble, Elizabeth Gish, Jean Johnson, and Keith Melville, memorandum to David Mathews, "John and Jane Q. Public Reactions to the 'With' Idea," October 30, 2020. This document can be found in the David Mathews collection, Kettering Foundation archives. For more information, contact archives@kettering.org.

9. There is a survey of the negative perceptions that Washington officials have of citizens in Jennifer Bachner and Benjamin Ginsberg, *What Washington Gets Wrong: The Unelected Officials Who Actually Run the Government and Their Misconceptions about the American People* (Amherst, NY: Prometheus Books, 2016), 9-10, 15-18.

10. In Latin, "*bellum omnium contra omnes.*" Hobbes, *Leviathan*, ed. C. B. Macpherson (New York: Penguin Books, 1968), 185.

11. Abraham Lincoln speaking to the Illinois Republican State Convention, Springfield, IL, June 16, 1858.

12. Jeffrey M. Jones, "Record-High 77% of Americans Perceive Nation as Divided," Gallup, November 21, 2016, https://news.gallup.com/poll/197828/record-high-americans-perceive-nation-divided.aspx; Rick Hampson, "As Trump Hits 100 Days, Americans Agree: We're Still Divided," *USA TODAY*, April 28, 2017; Natalie Jackson and Ariel Edwards-Levy, "Huffpollster: The One Thing Americans Can Agree On Is That They're Divided," *Huffington Post*, November 29, 2016, https://www.huffingtonpost.com/entry/americans-agree-divided_us_583d8036e4b04b66c01ba9af; John Wagner and Scott Clement, "'It's Just Messed Up': Most Think Political Divisions as Bad as Vietnam Era, New Poll Shows," *Washington Post*, October 28, 2017, https://www.washingtonpost.com/graphics/2017/national/democracy-poll/?utm_term=.d5c34dde0090.

13. "USA TODAY Network and Public Agenda to Explore the 'Hidden Common Ground' Among Citizens Leading to the 2020 Election," USA TODAY Network Pressroom, November 11, 2019, https://www.usatoday.com/ story/news/pr/2019/11/11/multi-platform-partnership-include-local-community-forums-sponsored-national-issues-forums-institute/2561645001/. Also see the National Issues Forums Institute website, www.nifi.org, for more information on how to participate in local forums, many of which are online.

14. See the 118,951 responses to @s.nesquik, "If you're a Democrat, say one nice thing about Republicans; If you're a Republican, say one nice thing about Democrats," (January 25, 2021), https://vm.tiktok.com/ZMeJdftwf/.

15. The *Christian Science Monitor* noted constructive work being done by: "Braver Angels, the Hidden Common Ground 2020 initiative, America Amplified, the Bridge Alliance, and the National Issues Forums." Editorial Board, "Nudges to

American Unity," *Christian Science Monitor*, October 26, 2020, https://www.csmonitor.com/Commentary/the-monitors-view/2020/1026/Nudges-to-American-unity.

16. Kristopher M. Smith, Tomás Larroucau, Ibrahim A. Mabulla, and Coren L. Apicella, "Hunter-Gatherers Maintain Assortativity in Cooperation Despite High Levels of Residential Change and Mixing," *Current Biology* 28 (October 8, 2018): 3152-3157.

17. Laurie Kellman and Emily Swanson, "AP-NORC Poll: Three-Quarters in US Say They Lack Influence," Associated Press, July 12, 2017, https://www.apnews.com/a3eac6255194410eb2ab2166f09cd429/AP-NORC-Poll:-Three-quarters-in-US-say-they-lack-influence.

18. The Harwood Group, *Citizens and Politics: A View from Main Street America* (Dayton, OH: Kettering Foundation, 1991), 19.

19. See the discussion of overlapping powers in Matthew Spalding and David F. Forte, eds., *The Heritage Guide to the Constitution* (Washington, DC: Regnery Publishing, 2014), 231-236; and Jon D. Michaels, "An Enduring, Evolving Separation of Powers," *Columbia Law Review* 115, no. 3 (April 2015): 515-597.

20. James M. Smith, review of *The Rise of the Unelected: Democracy and the New Separation of Powers,* by Frank Vibert, *Political Psychology* 29 no. 2 (April 2008): 297-300.

21. Lyons, "Refusal of Many to Heed Government Health Advice Is Linked to Growing Distrust of Authority."

22. Aaron Leavy, "Fort Collins, Colorado: An Expectation of Public Engagement," *National Civic Review* 105, no. 1 (Spring 2016): 48-53.

23. Leavy, "Fort Collins, Colorado."

24. Daniel Yankelovich and Isabella Furth, "Public Engagement in California: Escaping the Vicious Cycle," *National Civic Review* 95, no. 3 (Fall 2006): 3-11.

25. Ellen Knutson, "It's Our Turn to Decide: Participatory Budgeting in Chicago's 49th Ward," *National Civic Review* 105, no. 4 (Winter 2016): 14-22.

26. Brian J. Cook, *Bureaucracy and Self-Government: Reconsidering the Role of Public Administration in American Politics* (Baltimore, MD: Johns Hopkins University Press, 1996), 134-135.

CHAPTER II

A *WITH* STRATEGY

There may be better ways to begin restructuring what has become a deeply troubled relationship between the public and public institutions, ways that would strengthen our democracy.

WHY NOT TRY MORE GOVERNING *WITH* THE PEOPLE?

One possibility for doing that is captured in the word *with*. The idea behind a *with* strategy was inspired by Abraham Lincoln (*Figure 4*). At the dedication of the Gettysburg National Cemetery on November 19, 1863, President Lincoln closed his address with these words: "This nation, under God, shall have a new birth of freedom—and that government of the people, by the people, for the people, shall not perish from the earth." I believe that is still what most Americans hope for.

But today, do Americans agree that we have a government that is "of" the people? That's debatable. "By" the people? Doubtful. "For" the people? Perhaps for some, sometimes. So why not add another preposition—governing *with* the people? Maybe that would help bridge the divide separating the people of the United States from their government and from many of the

FIGURE 4. *At the dedication of the Gettysburg National Cemetery on November 19, 1863, Abraham Lincoln closed his address with these words: "[T]his nation, under God, shall have a new birth of freedom—and that government of the people, by the people, for the people, shall not perish from the earth." (Lincoln's address. Gettysburg, Pennsylvania, ca. 1905. Chicago: Sherwood Lithograph Co. Photograph. Library of Congress, https://www.loc.gov/item/2003674448/.)*

country's other governing institutions. Maybe that would also help citizens make the difference they would like to make. Fortunately, we already have some indications of this happening, which I'll discuss later. I am suggesting that we build on these to create the type of collaboration that would have all governing institutions working more *with* citizens, not just *for* them. In fact, I believe that working *with* citizens is the best way of working *for* them.

What I am proposing—a *with*-the-people strategy—isn't a sweeping, fix-everything-now solution. It is rather a build-on-what-grows collaboration that could have a cumulative effect on the troubles our democracy faces. A *with* strategy doesn't have a model to copy or a set of best practices to follow. It's just a different way of thinking about the relationship citizens should have with their governing institutions. These institutions will have to find out the best applications of the idea.

Here is a simple, everyday example of this strategy in action: I live on a tree-lined lane where the local government removes the fall's leaves with a huge vacuum on a big truck. But the truck can't fit on the narrow driveways to our houses, so we get together with our neighbors to rake our yards; then we pile the leaves on the lane so the city's trucks can do their job removing them with the vacuum. This ordinary example has the basic characteristics of a *with* strategy. People work together to produce something useful, something the government needs to be effective in doing its job. That is collaboration between partners, where each contributes something unique to a collaborative enterprise.

A Democratic Strategy

A *with* strategy is, most of all, a strategy for strengthening our democracy. Saying that, of course, demands an explanation of what is meant by *democracy*. The word has many definitions. The most common is that democracy is a system of contested elections resulting in a representative government. Democracy can also refer to the institutions of the government: courts, legislatures, and administrative agencies. These are certainly valid. Another less precise definition is that a "democracy" is just what we are in the United States. And because some people don't like the way things are, they say they don't like "democracy."

Most troubling, a good many people don't think of democracy as "us." It's somebody else—maybe the politicians, maybe those who lead the institutions. But it's not you and me. A strong democracy, however, has to be "us." This understanding of democracy was captured in the words of a song: "We are the ones we've been waiting for."[1] In the most profound sense, *We the People, are* the democracy. That idea is at the heart of a *with* strategy.

The democracy that this book is about began long before the word itself was coined. It is rooted in the lessons ancient humans learned in order to survive. Our ancestors were hunter-gatherers living in bands, tribal enclaves, and, later, villages. This was before there were kingdoms and nation-states.[2] As humans spread out around the globe, they carried with them a "political

DNA" developed in the struggle to stay alive. As noted earlier, one principal survival lesson was that we needed to work together, even with those from different bands or tribes, in order to live. The first *with* strategy was people working *with* people.

Other survival imperatives included the security needed to protect people from danger, the freedom to forage, fair treatment in the distribution of the goods made by collective efforts, and enough control to act on these imperatives. These imperatives are interdependent. They don't stand alone. If people had no control, to be secure from danger they had to be willing to work together. In time, imperatives such as these evolved into democratic values like freedom and justice.

Much, much later, the ancient Greeks captured some of this survival legacy in their language with terms like *democracy*. You'll notice this word has two roots. The first part, *demos*, means "the people in a village or community." The second is *kratos*, "sovereign power," which implies the capacity to act with authority in ways that make a real difference.[3] Modern representative government rests on this earlier civic foundation of shared decision-making leading to collective actions taken for the well-being of all.

Citizens as Producers

From this perspective, democracy is both a way of life and a political system in which, at the most fundamental or organic level, citizens must work with other citizens to produce things—public goods—that make life better for everyone. Our ancestors went on to form governments and other governing institutions to create more and different public goods. These two systems, one governmental or institutional and the other civic or organic, are dependent on each other in the ecosystem of democracy (which is the subject of another Kettering Foundation Press book, *The Ecology of Democracy*[4]).

I realize this concept of the role of citizens as producers isn't the conventional one, yet I was encouraged when the World Economic Forum, an organization of business leaders, issued a report that recognized the value of citizens being regarded as creators and producers rather than just consumers or clients.⁵ The notion of citizens as producers is at the heart of a *with* strategy.

Reciprocity and Complementary Production

"Working *with*" is based on reciprocity, another practice that developed early on in our struggle to survive. Reciprocity makes me think of a scene from my childhood. Where I am from, pine trees grow so rapidly that they are treated as a crop like corn, which is harvested and replanted. Today, seedlings are set out in neat rows so the timber can be gathered easily by machines. Before this equipment was available, the trees were cut by long crosscut saws, with two workers reciprocating by pulling the blade back and forth (*Figure 5*). Their efforts produced a result that neither laborer could have achieved by working alone. They worked *with* each other.

A *with* strategy also fosters reciprocity between what citizens do on their end of the "saw" and what governing institutions do on the other end.⁶ The strategy is based on evidence that most major institutions can't do their jobs as effectively without support from the things that people produce by working *with* other people.⁷ That is because some things can be done only by citizens or are best done by them. Neighbors organizing a "club" to encourage one another to walk more is a common example of what citizens do best. Their efforts draw on the unique healing power of human care and compassion, which has been clinically verified.⁸

The case for complementary efforts was made persuasively in Elinor Ostrom's Nobel Prize-winning research on what she called "coproduction." Citizens can't be left on the sidelines, she said, because their work is needed to reinforce and complete the work of governments, schools, hospitals, and other institutions. Here is Ostrom's very practical argument:

> If one presumes that teachers produce education, police produce safety, doctors and nurses produce health, and social workers produce effective households, the focus of attention is on how to professionalize the public service. Obviously, skilled teachers, police officers, medical personnel,

FIGURE 5. *A crosscut saw is used to cut a felled tree into sections as part of a "Logs for Victory" drive sponsored by the War Production Board during World War II. ("Girls longsaw fallen tree in woods," by Bettmann, image #515297290.)*

and social workers are essential to the development of better public services. Ignoring the important role of children, families, support groups, neighborhood organizations, and churches in the production of these services means, however, that only a portion of the inputs to these processes are taken into account in the way that policy makers think about these problems. The term "client" is used more and more frequently to refer to those who should be viewed as essential co-producers of their own education, safety, health, and communities. A client is the name for a passive role. Being a co-producer makes one an active partner.[9]

Products from the work of citizens can complement what institutions do because civic work is different from the work of institutions. Yet even when the work is the same, the effects of the work are different because of who does it. My neighbors joining together to clean up the lane in front of our houses has a different effect than what a city crew does. People working *with* people builds a sense of community.

Things Only Citizens Can Do

I want to focus now on the projects that make use of people doing the things professionals don't—and sometimes can't—do. That's why I prefer the term *complementary production* rather than *coproduction*, a term that might suggest that institutions' and citizens' work are the same. There are usually significant differences.[10]

A good example of complementary production is captured in a story a colleague told me about a conversation between a group of citizens in her community and their local government. The citizens had organized their fellow citizens to start a cultural project. The project's biggest assets were a sense of ownership and community responsibility, assets that are different from those of institutions. When the founders met with municipal officials, they didn't ask the officials to take over the project. They simply said, "Here is what we have done. Now what can you do?" Town officials then offered assistance, using resources that the citizens didn't have. This reciprocity is central to a *with* strategy. Citizens take an initiative; they work together to make things (public goods) that serve the common good. Then a governing institution adds the kind of resources it has.

Obviously, a relationship involves at least two parties, and a *with* strategy has implications for both. The relationship between institutional and civic democracy can't benefit both if citizens delegate much of what they must do to governing institutions. And the same will happen if institutions are influenced wholly by what professional expertise offers and don't make use of what citizens alone can provide.

I need to ring a bell or turn on a light here, but having neither, I'll just use bold print. The case I am trying to make in this book is that institutional democracy depends on its foundation in citizen, or civic, democracy. But I worry that this connection has come loose. To use a

navigation metaphor, it is as though the rudder of the ship isn't connected to the ship's steering wheel. Without being reconnected, institutions can't regain the public's confidence and citizens can't make the difference they want to make.

There are many other things that can be accomplished *only* by citizens working *with* citizens. In a democracy, public institutions can't create their own legitimacy. They can't unilaterally define their purposes or set the standards by which they will operate. And governing institutions can't sustain, over the long term, decisions that citizens are unwilling to support. Governments can build common highways but not common ground. And none of the governing institutions—even the most powerful—can generate the public determination required to keep a community or country moving ahead on difficult problems. This determination or political will is especially necessary for attacking those problems that grow out of a lack of community and then destroy that community. Also, only citizens have the local knowledge that comes from living in a place 365 days a year. Because of this knowledge, people know how to do things that are different from what professionals can and should do. Finally, institutions, governmental or nongovernmental, can't create citizens—at least not a democratic citizenry capable of governing.

What Isn't Being Proposed

As Kettering has watched readers react to the suggestion that a *with* strategy could be useful, the initial response to the idea is often, "Yes, that's just common sense." However, what *with* is interpreted as meaning is often just another form of public engagement rather than a reciprocal working relationship. It is the reciprocity and partnerships that are needed to gain the benefits that a *with* strategy can have for professionals and their institutions.

A *with* strategy isn't simply another form of public participation. And at the federal level, it doesn't mean just partnering with state and local governments. A *with* strategy also goes beyond consulting with citizens who are beneficiaries of programs. Moreover, it isn't the same as transferring government responsibilities to nongovernmental organizations; it isn't devolution.

And it is more than recruiting volunteers to help institutions like schools and hospitals do their jobs, valuable as that assistance is. I am not critical of any of these efforts; they are certainly helpful. I just believe more of the things only citizens can provide must be added. I'm joining the Ostrom chorus, with the slight difference between "co" and complementary production.

From early readers of this manuscript, we learned that we needed to give more attention to misunderstandings like those just listed above because a *with* strategy was sometimes written off as a simple idea that could be implemented by doing more of the same—institutional officials listening more carefully, holding more open meetings, consulting more with stakeholders. All of that is fine, but it isn't enough to restore public confidence or provide opportunities for people to make a significant difference and take responsibility. A *with* strategy treats citizens as producers, and few institutions have been "built" to do that. Without that understanding of citizenship, however, democracy isn't likely to be strong enough to meet its challenges.

A LEGACY FROM OUR HISTORY

Maybe a page from American history would help prevent some misunderstanding. History, as I think of it, isn't about the past so much as it is about the present interpreting the past. And the present changes constantly. I started working on this and the other historical sections in the book some time ago. The perspective on the past is different now. Nonetheless, I have kept what I had written earlier because it is what many, not all, Americans still see as their legacy. The more recent interpretations of our history are valuable. But this history of our history may also be useful.

Although a *with* strategy is idealistic in that it is democratic, it isn't a pie-in-the-sky fantasy. The United States has long recognized the need for what citizens produce with laws allowing tax exemptions for nongovernmental institutions serving a public purpose.[11] And public-government interaction is, in fact, very common in some situations. Think about communities hit by natural disasters—fires, floods, and storms. Neighbors on the scene start the work that relief workers finish.

The Origins of a Democratic Citizenry

American colonial society did not have today's consciousness of the political importance of women or minorities, certainly not of those who were enslaved. And the colonists themselves were the immigrants. Nonetheless, an embryonic understanding of what would become American democracy and the importance of all citizens began to develop soon after the first settlers arrived.

When I was teaching American history, one of my favorite stories wasn't the usual one about the Pilgrims and the *Mayflower*, which landed in 1620. That story does have implications for democracy. The passengers created a "civic body politic" by agreeing to abide by a compact with certain rules. The story I liked better occurred later, in 1633, in Dorchester, Massachusetts. The lead character was a clergyman, John Maverick. He was involved in creating a distinctly American form of democratic governance.

Just outside Boston, the town of Dorchester had a village green that must have attracted livestock because, as often happens and must have happened then, the animals went through the fences and onto the green to graze. That led to two problems: first, how to protect the green, and second—the issue behind the issue—*how to decide* how to protect the green. People gathered for church services, but Sunday may not have seemed an appropriate time to take up such worldly matters as livestock.[12]

At this point, the minister, John Maverick, intervened. What he said was not written down, but we can imagine its substance: Perhaps it was something like: "We have a problem. We need to solve it. Let's meet later and decide what to do." In school, we are taught stirring phrases like, "Give me liberty or give me death." However, what Maverick said in effect—we have a problem; let's talk about it—should go down in our history as the quintessential American political speech. I keep a copy of the notice of the meeting (a "warrant") on my wall.

What made this incident into a political tradition was that colonists began meeting every month, not just when the livestock were causing trouble. These gatherings throughout the New England colonies led to an institution that became a foundation for US democracy—the town meeting. This wasn't today's meeting *in* a town; these were meetings *of* a town. The colonists didn't adopt what might have been expected, the municipal form of government they had in England. Instead, they ran the colony using town forums. The authority behind them was in the promises people made to one another. This gave people power, which they sustained by means of covenants or mutual promises.[13] Respect for the authority of the citizenry was evident as early as 1644, when Roger Williams in Rhode Island argued that power should lie with the people.[14]

The American Revolution

Militias were another colonial institution having implications for a *with* strategy. Settlers produced something tangible, a military force, by working together. Men formed these militias, often electing their own officers.[15] Militias provided many of the soldiers who fought in the revolution.

Citizens were in the front line in other ways as well. In time, Massachusetts and other colonies created a civic network for political action that would lead to the revolution. This network began to take shape in 1772 when Samuel Adams established a 21-member "committee of correspondence." They created ties to other towns and generated a "public voice" that explained the colonists' position to the world.[16] The practice was so appealing that, within 15 months, all but two of the colonies had established their own committees of correspondence. In this way, the tradition of the town meeting grew even stronger. And the practice of uniting the small towns and drawing both authority and support from the people set a powerful democratic precedent.[17]

I am not sure that all colonists were democratically inclined, but I emphasize this part of our history here because I believe it shows a basis for thinking that there can be a public capable of acting in tandem *with* the government. That recognition is important because of the tendency to see the public as hopelessly incompetent in an age of professionalism.

A New Nation

A *with* strategy assumes that people can be responsible and able citizens. Confidence in citizens became even more evident on the eve of the revolution. The public debate, in 1776, turned to the question of whether a war for independence could be successful against what was then one of the world's greatest superpowers. John Adams, from the town meetings of Braintree, took on the task of defending the proposed Declaration of Independence.

Daniel Webster recalled that Adams had responded to doubters by insisting that citizens were not fickle but would stay the course in the resistance to British control. Perhaps influenced by his own era's democratic spirit, Webster imagined Adams rising to rhetorical heights to capture the spirit of 1776: "But we shall not fail. The cause will raise up armies; the cause will create navies. The people, the people, if we are true to them, will carry us, and will carry themselves, gloriously, through this struggle."[18] Whether this was actually Adam's rhetoric or that of Webster is open to question. (Adams was less than positive about the citizenry on other occasions.) Whoever gave the speech, it is a valid example of the democratic spirit of the era. This was the same citizenry that Abraham Lincoln placed his faith in at Gettysburg.

Having cited Adams as interpreted by Daniel Webster, I want to add what he wrote to his wife and advisor, Abigail, in 1776. (Her important role suggests that women did much more than has been recognized.) Reflecting on what he had learned about people and the power of their "public halls," John said in his letter to her:

Time has been given for the whole People, maturely to consider the great Question of Independence and to ripen their Judgments, dissipate their Fears, and allure their Hopes, by discussing it in News Papers and Pamphletts, by debating it, in Assemblies, Conventions, Committees of Safety and Inspection, in Town and County Meetings, as well as in private Conversations, so that the whole People in every Colony of the 13, have now adopted it, as their own Act.—This will cement the Union, and avoid those Heats and perhaps Convulsions which might have been occasioned, by such a Declaration Six Months ago.[19]

The continuing influence of the body politic is clear in the history of the Massachusetts Constitution, which was a precursor to the United States Constitution. After the revolution, the Massachusetts General Court attempted to write a constitution for their state. But the people in the town meetings rejected it. Only after it was redrafted and reviewed again in the meetings, literally line by line, did the people of the state adopt it.[20] There were discussions and votes at every step, not only on whether the proposed constitution was valid, but also on whether the General Court should have the authority to draft it. As Elliot Richardson said much later, reflecting the history he had been taught, "The people literally came together and decided what powers [they] wanted government to have."[21] Their actions gave validity to Thomas Paine's observation that "a constitution is not the act of a government, but of a people constituting a government."[22]

A New Sovereign: The Public

Following the victory over the British, Samuel Cooper, a Boston minister sympathetic to the American rebels, gave a sermon in 1780 at a ceremony recognizing the creation of the new constitution for Massachusetts (*Figure 6*). He compared the constitution that had been passed to the fruits that farmers produce by their labor. The revolution, Cooper said, had spawned a new framework of laws—"the regulations under which I live." He meant that the victorious rebels were entitled to claim that "I am not only a proprietor in the soil, but *I am part of the sovereignty of my country*" (emphasis added).[23] Cooper's generation had a right to this sense of sovereignty because they had, in fact, made something quite significant—a victory over the British that led not just to a new state constitution, but, eventually, to a new nation.

Thomas Jefferson, whose career was and still is marked by controversies, made a related and very telling point in 1820 in responding to a letter from William Charles Jarvis, who expressed doubts that most people were informed enough to make sound judgments. Jefferson replied, "I know no safe depository of the ultimate powers of the society but the people themselves; and if we think them not enlightened enough to exercise their control

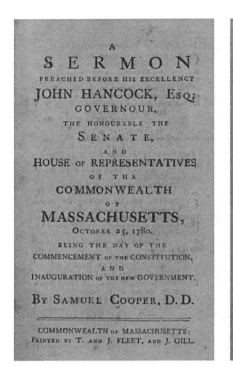

FIGURE 6. *Samuel Cooper's sermon. (Image courtesy of HathiTrust, https://hdl.handle. net/2027/mdp.35112203487782.)*

with a wholesome discretion, the remedy is not to take it from them, but to inform their discretion by education. This is the true corrective of abuses of constitutional power."[24]

In an earlier letter to Joseph Cabell in 1816, Jefferson had argued, in a similar vein, that community deliberations in what he called "little republics" had not only energized the revolution but would also continue to engage every citizen in the collective experience of self-government. And "where every man is a sharer in the direction of his ward-republic, or of some of the higher ones, and feels that he is a participator in the government of affairs not merely at an election, one day in the year, but every day; when there shall not be a man in the state who will not be a member of some one of it's [sic] councils, great or small, he will let the heart be torn out of his body sooner than his power be wrested from him by a Caesar or a Bonaparte."[25] Participation builds ownership, and ownership builds responsibility.

The Frontier

A *with* strategy requires, as I've said, a working citizenry. After the colonial and revolutionary years, that citizenry grew and spread to the vast frontier to the south and west. In the early 19th century, the central government was small and far away. And even though many of the authors of the Constitution wanted a republic with a limited role for citizens and not a democracy, the frontier bred its own form of self-rule. The absence of government opened the door wider to what I think of as civic democracy.

Frontier life was harsh, even brutal, and sometimes brought out the worst in people. (I know about that from all the Westerns I watched growing up.) Our forebearers were well aware that people weren't always responsible and that they sometimes abandoned themselves to what Alexis de Tocqueville called "the disinterested and unreflective sparks that are natural to man."[26] Yet the frontier also demanded collective efforts for people to survive. Settlers had little to rely on except one another, and they had to cooperate to launch common projects like providing education for their children. The frontier also gave us many of the civic associations that I'll talk about in the discussion in chapter XV of the sources of power that citizens can draw on.

During the 19th century, citizens linked arms to found communities, build schools, and raise militias. This was the America where Tocqueville found civic associations doing everything from promoting religion to combating alcoholism. People's participation in the work of these associations nurtured their appreciation for their fellow citizens' good judgment, fortitude, and ingenuity.[27] Tocqueville also noticed that Americans, unlike Europeans, were more inclined to go to their neighbors than the local authorities when there was a common problem to solve.[28] Historian Robert Wiebe wrote, "The driving force behind 19th century democracy was thousands of people spurring thousands of other people to act."[29]

Among the driving forces for democracy, the common or public school movement stands out. Education was seen as the best means for creating a more perfect union. That conviction was also reflected in establishing institutions of higher education. State universities were founded to create a new class of democratic leaders. Land-grant colleges were to serve farmers and mechanics. Later, African Americans, women, and Native Americans created their own institutions.[30] Even private colleges and universities took on public missions.

The democratic faith that was born on the frontier, as I see it, wasn't so much that The People were always *right*, but that they had *the right* to rule themselves, to judge what was in their best interests. The democratic faith is also that we, collectively, can, over the long haul, make better decisions about our future than any one person or any elite group can make for us.

An Era of Reform

My Kettering colleague Alex Lovit has noted that the 1830s marked the height of an antebellum reform movement, which stretched from the religious Second Great Awakening around 1800 until the Civil War. These reforms often worked through the citizens' associations that Tocqueville described. The aims of these associations varied: to abolish slavery, promote religious and moral learning, care for those who were blind or deaf, and make the prison system more humane. Reformers also championed democratic institutions like common public schools.[31]

The government began to work *with* the citizenry and their associations in these early reform efforts. When people came together in frontier communities to establish schools, the federal government pitched in to provide land. The educational culture promoted norms of mutual assistance, reciprocity, social responsibility, and commitment to the common good. At the same time, there was a premium placed on industry, hard work, enterprise, and personal responsibility.[32] The objective was to develop a citizenry capable of strengthening the economy and doing its share of the governing.

The Politics of Protest

The United States was born in revolutionary protest, which continued through the reform era, the Civil War, and on into the late 19th century. American democracy has always been turbulent but able to bounce back from adversity. The age of democratic reform of the 1830s had ended tragically in a bloody war, followed in the final decades of the 19th century that were marked by economic misery and racial injustice. Slowly, painfully, the US moved into the Industrial Age, which would eventually make it the world's leading economic power, though that transition was not easy.

This transition was particularly difficult for farmers. In the late 19th century, they attempted to join forces across racial and regional divisions, give women a more prominent role, and promote cooperative economic enterprises. Organizations like Granges gave people opportunities to air their concerns, and the Farmers' Alliance provided political education programs that were unlike the electoral programs designed to win at the polls.[33] These programs were designed to develop the skills of citizenship. The self-organizing in these efforts is an example of one of the necessary elements of a *with* strategy—citizen initiative.

Charles Postel writes about this duality of supporting public schools while simultaneously maintaining independent educational efforts as the backbone of the reforms: "Farm reformers believed that closing the rural education gap was a prerequisite for improving rural life. Like many other Gilded Age Americans, they subscribed to the notion of progress through education." Postel concludes, "Education served to agitate, mobilize, and organize at the grass roots."[34] That is one of the ways a public of producers generates the power needed to collaborate *with* the government.

The Progressive Era

The next reform era saw the creation of many of the nongovernmental civic organizations that are prominent today, such as the General Federation of Women's Clubs, the League of Women Voters, the Sierra

Club, the American Civil Liberties Union, the National Association for the Advancement of Colored People, and the Urban League. These civic organizations were intermediaries intended to help citizens come together to improve society and to link people to electoral democracy. The significance for *with* is that these civic organizations enlisted and connected people, making them more powerful.

Progressive organizations furnished some of the benefits later provided by governments. Settlement Houses, for instance, provided services for the poor, which government professionals would come to offer. These organizations also supplied forms of assistance that the government could not. For example, volunteers offered a neighborly relationship with residents in the houses, which was different from the relationship with professional caseworkers. Settlement Houses also acted like modern pressure groups. To build public support for reforms, they informed the general public about the painful consequences of unemployment, the roots of poverty, and the exploitation by landlords. As economist Richard Ely reported in 1891, the main goal of social reform espoused by the Settlement Movement was to foster "the helpful cooperation of citizens with public authority, particularly with those of the city."[35] His comments could be a motto for a *with* strategy.

I won't go on into 20th-century history. My purpose was to show the historical grounding for a *with* strategy.

WHAT'S NEXT?

I've noted in bold print that a major objective of a *with* strategy is overcoming the problems that weaken our democracy. One of those is the lack of a mutually beneficial interplay between our governing institutions and citizen, or civic, democracy. Institutions can't be effective or democratically relevant without the benefit of what a citizenry of producers can provide. But in saying this, I want to be realistic about the obstacles to that collaboration as well as the benefits. Chapter III begins that discussion.

NOTES

1. In 1995, Bernice Johnson Reagon was commissioned to compose the work, "Anybody Here? Song Journey in Seven Movements," with text by June Jordan from the "Poem in Honor of South African Women." The recessional of the work is called "We Are the Ones We Been Waiting For." The song appears on Sweet Honey in the Rock's 1998 album *Twenty-Five.*

2. The foundation has been reading the literature in paleo-political anthropology for many years (reviews on file) as well as examining the work of scholars who found what we know of prehistoric times useful in understanding the earliest forms of politics. See Francis Fukuyama, *The Origins of Political Order: From Prehuman Times to the French Revolution* (New York: Farrar, Straus, and Giroux, 2011).

3. See Robert Beekes, *Etymological Dictionary of Greek*, vol. 1 (Boston: Leiden, 2010), 325, 772 and Henry Liddell and Robert Scott, eds., *A Greek-English Lexicon* (Oxford: Clarendon Press, 1968), 386-387, 992.

4. David Mathews, *The Ecology of Democracy: Finding Ways to Have a Stronger Hand in Shaping Our Future* (Dayton, OH: Kettering Foundation Press, 2014).

5. Global Agenda Council on the Future of Government, *Government with the People: A New Formula for Creating Public Value* (Cologny, Switzerland: World Economic Forum, February 2017).

6. Robert Putnam makes this same point in his work on social capital, finding that "a society that relies on generalized reciprocity is more efficient than a distrustful society." Robert Putnam, "The Prosperous Community: Social Capital and Public Life," *American Prospect*, December 19, 2001.

7. Elinor Ostrom, "Covenanting, Co-Producing, and the Good Society," *PEGS* (Committee on the Political Economy of the Good Society) *Newsletter* 3, no. 2 (Summer 1993): 8.

8. Bobby Milstein, *Hygeia's Constellation: Navigating Health Futures in a Dynamic and Democratic World* (Atlanta, GA: Centers for Disease Control and Prevention, April 15, 2008), 54-57.

9. Ostrom, "Covenanting, Co-Producing, and the Good Society," 8.

10. For more examples, see John McKnight, "Neighborhood Necessities: Seven Functions That Only Effectively Organized Neighborhoods Can Provide," *National Civic Review* (Fall 2013).

11. Paul Arnsberger et al., "A History of the Tax-Exempt Sector: An SOI Perspective," *Statistics of Income Bulletin* (Winter 2008): 106, 124.

12. Dorchester Antiquarian and Historical Society, *History of the Town of Dorchester, Massachusetts* (Boston: E. Clapp Jr., 1856), 30-33; Maude Pinney Kuhns, *The*

"Mary and John": A Story of the Founding of Dorchester, Massachusetts, 1630 (Rutland, VT: Tuttle Pub. Co., 1943); and James Henry Stark, *Dorchester Day: Celebration of the Two Hundred and Seventy-Ninth Anniversary of the Settlement of Dorchester, June 5, 1909* (Boston: Municipal Printing Office, 1907). Most New England settlements governed themselves through town meetings. The October 1633 document describing a town meeting in Dorchester was not the first town meeting, but it was the first recorded case of a locally elected town "selectmen." Joseph Zimmerman, *The New England Town Meeting: Democracy in Action* (Westport, CT: Praeger, 1999), 21.

13. John Locke, *Two Treatises on Civil Government* (London: George Routledge and Sons, 1884), 277-278. See also Hannah Arendt, *On Revolution* (New York: Penguin Books, 1963), 176. The democratic impulse behind these town meetings is illustrated by a certain inclusiveness in that they weren't limited just to those who were eligible to vote. Voting eligibility in the 17th century was quite restricted. The town meetings, on the other hand, were more open. Property ownership, for example, was rarely a prerequisite for inclusion. Even common "debtors and laborers" often participated. Robert E. Brown, *Middle-Class Democracy and the Revolution in Massachusetts, 1691-1780* (Ithaca, NY: Cornell University Press, 1955), 78-99. Also see Bruce C. Daniels, *The Connecticut Town: Growth and Development, 1635-1790* (Middletown, CT: Wesleyan University Press, 1979), 64-93. Most important, the town meetings did not deal exclusively with problems of governing—as in the uses of the greens. They served more basic public purposes. They were forums for people to decide on their common, shared interests. I am not saying that the town meetings were perfect. Attendance was sometimes poor. They didn't always promote free expression. Dissenters like Roger Williams and Anne Hutchinson could be banished. The town meetings reflected all the limitations of Puritanism. Michael Zuckerman, *Peaceable Kingdoms: New England Towns in the Eighteenth Century* (New York: Knopf, 1970), 19. The important point here is that these community meetings were *public* institutions. The public preceded the government in this country, just as democracy preceded representative government. The difference between the civil bodies politic—the public—and the government can be seen in their disagreements. The ill-tempered complaint of William Shirley, colonial governor of Massachusetts, is a good illustration. With obvious irritation, he wrote that a Boston town might be called "upon the Petition of ten of the meanest Inhabitants, who by their constant attendance there generally are the majority and outvote the Gentlemen, Merchants, Substantial Traders, and all the better part of the Inhabitants; to whom it is Irksome to attend at such meetings." Newton Edwards and Herman G. Richey, *The School in the American Social Order* (Boston: Houghton Mifflin, 1947), 83-84. As cited in Leonard P. Oliver, *The Art of Citizenship: Public Issues Forums* (Dayton, OH: Kettering Foundation, 1983), 7.

14. Thomas E. Ricks, *First Principles: What America's Founders Learned from the Greeks and Romans and How That Shaped Our Country* (New York: Harper, 2020).

15. This example also shows that all citizen-formed associations were not benign. Take the case of South Carolina during the Revolution. Every able-bodied white male was expected to provide military service to the colony. However, when the Revolution reached the backcountry, the militias divided into Whig/rebel and Tory/loyalist forces. They fought a war notable for atrocities on both sides. These partisans did not follow the rules observed by standing armies. War is horrible, and the clashes of militias could be especially so. John Gordon, *South Carolina and the American Revolution: A Battlefield History* (Columbia, SC: University of South Carolina Press, 2003), 11.

16. G. Edgar White, *Law in American History, Vol. 1: From the Colonial Years through the Civil War* (New York: Oxford University Press, 2012), 121.

17. Richard D. Brown, *Revolutionary Politics in Massachusetts: The Boston Committee of Correspondence and the Towns, 1772-1774* (New York: Norton, 1970), 57.

18. Webster's imagining what Adams said in his defense of the Declaration of Independence is recorded in Daniel Webster, *Discourse in Commemoration of the Lives and Services of John Adams and Thomas Jefferson, Delivered in Faneuil Hall, Boston, August 2, 1826* (Boston: Cummings, Hilliard and Co., 1826), 40-41.

19. L. H. Butterfield, Marc Friedlaender, and Mary-Jo Kline, eds., *The Book of Abigail and John: Selected Letters of the Adams Family, 1762-1784* (Cambridge, MA: Harvard University Press, 1975), 142.

20. Robert J. Taylor, ed., Introduction to *Massachusetts, Colony to Commonwealth: Documents on the Formation of Its Constitution, 1775-1780* (Chapel Hill, NC: UNC Press, 1961), ix-xi.

21. Elliot Richardson, "We Delegated Our Powers" (remarks presented at the Fourth Presidential Library Conference on The Public and Public Policy, Ann Arbor, MI, March 18, 1986), 1.

22. Thomas Paine. As quoted in Arendt, *On Revolution*, 143.

23. Samuel Cooper, *A Sermon Preached before His Excellency John Hancock, Esq., Governour, the Honourable the Senate, and House of Representatives of the Commonwealth of Massachusetts, October 25, 1780: Being the Day of the Commencement of the Constitution, and Inauguration of the New Government* (Boston: T. and J. Fleet, and J. Gill, 1780). See also Charles W. Akers, "Religion and the American Revolution: Samuel Cooper and the Brattle Street Church," *William and Mary Quarterly* 35, no. 3 (1978): 477-498.

24. Edward Dumbauld, ed., *The Political Writings of Thomas Jefferson: Representative Selections* (New York: Liberal Arts Press, 1955), 93.

25. Thomas Jefferson to Joseph C. Cabell, February 2, 1816. Retrieved from the Library of Congress, http://hdl.loc.gov/loc.mss/mtj.mtjbib022312.

26. Alexis de Tocqueville, *Democracy in America*, trans. Harvey C. Mansfield and Delba Winthrop (Chicago: University of Chicago Press, 2000), 501-502.

27. Robert H. Wiebe, *Self-Rule: A Cultural History of American Democracy* (Chicago: University of Chicago Press, 1995), 71.

28. Tocqueville also observed, "Everywhere that, at the head of a new undertaking, you see the government in France and a great lord in England, count on it that you will perceive an association in the United States." Tocqueville, *Democracy in America*, 489.

29. Wiebe, *Self-Rule*, 71.

30. David Mathews, *Why Public Schools? Whose Public Schools? What Early Communities Have to Tell Us.* (Montgomery, AL: NewSouth Books, 2003).

31. I have had a personal interest in the history of the 1830s for some time. The first book I read, perhaps as an undergraduate, was Alice Felt Tyler's *Freedom's Ferment: Phases of American Social History to 1860* (Minneapolis: University of Minnesota Press, 1944). From that, I went to Henry Steele Commager's books like the little collection of original documents in *The Era of Reform, 1830 to 1860* (New York: Van Nostrand Reinhold, 1960); then to Vernon L. Parrington, *The Romantic Revolution in America, 1800-1860* (New York: Harcourt, Brace, 1927); and Daniel J. Boorstin's three volumes about the Americans (for which I paid $3.93 a book): *The Americans: The Colonial Experience* (New York: Random House, 1958); *The Americans: The National Experience* (New York: Random House, 1965); and *The Americans: The Democratic Experience* (New York: Random House, 1973). For a more recent account, see Steven Mintz, *Moralists and Modernizers: America's Pre-Civil War Reformers* (Baltimore: Johns Hopkins University Press, 1995).

32. Malcolm J. Rohrbough, *Trans-Appalachian Frontier: People, Societies, and Institutions, 1775-1850*, 3rd ed. (Bloomington: Indiana University Press, 2008).

33. Theodore Mitchell, *Political Education in the Southern Farmers' Alliance, 1887-1900* (Madison: University of Wisconsin Press, 1987), 16.

34. Charles Postel, *The Populist Vision* (New York: Oxford University Press, 2007), 48.

35. Louise C. Wade, "The Heritage from Chicago's Early Settlement Houses," *Journal of the Illinois State Historical Society* 60, no. 4 (Winter 1967): 412.

CHAPTER III

RECONNECTING CIVIC AND INSTITUTIONAL DEMOCRACY

A *with* strategy can have significant benefits for institutions and citizens, as well as for democracy. But it faces obstacles that I want to acknowledge. One has to do with the lack of alignment between two forms of democracy. Democracy was originally citizens working with citizens to survive. A more recent form is used in governing through such institutions as legislative bodies, courts, schools, NGOs, foundations, and the media. These two democracies are interdependent. As Elinor Ostrom found, institutional democracy can't do its job effectively without the complementary work of the citizenry. And citizens can't live the lives they want to live without the assistance of the governing institutions in the economy, in health, in education, and so on. How much of that assistance there should be, how involved the government institutions should be, and how much control the citizenry should have over those institutions have always been debated. Nonetheless, institutional democracy will always be a necessary part of our lives. That leaves us with the question of what the relationship between these two forms of democracy, which is currently not good, should be.

MISALIGNED

Why is that so? The two democracies appear to be badly misaligned, which is reflected in the mutual distrust. Rather than being complementary, they often rub against each other the way two parts of an engine can squeak and clank when they don't fit as they should. Ironically, that can happen in politics even when institutional democracy tries to aid civic democracy.

The Blobs and the Squares

Here is a case of what can go wrong: Some years ago, some grantmaking foundations that Kettering was working with were troubled because their grants to community groups weren't having the effects they had hoped they would have. As one of the grantmakers said, the problems they were trying to help solve were getting worse despite years of funding what were supposed to be solutions. Could Kettering research help understand why?

In talking with the community groups, Kettering noticed that the grantmakers had distinctive ways of going about their business that were quite different from the way the grassroots organizations worked. The two weren't compatible. Kettering called the grassroots groups "Blobs" because they were often loosely organized. We labeled the grantmakers, which were highly structured, Squares.

Some years later, the creator of Time Banking, Edgar Cahn, picked up and expanded on our research in his book, *No More Throw-Away People,* and in a very clever animation, "The Parable of the Blobs and Squares."[1] Cahn saw that Blobs had the energy and networks that could be useful in combating many community problems. They recognized community resources and knew how to use them. Squares, on the other hand, knew how to manage money and organize institutional action. They had equipment and professional expertise. The problem was that no matter how much the Squares reached out in a community to get at the root causes of problems, they seldom succeeded. Equally problematic, they couldn't mobilize the energy of a community.

The Squares tried to meet these challenges by giving money to the Blobs. Naturally, this meant that the Blobs had to show financial accountability. Many Squares also insisted on measurable results to show accountability. "Grass roots groups," Cahn wrote, "were taught to develop mission statements and strategic plans in order to remain 'true' to mission. Neighborhood leaders were trained in how to be Board members, how to conduct 'proper' meetings, [and] how to write and amend by-laws."[2] The sad result was an unintended consequence: The Blobs became colonized and lost the very qualities that made them effective at the grass roots.

Although Cahn was describing nongovernmental Squares, what he observed can be just as true for some government agencies. For any kind of Square to work *with* Blobs, ways to minimize colonization have to be found. A *with* strategy helps do that by recognizing the distinctive characteristics of the way Blobs work.

I have to admit that I don't know of any perfect solution to this problem of unintended consequences. However, a possibility might be for Squares to support Blobs in what they can uniquely create. For example, Blobs have created in some communities an environment that has allowed opposing groups to identify common objectives or "superordinate" goals outside their conflicts where some progress could be made. Blobs did that in the school integration crises in the 1960s and 1970s when citizen-initiated, multiracial groups formed to bring opposing factions, if not to work together, to at least avoid violence when schools complied with court orders to desegregate. (There is more about that in chapter XII.)

Admittedly, improvement in the political climate is difficult to evaluate using quantitative standards. How could one measure creating opportunities for opposing factions to find and work on compatible objectives in a hostile political environment?[3] That, by the way, is a challenge for evaluating much of what is truly important in community life.

Avoiding unintended consequences, however it is done, and recognizing the unique contributions of Blobs are crucial because they play essential roles in democratic life. Not only can they convert energy, even cynicism, into constructive action, they can connect and engage people despite their differences. They also promote values that are essential to a democratic culture, norms like cooperation and respect. Blobs are self-generating because human beings are social creatures. People are continuously building ties to one another and forming all kinds of Blobs, from neighborhood associations to gangs. We ignore their importance—for good or ill—at our peril.

Why the Lack of Alignment?

I have tried to understand the reasons institutional democracy has become divorced from civic democracy. After all, why should there be such a separation? The bureaucrats in institutions are our fellow citizens. But, these citizens play different roles when they are in their professions. Judges are citizens, but when they are on the bench, we address them as "Your Honor."

Can Differences Be Used Constructively?

One of the reasons for the misalignment may be the differences between the way citizens do their work and the ways governments and large institutions do theirs. These differences could be an obstacle to a *with* strategy. On the other hand, the tasks that make up any kind of work are similar. Recognizing that similarity could also be the basis for collaboration. Most all work involves identifying problems, making decisions about what needs to be done, finding the necessary resources, organizing the efforts, and evaluating what happens. Nothing exceptional about that. Nonetheless, civic and institutional ways of working not only may fail to mesh, but the way governing institutions work may also adversely affect what citizens are trying to do. That was true in the parable of the Blobs and Squares. So, bringing about a better alignment is no cake walk. Blobs have a more organic way of organizing, such as by building associations. Institutions, on the other hand, take on tasks in ways that resonate with institutional culture, which is bureaucratic. Bureaucratization brings with it certain mind-sets and values that are problematic for a democratic *with* strategy.

An Inevitable Tension

It's popular to blame bureaucrats for all we don't like about large institutions. I don't want to do that. Nonetheless, there are reasons that public administrators and citizens wind up on different pages when it comes to serving democracy. Before he was president, Woodrow Wilson was a young scholar in what was then the new field of public administration. He recognized an inevitable clash between values implicit in the canons of effective administration and democratic values.[4] That was particularly true as government administration became more professional and expert. Bureaucracies were to be objective and above the political fray, which would allow them to be better able to see and serve the true public interest. Yet those worthy ambitions clashed with democratic values like rule by the people—people who consider themselves the rightful judges of their own best interests.

A friend of mine who was a prominent political figure (I won't name him because I want to keep him as a friend) once thought he could quell antigovernment outrage by comparing the government to a store that was dedicated to good customer service. But the analogy didn't work. A still-outraged citizen told me to let my friend know that he wasn't a customer. He and his fellow citizens *owned* the darn store! (He didn't actually say "darn," but you can imagine what he did say.)

Although people are supposed to have a voice in the decisions being made on their behalf, that is less likely to happen if citizens are seen only from a professional point of view. The easy but erroneous assumption is that what most people should say and do should be the same as what is said and done from a professional perspective. Administrators may believe, with some justification, that if citizens knew what professionals knew, they would support what the professionals were doing. This, of course, assumes that the problem to be solved, as experts see it, is the same as the problem that citizens experience.[5] That is not necessarily true.

The Influence of Special Interest Groups

It also may be that alignment with civic democracy isn't a priority for institutions because they are responding to another "public" made up of special interest groups. These groups have found a powerful way to align what they do with the way institutions, especially in governments, go about their work.

Not only is institutional administration in tension with democracy, its claim of independence from political manipulation is questionable. Well-organized and well-funded special interest groups of all types have been able to exercise considerable political clout.[6] They have formed alliances with the staffs both in government agencies and in Congress. Interest groups with allies in the bureaucracy as well as in the legislative branch can shape laws and regulations, even, in some cases, bypassing open debate in Congress. (See chapter X.) The role these groups play is rarely visible to the public. Collaboration with citizens who aren't in interest groups is nearly impossible when the legislative process takes place out of public view.

THE COSTS OF A WITH STRATEGY

Committed as I am to a democracy where the *demos*, the citizenry, is central, my experiences with governments at the state and local levels have taught me that changes in institutions usually have costs that can go beyond those that are financial. Citizens also have costs in a *with* strategy. They have work to do with other citizens. (That's the subject of chapter IV).

Despite potential benefits to the governing institutions and their professionals, a *with* strategy poses risks. Citizens need to be aware of these. When institutional officials try to engage a citizenry of producers, professional colleagues may not only fail to be supportive but may be quite critical. Furthermore, entering a collaborative relationship with citizens can be perilous if citizens don't deliver on their share of the work. Because of this uncertainty, professionals can be hesitant to commit their institutions to collaborate. Even when people are productive, integrating what they produce into institutional ways of working can be difficult. For instance, citizens and their communities can educate. But how can their "lessons" fit into a standard curriculum? That will take extra effort and considerable ingenuity.

One of the greatest hesitations officials have to working *with* citizens is that people have different expectations and make conflicting demands on their institutions. That often happens to school administrators. In the 2020 academic year, the demand that schools stay open despite the coronavirus pandemic was countered by the insistence that they stay closed and go online. If parents didn't have access to the internet or had to work outside the home, their circumstances were quite different from those of families who were in the opposite situation. What were educators to do? For school administrators, the costs of trying to engage all these citizens and being caught in the crossfire seemed enormous.

Despite these unlikely circumstances, there may be possibilities for a mutually beneficial collaboration. If parents and other citizens have opportunities to weigh the trade-offs and see the complexity of issues, it might help achieve what happened in our country's early town meetings—allowing hasty first reactions to mature into sound judgments. Today, families may not agree, but the deliberations might help them appreciate the complexity of the decisions the schools have to make, and that might change the tone of the dispute. However, that would require other community organizations to hold deliberative town meetings. The schools can't do what needs to be done alone; they must have help from others in the community. Libraries, for example, have played the role of sponsors for such deliberations.

A BETTER ALIGNMENT

As was highlighted in bold type in chapter II, one of the main objectives of this book is to encourage a more effective alignment between citizens and bureaucracies because both can benefit. Sure, there are doubts whether this is possible, many having to do with people's willingness and ability to be productive citizens. Institutions also have challenges because they weren't usually designed to deal *with* citizens as producers.

However, institutions may see benefits to a more constructive relationship with the citizenry, provided they aren't put on the defensive by being labeled incompetent bureaucracies. The professionals I worked with in the government were able, intelligent people who were dedicated to serving what they saw as the public interest. The difficulty is more the opposite. Bureaucrats are such expert professionals, it is only natural that they would be tempted to tell citizens to sit down and "leave the driving to us." The so-called "populist" revolt that has taken place around the world shows that isn't going to happen. People aren't sitting down; they are standing up, wisely or not.

Not More, Just Different

As I've said, I believe that governing institutions can benefit from realigning their ways of working so they can take greater advantage of what citizens alone can produce. This realignment doesn't depend on overhauling all established ways of working. I will look at some cases in the following chapters in which neither citizens nor professionals have to do something altogether different; they just have to consider doing what they do differently. That can allow different ways of working to mesh better.

I believe there is a path to moving forward, and it begins in recognizing that while there are differences between the way institutions work and the way the citizenry works, the tasks are similar. That means they can complement each other. To be more specific, citizens and institutions each give names to problems, even though the terms aren't identical. For example, citizens want to feel that they are safe in their homes, and this feeling of security is less quantifiable yet more compelling to them than the crime statistics professionals use. It shouldn't be too difficult for professionals to incorporate the names people use when describing problems. That is one example of a better alignment. Also, as people decide what to do about their problems, they draw on their experiences, not just data. Admittedly, experiences can be misleading, but the memories of the experiences usually reflect what people consider valuable. Knowing that can help institutions to be more effective in communicating with citizens on controversial issues like taking vaccinations.

A better alignment can begin, too, when citizens and professionals deliberate to make decisions. Both professionals in governing institutions and citizens have to weigh various options for action against their costs and consequences. They both must deal with tensions among the things they consider valuable as they weigh pros and cons. And they both should deliberate to move from first impressions to a more shared and reflective judgment. Each has to do its own version of this choice work. (There is more about deliberative decision-making in the next chapter.)

When institutions, governmental or nongovernmental, sit down with a deliberative citizenry to compare the outcomes of their respective efforts at choice work, they are collaborating *with* one another. This has happened in Hawaii on issues like legalizing gambling.[7]

WHAT'S NEXT?

Despite a *with* strategy's benefits, doubts about the citizenry run deep. People are often thought to be apathetic, selfish, uninformed, biased, hopelessly divided, and easily manipulated, and these are just a few of the doubts. Complementary producers? That doesn't seem likely. The hard truth is that many of these criticisms are justified; human beings have all these failings and more. Yet that isn't the whole story, and that is the subject of the next chapter.

NOTES

1.   Edgar S. Cahn, *No More Throw-Away People: The Co-Production Imperative*, 2nd ed. (Washington, DC: Essential Books, 2004). The video, "The Parable of the Blobs and Squares," by James Mackie, can be viewed at https://www.kettering.org/blogs/parable-blobs-and-squares or on Vimeo at https://vimeo.com/42332617.
2.   Cahn, *No More Throw-Away People*, 83–84.

3.   There is an excellent example of an organization in Israel called the Citizens' Accord Forum that creates such opportunities.

4.   Woodrow Wilson, "The Study of Administration," *Political Science Quarterly* 2 (June 1887) as reproduced in Jay M. Shafritz and Albert C. Hyde, eds., *Classics of Public Administration*, 2nd ed. (Chicago: The Dorsey Press, 1987), 22.

5.   John Doble, a senior research fellow at Public Agenda, reports, "In terms of my own experience, the vast majority of experts I've interviewed over the years in all kinds of fields such as foreign policy . . . , health care, the environment, criminal justice . . . , education (especially school board members and principals), science policy . . . , journalism, etc.—think that 'if only the public understood the issue as well as we do, they'd agree with us.'" John Doble, memorandum to David Mathews, "Examples of Disdain Toward Ordinary Citizens," September 14, 2018.

6.   Theda Skocpol, "The Narrowing of Civic Life," *American Prospect* (May 17, 2004), http://prospect.org/article/narrowing-civic-life.

7.   Delores Foley, *Sustaining Space and Developing Leadership for Public Deliberation Workshop: History and Impact of the Deliberative Dialogues Project at the University of Hawaii at Manoa* (Dayton, OH: Report to the Kettering Foundation, July 11, 2006).

CHAPTER IV

THE POWER OF THE PEOPLE?

The most common argument against the suggestion that the country would be well served if there were more emphasis on people working *with* others and *with* their institutions is that regular folks don't have enough power to be effective. It has been said that the average person is a hopeless amateur in a world that is now so complex that it can be governed only by professional expertise.[1] The unstated assumption behind these criticisms is that citizens don't have anything to offer those in positions of real authority and power except their support. The only role citizens should play is as voters, and to play even that role, they really ought to be better informed.

I don't agree with these criticisms for reasons I will explain, but neither do I dismiss them out of hand. They have to be taken seriously. This jaundiced view of the citizenry goes so deep and is so widespread that I worry that if I don't speak to it up front, the negative perceptions could put a distracting cloud over what the book has to say about a *with* strategy. That strategy calls for collaboration between citizens and governing institutions. If citizens can't do their part, there can't be a *with* strategy.

It is also important to speak to the people who think of themselves as powerless. Power is associated with legal authority, expertise, and money. Those are difficult for most people to come by. This chapter proposes rethinking what power is and how "average" (whatever that means) citizens can generate it themselves. It is about how a democratic citizenry can be self-empowering.

I hope that political leaders and professionals in our governing institutions are willing to consider a different definition of citizenship and a different understanding of the work that people can do and how they do it. This could help our institutions develop a more constructive relationship with a public that they often see as divided, demanding, and unreasonable.

POWER RECONSIDERED

The powers of citizens aren't like the powers that institutions and established authorities have. Harry Boyte, founder of Public Achievement and senior scholar of public work philosophy at Augsburg University, thinks of power as the ability of citizens to make public goods by joining forces with other citizens.[2] That is "power with," rather than institutional or authoritative "power over," a distinction made by Mary Parker Follett.[3] We know governments have power over people. Large corporations have this kind of power, too. But most citizens don't have any such power. So, by conventional definitions, they appear powerless, even to themselves. When people doubt that they can make a difference in the political system, many don't see any point in participating in it.

What helps change this perception is recognizing that there is more than one kind of power. People have innate power, which is in the talents, the skills, and the knowledge they develop from their experiences. These individual powers are amplified by people's ability to form groups and work together with others. Alcoholics Anonymous is an example of what people can accomplish by joining forces. The members don't have the legal authority to control what others do, but they have been effective in changing harmful behaviors by supporting one another.

Supporting and cooperating with others who aren't like us—who aren't part of our kinship group—has been the key to our survival. Humans have covered the globe because we could work together.[4] And we have survived because we've exercised good judgment more times than not about what that work should be—what actions are or aren't in our best interest. To be sure, humans are competitive, often selfish, and prone to violence. We don't have to look far to find evidence of that. Still, overall, as I noted earlier, cooperation has won out. Proof? We are still here and in greater numbers than ever.[5]

The Power in Associating

Individual abilities and knowledge have been brought together in countless associations, informal and formal. Neighbors who drink coffee together regularly and discuss problems on their street. That is an informal association. Women who banded together to create an organization called Mothers Against Drunk Driving (MADD) to stop people from driving while impaired. That is a formal association. Associations are to civic life what cells are to biological life. They are the basic organisms of a political ecology.

John McKnight has spent a career studying what civic associations do, particularly in neighborhoods.[6] They care for the elderly and the vulnerable young. They develop leadership because everyone has to play a role. They are problem solvers and encourage initiative and enterprise. Not being bureaucratic, they can respond quickly when there are emergencies. Most significant of all, McKnight reminds us, associating is different from voting, which delegates power to others. Associating *generates* power.

The importance of associations was evident in a 2018 study of what has allowed some cities to lower their crime rates when others couldn't.[7] These cities had generators of civic energy in a multitude of associations of citizens working to improve their community (*Figure 7*). Researchers found that "every 10 additional [civic] organizations in a city with 100,000 residents . . . led to a 9 percent drop in the murder rate and a 6 percent drop in violent crime."[8] These civic groups didn't necessarily see their work as preventing violence, but "in creating playgrounds, they enabled parents to better monitor their children. In connecting neighbors, they improved the capacity of residents to control their streets. In forming after-school programs, they offered alternatives to crime."[9] Even if not directly related to crime, these efforts helped turn negative emotions into positive energy.

FIGURE 7. *Civic associations have helped to lower crime rates in some cities by creating playgrounds and offering after-school programs. ("Teamwork by community volunteers to rebuild a children's playground," by Billy Hustace, in the Corbis Documentary collection, image #523425090.)*

Small Is Beautiful

Associations don't have to be big or formal to have the power to bring about change. Peter Block said it well: "We change the world one room at a time."[10] Small groups are powerful in their own right. Typically, they are of between 3 and 12 people, which allows everyone to be heard. They also depend on everyone to act. And they are indispensable bridges between individuals and the community. Linked together, they strengthen civic infrastructure.

I believe Block is right about the power of small groups without scale but with strong connections. They are like glue; they have adhesive strength. And the more they connect different people with a range of abilities and ties to others, the more powerful they are.

The Power in Networking

Associating encourages more associating. Small groups extend their power by networking with other small groups that have related concerns and purposes. These networks allow associations to reinforce one another, which makes the sum of their efforts much greater than the parts or individual projects can be.

Citizens can build networks to connect to others they need but don't totally agree with. I recall a community that was having terrible difficulties: the economy was stagnant, race relations were terrible, and the schools were far below par. The situation didn't change until a small group of citizens began to ask who wasn't present when community problems were being discussed—people who needed to be there if the problems were going to be solved. That question led the group to a surprising conclusion: The people they needed most weren't the mayor or the leading business owners. They were the SOBs down the street—people who certainly didn't like them. These people were nonetheless crucial because they weren't contributing to problem solving; they were blocking it. Why weren't these malcontents at the table? No one had invited them. If they had been invited, would they have come? Probably not. So, the group began looking at what discussions the SOBs were in and how to connect to the associations where they talked. That's when the community began to change.

Networks are effective because they aren't shaped like a wagon wheel with all the spokes connected to a central hub.[11] They have multiple, interconnected nodes rather than centralized controls. Anyone can communicate with anyone else. Knowledge spreads rapidly.

People who bring about change are usually connected in any number of overlapping networks. These networks provide support, encouragement, and more. People share resources essential to their work. Power multiplies. A classic study of networks is Mark Granovetter's "The Strength of Weak Ties."[12] He points out that, although there must be enough commonality for networks to be coherent, broad and loose ties are indispensable.[13] Strong ties, on the other hand, while fostering initial cohesion, ultimately lead to fragmentation, with multiple enclaves or exclusive cliques.

The Power of Examples

Another source of power that citizens have is the power of example. Some people don't like to have trash in their cars, so they throw it out on the roads. In one town, few seemed bothered by the trash until a good citizen decided something had to be done. He began to pick up the litter. That encouraged other people to do the same. Trash throwers became hesitant about tossing cans and paper out of their cars because they were afraid of running into one of the trash pickers. Later, the county government got involved and started an antilitter program. It all began by a few people exercising the power of an example.

As in this case, examples don't have to be heroic; they can be quite ordinary. I once saw how effective a personal example could be when, in response to a question about what a lone individual could do to solve a school problem, an administrator said simply but profoundly, "I can change the way I do my job." That is power.

Some of the power that citizens can draw on is obvious in everyday life but below the radar of what is usually considered political. In *Life as Politics: How Ordinary People Change the Middle East*, Asef Bayat coined the term *social nonmovements* to describe the "seemingly mundane practices" that can precipitate social and political change.[14] These nonmovements are "the collective endeavors of millions of noncollective actors, carried out in the main squares, back streets, court houses, and communities."[15] He describes changes in everyday behaviors that add up to changes in social norms. They have been as simple as changes in dress—maybe nothing more than a colorful scarf over the head. These kinds of changes are not confrontational; they are quite ordinary. Yet, as the fashion changes caught on, people recognized they did, indeed, have power. It was within them.

An example of noncollective action in the United States is the "pay it forward" phenomenon. People began assisting others, often strangers, as though they were reciprocating for a past gift, which they hadn't received. Acts of unprovoked generosity have caught on and spread worldwide, long before a foundation was created to support this nonpolitical movement.[16]

The Civil/Human Rights Movement in the United States is perhaps the best-known case of the power of the examples set by citizens when they join forces with other citizens. People often think of the Movement as something that took place in the 1950s and 1960s. That was because the events then were so unforgettably tragic: dogs attacking protesters, fire hoses turned on crowds, children dying when their church was bombed. These tragedies galvanized a response that its founders insisted was a human rights campaign, which was to be broad based and inclusive.[17] That campaign actually began much earlier in work by African Americans who had joined forces to create schools for newly freed slaves and, later, to insist on the right of their children to have the same quality of education that white children had. They left a history of powerful examples set by a thousand nameless people and a thousand nameless acts.[18] These examples inspired others later to set examples by registering as voters to claim their rights at the polls. These examples changed not only communities, they changed the country. (Local isn't necessarily parochial.)

CITIZENSHIP RECONSIDERED

Citizens as Producers with Agency

Citizens aren't typically seen as producers of public goods. More often they are thought of as consumers of goods others provide. And we are constantly consuming; we have the power of our purses. However, a citizenry of consumers has far less power than a citizenry of producers making things, both tangible and intangible. Changing a political climate is intangible. Joining forces to build schools for formerly enslaved children is tangible.

There is a long history of citizens as producers. Since the American Revolution, people have made a difference by protesting and pressuring officials to meet their demands. Citizens have also made a difference by joining forces to make things that improve life for everyone. On the frontier, they came together to construct houses, harvest crops, and build cities. In the modern era, productive citizens have established neighborhood watches and collected material to fashion face masks when a pandemic hit.

What citizens have produced has made them the sovereign power in the United States: "The People" who authored the Constitution. Recall Samuel Cooper's sermon in which he explained how he and his fellow citizens became sovereign through the constitutions they ratified.

Empowering Institutions

Citizens can't be left on the political sidelines, not only because they have the right to govern and are indispensable in combating our most difficult problems, but because their work is needed to complement the work of governments, schools, and other institutions. As noted, this was Elinor Ostrom's argument for citizens as coproducers. People enhance their power as producers when what they produce makes governing institutions more effective.

Look at the research on what happens in the first days after many natural or human-made disasters strike. Survival depends largely on people helping people. One study concluded that "successful remedies and recovery for communitywide disasters are neither conceived nor implemented solely by trained emergency personnel, nor are they confined to preauthorized procedures."[19] Rather, "family members, friends, coworkers, neighbors, and strangers who happen to be in the vicinity often carry out search and rescue activities and provide medical aid before police, fire, and other officials even arrive on the scene."[20] Disasters reveal what only citizens can do. We saw that happening when coping with multiple crises in 2020.

In some cases, institutions and their professionals are happy to have the needed help. But not always. Citizens' initiatives have made some professionals feel defensive, as though nonprofessionals were taking over their jobs. That could be the case if citizens were interfering, but that isn't what was happening in the study just cited.

A Different Way of Working

In the last chapter, I noted that the tasks in the work of citizens and institutions are very similar. They both involve identifying problems, deciding what to do, organizing actions, and so on. That creates opportunities to collaborate, not because citizens and institutions go about their work the same way, but because there are differences. And those differences create the opportunities for one way of working to add to another. I gave a few examples earlier. But because this chapter is about the power citizens have,

I need to say more about how distinctive the way citizens work is and how valuable the differences are.

As I said in chapter III, unlike institutions and people in their professional roles, most citizens don't identify problems in expert terms. They are more prone to take into account what their experiences tell them is most valuable and should be held dear when deciding on how to combat problems. People also have access to local knowledge that comes from years of direct experience with problems. The options for actions to solve these problems go beyond what can be done by institutions. And, as has just been discussed, citizens act through their families and friends and the associations they form. Furthermore, citizens don't make decisions about which options are best by using institutional methods, such as cost-benefit analysis. The resources citizens draw on to act, such as personal talents and family strengths, are different from institutional resources. Citizens also organize their work less bureaucratically than institutions do.

Even when the work institutions do is the same as the work done by citizens, people working with people has a distinctive quality. Recall the leaf-raking example. My neighbors could have hired a road crew to keep our lane clean. Yet, when the people living around me work together in the cleanup, it builds a stronger sense of community.

The contributions that citizens can make are distinctive in other ways. Governing bodies can't create their own legitimacy. They can't, on their own, define their purposes or set the standards by which they will operate. They can't sustain decisions that citizens are unwilling to support. As I said earlier, they can build common highways, but not common ground. Furthermore, institutions—even the most powerful—can't generate the will required to keep moving ahead to combat stubborn problems.

THE POWER TO DELIBERATE

The people's power to act isn't enough in itself. The actions must be in the best interest of all the community. Citizens have the power to exercise the good judgment that results in sound decisions—provided they use it. It is the power to deliberate. Deliberating is what juries do. It is what we hope legislative bodies will do. It is what we do when we have to decide what work we should do together. And, individually, we use it when we have to choose where to go after high school or what career to pursue.

To deliberate is to weigh various options for action carefully to determine their value. In ancient Greece, deliberating meant the talk people used to teach themselves before they acted.[21] Earlier, I said that human beings have survived by working together across differences—by doing work that is based on sound collective decisions about what should be done in the best interest of all.

In a democracy, as you'll recall, the people collectively are the *demos* with the sovereign power (*kratos*) to decide. They act by joining forces civically and through representative governments. Deliberating brings people together to inform their judgment about what is best to do. Whether or not they use it, people have a natural faculty for deliberating. A deliberative democracy is self-empowering.

Because it is so essential to a *with* strategy, the next section of this chapter elaborates on what deliberating does and how it works to bring people together to act as wisely as possible. Public deliberating on public issues with the people around us doesn't have the same purpose as jury or legislative deliberations. Its objective is to inform public actions, and there can be more than one of these. Whoever deliberates, it isn't foolproof.

The Public Isn't Always Right

Citizens may be given useful information to help in decision-making, but numerous studies show that people are easily swayed by biases and other distractions. And there are cases in which collective decisions have proven to be terribly wrong. In some instances, individuals are too divided and antagonistic to decide anything together. Still, when people with different experiences and concerns are together deliberating, as they are in public life, they can often (not always) improve the decision-making.

When our experiences and perspectives differ, as they do, drawing on all of them in deliberating can gives us a broader, more complete understanding of the reality around us—and of ourselves. This understanding improves the decision-making.

Evidence of Deliberation's Effects

The human brain is hardwired for deliberation. And if we use this faculty as we should, it doesn't have to get up to scale; it is already innate.[22]

For 40 years, my colleagues and I have seen people try to bring deliberation to bear on a wide range of difficult issues, indeed on the country's most controversial issues: abortion, gun policy, freedom of speech. Sometimes these efforts to deliberate have failed. Still, enough haven't for us to see that deliberation can work. The public deliberations we have seen most often have been those in National Issues Forums (NIF). These forums are nonpartisan and are sponsored by a diverse network of local organizations ranging from libraries to schools, to senior citizen centers and religious congregations. Even some prisons have used these deliberative forums for "civic rehabilitation." Reports on the outcomes of hundreds of NIF deliberations are available in the Kettering Foundation archives, and some examples are given in this book.

Making Everyday Talk More Deliberative

The NIF forums are designed to prompt deliberation, but their greatest contribution is to strengthen deliberation wherever public decisions are made—in civic associations, boards, legislative bodies, and administrative agencies. The forums work in the same way a healthy diet does to boost a body's immune system. They boost the deliberative system.

The Kettering Foundation works with the NIF network in three ways: by framing major issues selected by forum sponsors to encourage deliberation, by analyzing the outcomes of the NIF deliberations, and by presenting the results nationally. (Local forums report their outcomes locally.)

Public Agenda initially "subcontracted" the work of framing issues. Dan Yankelovich, a founder of Public Agenda and one of the country's leading public opinion analysts, had discovered that in some elections there was a shift from ever-changing opinions to more stable ones. He wanted to see whether it was possible to jump-start this movement from first impressions to more shared and reflective public judgment. He thought that creating a citizens' briefing book would do this, and Public Agenda prepared the first ones. Kettering eventually assumed responsibility for these books, using its research on issues selected by forum sponsors. In return, Kettering draws on the forum outcomes in its studies of the role of the citizenry in a democracy.

The first NIF issue book had to do with Social Security, which was in financial trouble. These forums demonstrated the validity of the Yankelovich thesis. First reactions did begin to give way to more considered opinions. The results were presented in 1983 at a conference at the new Gerald R. Ford Presidential Library, a conference led by former presidents Ford and Carter.

Deliberation and Judgment

Public deliberation is crucial in dealing with issues that require sound decisions or good judgment. We have to use our best judgment when faced with decisions that have no certain technological or scientific answers. When there are a number of possible answers, we have to decide which best fits with the things we consider essential to our well-being, things we hold dear.

Political decision-making requires judgment because most political decisions ultimately have to do with what *should* be done or what is the *right* thing to do. How free should free speech be? Should the health of my community outweigh my right not to wear a mask or refuse a vaccination? These are normative matters and can't be answered with expert, factual information alone. At issue in nearly every issue is what is deeply valuable to people. I don't mean "values"; I mean the ends and means of life itself.[23] There are many things people hold dear that lie at the deepest level of human motivation. I mentioned these ancient imperatives earlier—security, freedom, fairness, and control. They are important to everyone. When faced with a threatening problem, people want to know whether they have the support of others that will make them secure from danger. They want to be sure that they will be free to act as they think best. And they want to be confident that they are going to be treated fairly. People are also greatly concerned about what control they will have in shaping their future.

Tensions and Trade-offs

Although everyone has the same primal concerns about their well-being, people live under different conditions, so they put different priorities on what they hold dear. Because of their circumstances, some people may consider safety more important than some personal freedoms. As people become more aware of what they all hold dear, as well as how they differ in circumstances and experiences, they are more likely to recognize the complexity of issues.

Because circumstances can vary a great deal, deliberation requires giving a "fair trial" even to options that some may have reason to oppose. That is one of the key principles of deliberation. Admittedly, considering what is good in an option labeled as bad is a challenge. Although it's tempting to avoid what could be an unpleasant conversation, it is imperative to hear opposing views and recognize the inevitable tensions among all that people hold dear. As just noted, these tensions show how complex a problem is, even a problem that may have appeared to be a no-brainer to solve. Such tensions can't be resolved by no longer caring about things that are deeply valuable, so people have to find a way to balance or harmonize competing concerns. That is what deliberative decision-making encourages.

Disagreement without Divisiveness

Realizing the tensions among things that are valuable helps change the decision-making from one of people against people to people against a complex problem. When deliberating, people don't necessarily come to agree or like one another, yet they can see that others, however mistaken they may appear to be, are not evil. Deliberation recognizes that there will be inevitable tensions over what should be considered most valuable. These aren't justifications for mortal combat, but rather the result of differences in circumstances and experiences.

This shift away from divisiveness has occurred in the National Issues Forums and been affirmed in an experiment in Finland on a very polarizing issue. The Finnish researchers found that clashes in opinions decreased in forums where deliberative principles were respected. These principles included giving a fair hearing to unpopular options. When there were just discussions without such precepts, polarization actually increased.[24]

Deliberation counters divisiveness in several other ways. One of the most important is focusing on the practical side of problems. Take the case of one community where sewage was flowing into streets and homes.[25] People clashed over which neighborhoods were getting "most favored nation" treatment and which were routinely neglected. That was a legitimate question, but trying to reach a conclusion wouldn't stop the sewage. The urgency and rankness of the problem—sewage leaks were likely to occur anywhere, anytime—demanded a practical solution, not a partisan debate. By working together to eliminate the problem, they set the stage for dealing with the problem of unequal treatment.

When people deliberate, they are more likely to recognize that they hold the same things dear, even though they disagree on the best way to secure them. That makes the problem they are trying to solve more of a shared problem. This insight is no small benefit in a polarized, political environment. When deliberating on controversial issues, the antagonisms don't go away but they may be less likely to dominate the political climate.

Looking for "Pivots"

The deliberation we have seen has prompted people to at least consider options they dislike. How does that happen? Kettering researchers wondered whether there was something like a trigger, or "pivot," that would open forum participants to considering unpopular points of view. Comparing notes from hundreds of forums over many years, we discovered a pivot that seems to be the catalyst. The precipitant wasn't a new set of facts (although introducing strategic information was helpful). And it wasn't a persuasive, logical argument. Rather, it was a very human story someone told about an experience that showed the complexity of an issue. An example: In one forum, a young woman, who was very much opposed to abortion, explained what it was like to have had an abortion herself. Hearing her story, and her anguish, didn't change the minds of those who championed the right to end a pregnancy. However, it made them more open to understanding the other side of the issue.

Not having to agree also makes a difference. Deliberative forums have helped turn some acrimonious debates into a search for an area somewhere between agreement and disagreement. Perhaps people recognize that they are seldom in total agreement with anyone, even those closest to them. Maybe healthy relationships are always in this gray area.

As the Kettering researchers looked to see whether there had been pivots on other issues, they found several. One occurred in a forum on AIDS. A minister, convinced that the disease was God's punishment, sat in the front row, ready to deliver his message. He had disrupted previous discussions of the issue by his vigorously insisting that not only was he right, but anyone who disagreed was morally derelict. In this forum, the moderator was wise enough to let the minister speak first. Then the moderator asked whether anyone else thought the AIDS issue had a moral dimension. Nearly everyone raised a hand. The response drew the minister into the group rather than pushing him out. He wasn't the only one who valued a moral order. While his point of view didn't change significantly, both the tenor of what he said and the way he participated did. He lowered his voice; he listened more. (After the forum, people commented on how the exchange with the minister was different from what it had been in less deliberative settings.) Conflict remained over which moral imperatives should direct decisions about AIDS policy, but it was more of a shared conflict. People went on to dig into the hard work of making a decision about how to deal with a possible AIDS epidemic. There was still a great deal of emotion though less antagonism.

Misunderstandings of Deliberation

Given the variety of meanings of *deliberation,* it is no wonder that there is some confusion about the kind discussed in this book. One misperception is that deliberation is a special, almost magical process or technique. Not so. Neither is deliberation just polite, informed discussion. It is hard choice work that requires grappling with tensions. And it seldom results in full agreement on solutions. Instead, it can show a range of actions that people will or won't take or support, which encourages them to look for middle ground or a balanced course of practical action that most everyone would be willing to live with—at least temporarily.

This kind of deliberation has also been confused with purely rational, fact-based decision-making. Certainly, factual information is essential. However, because many political questions are about what is the *right* thing to do, and facts alone don't provide absolute answers, people have to rely on the moral reasoning that deliberation employs. Moral reasoning recognizes that questions of what is right arouse strong emotions, and deliberation helps people come to terms with those feelings.

Because of the emphasis placed on facts and data, it is frequently assumed that only the well-educated can deliberate. That just isn't so. People from all walks of life have taken part in public deliberations, and there have been no reports of any groups who lacked the capacity for this choice work. For instance, Professor Bonnie Braun and a research team at the University of Maryland studied forums involving women from poor, rural communities. Their research did not show any lack of capacity for deliberating; neither have any of the NIF meetings.[26]

Public deliberation is also easily misunderstood when it is seen as one of the many techniques used in small groups and not a natural faculty of the human brain. The misperception that deliberation requires special skills, which only a few people have, often comes from being aware that working through tensions is hard work. Things that aren't easy, however, are still things that humans do all the time. That is true of public deliberation. It is both natural and challenging.

Although civil, informed discussions have benefits, they don't go far enough to produce deliberation. People have to face up to unpleasant tensions and trade-offs in order to trigger the brain to exercise its faculty for judgment. (Recall the Finnish study: Conventional discussions of a polarized issue can widen the differences.)

Still another common misconception has to do with the deliberative forums in which participants are self-selected, not chosen to create a demographically representative sample as polls do. That is useful, but the organizations holding NIF-type deliberations aren't trying to produce poll data. They are trying to encourage more deliberation wherever public decisions are made. And that isn't in demographically representative groups.

Most sponsors of NIF deliberations do make every effort to bring together as diverse a forum group as possible. Yet even people who are demographically similar may not all think alike. In deliberative forums, those who are alike in many ways have often discovered that they have quite different opinions. Also, although people take comfort in views they admire, they may be curious about contrary views, provided those aren't advanced in an offensive manner. Forum participants certainly try to persuade one another as they hold on to cherished beliefs. But deliberation encourages people to at least understand why the options they like are unappealing to others.

Deliberation and Action

Perhaps the most common misperception of deliberation is that it is just talk. But politics is about action, and so is deliberation. Deliberating doesn't stand alone; it is intertwined with acting. The experience of acting continually shapes the decision-making, just as the decision-making shapes the action.[27] It makes no sense to think of deliberation as separate from action. Past actions or experiences, when filtered through the things people consider most valuable, become some of the "facts" most relevant in making decisions. Public deliberation uses expert and professional knowledge but adds the knowledge people create. Deliberation "teaches." And the shared knowledge it uses makes the actions more effective.

Patterns to Watch For

One pattern is when people get trapped in the terms of bipolar debate. That happened during the Cold War with Russia. The political debate was over preventing nuclear war. One option was to put our nuclear bomb in aircrafts that were constantly flying. That was to protect us from attack because an enemy would know we could retaliate. Another option was to put the bombs underground. Then a third option was added that reframed the issue. It said that maybe the problem wasn't a technical one of armament deployment; maybe it was about security. The third option was to do things that would make the Soviet Union feel safe so the US could be safe—and vice versa. That option was added to the first NIF book on an international issue. It helped change the debate.

Another pattern: Look at the options that were considered after World War I. There weren't issue books, but if there had been, they might have followed the debate at the time. Option one was to punish Germany so severely that it would never start another war. Option two was the peace option: Strengthen the peace-serving institutions and develop a peace-loving culture. The third option wasn't very visible; it was to join all of Europe in a compact to promote unity. (That option eventually led to the EU.) The winning option was the first one—punishing Germany severely. It prompted the German nationalism that produced Hitler and WWII.

The lesson to be learned: Avoid issue framings that offer a villain to blame for all that is wrong. There is seldom one cause for a serious, completely wicked problem, even though one or more parties may be acting very badly.[28] Blaming stops public deliberating. The decision is fore-ordained—punish the villain.

EVERYDAY OPPORTUNITIES

No one needs to wait for a forum in order to deliberate. There are opportunities every day to make discussions more deliberative. When an important issue comes up in a community, such as a threat to public health, or a faltering economy, or instances of racial injustice, people will start talking to one another about what the problem is and what should be done to solve it. During the pandemic in 2020, those conversations took place all over the country. Should the schools stay open, or should all instruction be online? Should people travel? Who should decide? The list of issues goes on. Similar initiatives in public deliberation have occurred because public safety and the role of the police are continuing issues.

In these circumstances, the elements of deliberation that are in people's minds are reflected in the questions they ask one another. You can hear these conversations in waiting rooms and at tables in coffee shops. I have a friend who learns from what he hears in taxis. People speak in their own voices, and they aren't going to phrase questions the way I am about to do in this paragraph. But what I have heard and been told suggests people are thinking deliberatively when they ask questions somewhat like these: What do you think is the real problem? Is it something other than what everyone says it is? What is missing? Why should we care? What's at stake for you and your family? What should be done, what might be the consequences, and who should be acting? Is there anything you and I should do? Can we? Who else needs to act? Are we missing somebody? How is this decision going to be made? Who should decide?

In conversations with deliberative elements, a lot of people have solutions they advocate, but are there unwelcomed consequences to also consider? The question being asked is, in plain speak, "How much is what you are proposing going to cost?" Who is going to pay? Other questions may explore whether there are more resources that could be used and who has them. Do I have any that I would be willing to commit? How is all that needs to be done going to be organized effectively? Who's going to do the organizing? How will we know whether what will be done is effective and not just a waste of our money and time? Posing these kinds of questions as people ordinarily speak helps turn everyday conversations in a more deliberative direction.

Although there is an order to the questions I've just listed, I don't want to give the impression that everyday deliberation is linear. People move back and forth. When laying out various options for actions, they may go back and ask whether what they thought was the problem was really the problem. And they may appear to go off track from time to time. Deliberating can also be punctuated by pointless complaining, airing of biases, blaming others—all the things that don't appear at all deliberative. Still, there are opportunities to shift into a deliberative mode with variations of the generic questions I've described.

For instance, asking whether the "obvious" problem is the real problem moves a conversation in a deliberative direction. It opens the door to looking at how other people may experience a problem. Asking whether there are more ways of solving the problem encourages getting other options on the table. "How is the decision going to be made, by whom, where, and how?" invites consideration of how open and deliberative the decision-making will be. Asking, "What can we do ourselves?" recognizes that citizens, not just institutions and experts, can be actors. Questions about resources, organizing, and evaluating results also have the potential to make the decision-making more deliberative. These questions turn deliberative talk into deliberative politics—into deliberative democracy.

Deliberating is self-empowering when people discover that it is something they can do and that this ability improves with practice. Some forum participants have even taken what they have learned in public meetings back into their family conversations. People can draw on this innate power when they are troubled by doubt about their ability to make a difference.

WHAT'S NEXT?

This chapter has been about the powers citizens can draw on to do their part in collaborating *with* one another and the governing institutions. The book now moves to the other side of the strategy—the role of governing institutions.

The next three chapters go behind the scenes in Washington and a large cabinet department to describe the political culture and the way the federal government works. The book also looks at state and local governments. And it's about nongovernmental institutions. Most all of these governing institutions have similar ways of organizing what they do and similar mind-sets about their role. How compatible are these with a *with* strategy?

NOTES

1. That is exactly how citizens were portrayed in a 1998 article in the *Economist* that read, "When professionals dominate all complex subjects, from the forecasting of markets to the cataloguing of library books, perhaps it is too much to hope that public policy can ever be the province of the amateur." "American Democracy: Building the Perfect Citizens," *Economist* (August 22, 1998): 21–22. Interestingly, in 2020 the *Economist* featured an article on citizens' assemblies, "Citizens' Assemblies Are Increasingly Popular," *Economist*, September 19, 2020.

2. Harry C. Boyte, *Awakening Democracy through Public Work: Pedagogies of Empowerment* (Nashville: Vanderbilt University Press, 2018).

3. Mary Parker Follett, *Creative Experience* (New York: Longmans, Green and Co., 1924), 199-200.

4. See Kristopher M. Smith, Tomás Larroucau, Ibrahim A. Mabulla, and Coren L. Apicella, "Hunter-Gatherers Maintain Assortativity in Cooperation Despite High Levels of Residential Change and Mixing," *Current Biology* 28 (October 8, 2018): 3152-3157.

5. Joe Pinsker, "What Happens When the World's Population Stops Growing," *Atlantic* (blog), July 31, 2019; Robert Kunzig, "Population 7 Billion," *National Geographic* 219, no. 1 (January 2011).

6. John McKnight, "Associations and Their Democratic Functions" (Dayton, OH: Report to the Kettering Foundation), https://resources.depaul.edu/abcd-institute/publications/publications-by-topic/Documents/Associations%20and%20 Their%20Democratic%20Functions.pdf.

7. Patrick Sharkey, *Uneasy Peace: The Great Crime Decline, the Renewal of City Life, and the Next War on Violence* (New York: W. W. Norton, 2018).

8. Emily Badger, "The Unsung Role That Ordinary Citizens Played in the Great Crime Decline," The Upshot, *New York Times*, November 9, 2017, https://nyti.ms/2hlT3Mu.

9. Badger, "The Unsung Role That Ordinary Citizens Played in the Great Crime Decline."

10. Peter Block, *Community: The Structure of Belonging*, 2nd ed. (Oakland, CA: Berrett-Koehler Publishers, 2018), 98.

11. Sean Safford, *Why the Garden Club Couldn't Save Youngstown: The Transformation of the Rust Belt* (Cambridge, MA: Harvard University Press, 2009), 6.

12. Mark S. Granovetter, "The Strength of Weak Ties," *American Journal of Sociology* 78, no. 6 (May 1973): 1360-1380.

13. Granovetter, "The Strength of Weak Ties," 1378.

14. Asef Bayat, *Life as Politics: How Ordinary People Change the Middle East*, (Stanford, CA: Stanford University Press, 2013), 48.

15. Bayat, *Life as Politics*, x.

16. Pay It Forward Foundation, "About Us," https://www.payitforwardfoundation.org/about.

17. Numerous sources have made the point that the Civil Rights Movement was really a human rights movement. These include Carol Anderson, *Eyes off the Prize: The United Nations and the African American Struggle for Human Rights, 1944-1955*, (Cambridge, UK: Cambridge University Press, 2003) 1-2; Malcolm X and Alex Haley, *The Autobiography of Malcolm X* (New York: Random House, 1964), 207; Roy S. Johnson, "Our Black Elders Are Mad at Us," AL.com (March 5, 2021), https://www.al.com/news/2021/03/johnson-our-black-elders-are-mad-at-us.html.

18. Wayne Flynt used this characterization when speaking at the "Tuskegee 1963 Education and Democracy Symposium: Commemorating Desegregation in Alabama Public Schools." The forum was held on August 23-24, 2013, at the Tuskegee Human and Civil Rights Multicultural Center. It is an apt way of describing how a democracy works. I've also cited another historian, Robert Wiebe, who used it to describe what happened on the frontier. Robert Wiebe, *Self-Rule: A Cultural History of American Democracy* (Chicago: University of Chicago Press, 1995).

19. Monica Schoch-Spana et al., "Community Engagement: Leadership Tool for Catastrophic Health Events," *Biosecurity and Bioterrorism: Biodefense Strategy, Practice, and Science* 5, no. 1 (2007): 10-11.

20. Schoch-Spana et al., "Community Engagement," 11.

21. In the "Funeral Oration of Pericles," Pericles describes public deliberation as *prodidacthenai . . . logo*, or the talk Athenians use to teach themselves before they act. See Thucydides, *History of the Peloponnesian War* 2.40.2.

22. For an account of an everyday system somewhat like the one I describe, see Jane Mansbridge, "Everyday Talk in the Deliberative System," in *Deliberative Politics: Essays on Democracy and Disagreement*, ed. Stephen Macedo (New York: Oxford University Press, 1999), 211-239. In their review of the neurobiology of decision-making, Ernst and Paulus explain how deliberative decision-making is integrated into

the neurological process. See Monique Ernst and Martin P. Paulus, "Neurobiology of Decision Making: A Selective Review from a Neurocognitive and Clinical Perspective," *Biological Psychiatry* 58, no. 8 (2005): 597-604. In scientific terms, deliberation is closely associated with the functions of the right dorsolateral cortex and the orbitofrontal cortex. Other parts of the brain contribute emotional processing, which is critical in deliberation.

23. I've drawn largely from the work of Milton Rokeach and Sandra J. Ball-Rokeach, "Stability and Change in American Value Priorities, 1968-1981," *American Psychologist* 44 (5) (May 1989): 775–784.

24. Kim Strandberg, Staffan Himmelroos, and Kimmo Grönlund, "Do Discussions in Like-Minded Groups Necessarily Lead to More Extreme Opinions? Deliberative Democracy and Group Polarization," *International Political Science Review* (June 26, 2017): 1-17, http://journals.sagepub.com/doi/pdf/10.1177/0192512117692136.

25. Ahmed Naguib, video interview by Paloma Dallas, July 2014.

26. Bonnie Braun et al., *Engaging Unheard Voices: Under What Conditions Can, and Will, Limited Resource Citizens Engage in the Deliberative Public Policy Process?* (College Park, MD: Report to the Kettering Foundation, March 2006), 5.

27. Daniel Yankelovich, *Coming to Public Judgment: Making Democracy Work in a Complex World* (Syracuse, NY: Syracuse University Press, 1991), 95-96.

28. The classic reference on "wicked" problems is Horst W. J. Rittel and Melvin M. Webber, "Dilemmas in a General Theory of Planning," *Policy Sciences* 4 (1973): 155–169.

CHAPTER V

INSIDE WASHINGTON IN THE 1970s

The political environment in the nation's capital during the 1970s, although not like today, was hammered by turmoil. The country had witnessed the assassination of President John F. Kennedy in 1963, followed by the assassinations of Martin Luther King Jr. and Robert Kennedy in 1968. Protests against the Vietnam War on campuses and at the Capitol carried over into the 1970s. Then the world was traumatized by shocking scene after scene of political terrorism: bombings, kidnappings, murders. The turbulence continued with the resignation of President Richard Nixon in 1974.

Washington itself, although criticized for its policies, didn't seem as much a target as it would become later. And only a few perceptive scholars studying public opinion detected a growing loss of public confidence in government, which would eventually become a political pandemic.

When I arrived in Washington in 1975, politics had a competitive edge, yet I found that it was balanced by civility and pragmatic, collegial norms. The atmosphere would have been conducive to a *with* strategy had it not been for the perception on both sides of the partisan aisle that people in general were not that interested in politics except during elections. This perception was not considered prejudicial; it was just an unexceptional commonplace. Yet, for some reason, I found myself uncomfortable with this conventional wisdom.

BRINGING GOVERNMENT BACK TO THE PEOPLE

If there were ever a president who personified Washington at its best, it was Gerald Ford, the 38th President of the United States, who came to office in the wake of Nixon's resignation in 1974. President Ford asked me to replace Caspar Weinberger as Secretary of Health, Education, and Welfare (HEW) (*Figure 8*). I will always be grateful to him for that opportunity.

Ford repeated a pledge that goes back at least to Woodrow Wilson, which was, "to bring the government back to the people."[1] In Washington, that phrase usually meant returning government more to the state and local levels.[2] Although I would later think more was necessary in proposing a *with* strategy, "bringing government back" struck a responsive chord in me. As a member of the cabinet, my objective was to find ways HEW could respond to that challenge.

I don't claim that President Ford understood democracy exactly the way I do, but we did share a certain confidence in "The People." We also shared a pragmatic bent—working through conflicts, solving problems, getting the job done. Daniel Boorstin, who was Librarian of Congress during the Ford years, argued that, with the exception of political philosophers, Americans have been uninterested in the dogmas that preoccupied Europeans.[3] This aversion to ideology and the bent toward pragmatism, he believed, had been among the country's "peculiar strengths." That doesn't mean that pragmatists are relativists, that anything goes, or that whatever works is fine. Not at all. Many pragmatists are committed to the values that have emerged over our history, and their practical instincts operate within a framework of traditional American beliefs.[4]

For me, the American heritage boils down to solving problems in ways that respect opposing points of view, avoid coercion, and are guided by common sense (i.e., the shared sense of things that we have in common). Trying to find what works strikes me as more useful than depending on legalisms, citing bureaucratic rules, or navigating by partisan charts. I saw President Ford's approach to the presidency as consistent with this heritage.

FIGURE 8. *David Mathews is sworn in as Secretary of the Department of Health, Education, and Welfare, August 8, 1975. From left to right, Lucy Mathews, Chief Justice Warren Burger, Mary Mathews, David Mathews, Lee Ann Mathews, President Gerald Ford. (From David Mathews' photo collection at the Kettering Foundation. Photo by Norman J. Tavan, Department of Health, Education, and Welfare.)*

THE LEGACY OF AN ECONOMIC COLLAPSE AND A WORLD WAR

Before going further into the politics of the 1970s, it is important to first step back and look at the history that shaped the political environment of that decade. The environment was influenced by two catastrophic events: the Great Depression of the 1930s and the Second World War. Without recognizing these events, it is difficult to account for the role and scope that modern government has taken.

The Great Depression and the New Deal

By the 1970s, the scope of government programs had already grown considerably to relieve the distress caused by the Great Depression. This economic upheaval put a premium on the government working *for* the people. President Franklin Delano Roosevelt responded to economic hardship with the New Deal, offering a host of relief programs. As government grew, much of what civic groups once did in areas like social welfare and education was transferred to Washington and state capitals.

The Great Depression was a horrendous economic crisis for the United States, but it also created an opportunity for professionals to demonstrate the effectiveness of their "scientific" approach to government. With as many as a quarter of the US workforce unemployed, the nation's existing system of private philanthropies buckled under the strain.[5] The scale of the crisis challenged all preconceived understandings of appropriate government and economic policy. Many Americans came to see the federal government as the only institution sufficiently powerful to relieve the economic distress and assist the needy.

Supporters of the New Deal included veterans of the Progressive Movement, who had long advocated a stronger regulatory and administrative bureaucracy. The crisis of the Great Depression strengthened these convictions and also made new converts. For example, Hugo Black, whom I got to know in Washington, had been a senator from Alabama during the Roosevelt years and became one of the New Deal's most prominent supporters. Initially seeing government primarily as a legal mechanism to correct wrongs, he had not supported activist federal economic policies. Yet, as the Depression deepened and breadlines grew longer, Black came to believe that government "had to take the initiative, and be a positive instrument to help people."[6] When the Supreme Court struck down major elements of New Deal legislation, Senator Black supported Roosevelt's plan to expand the size of the court and appoint friendly judges. Though this plan failed, Black was rewarded for his loyalty by being appointed to the court, where he served for more than three decades.

The New Deal also altered the federal-state balance of power by using the federal government to fund and reform state governments.[7] However, programs for specific groups of people initiated in Washington created difficulties for the states in administering federally structured benefits. Jurisdictional disputes were common, and I was faced with some of them at HEW. Adding to the burden on the states, federal standards that had been one policy for all changed to "categorical" or specific policies tailored to divide funds among an array of groups.[8] That also made the administration of the programs more difficult.

World War II and After

After the Great Depression and before the Second World War, the concept of democracy, particularly as it had to do with the role of citizens, changed. The frontier was gone, and the federal government moved more to the center of the political world. Citizenship was being redefined more by people's relationship to the government and less by their ties to one another. That had major implications for a possible *with* strategy.

Faith in a democratic citizenry had been tested in 1927 in the disagreement between philosopher John Dewey and journalist Walter Lippmann. Dewey, considered by many the country's preeminent philosopher, valued citizens because they were central to his understanding of self-government, which was rooted locally, much like Thomas Jefferson's conception of "little republics." It was Dewey who said, "Democracy must begin at home, and its home is the neighborly community."[9] His opponent, Lippmann, thought that the idea of a self-governing public was preposterous. He called the public a "phantom."[10] Lippmann's critique is often the basis for rejecting the idea of a public capable of working *with* the government, except perhaps as individual volunteers who are trained by professionals.

Lippmann notwithstanding, democracy became more popular during World War II, which was seen as a battle against fascism. That reaffirmed the value of self-rule. Allegiance to democracy was high, and citizens were important because of their service in the war effort, not just in the military but also in the work they (often women) did in the defense industry. Citizens were valued, too, for their willingness to buy government bonds to finance the war and for planting "victory gardens." My mother aided civil defense by serving as a lookout for enemy planes and ships when we were living on the Florida coast.

Citizens in the Post-War Era

The post-World War II era was marked by continued military conflict in Korea and the Cold War with the Soviet Union. The importance of citizens and their work, however, wasn't always recognized in the way it had been when the country was united in a worldwide struggle against Nazi aggression.

General Dwight David Eisenhower became President in 1953, followed by Kennedy, Johnson, and Nixon. The federal government continued to grow no matter which party was in power.[11] And some elements of a *with* strategy surfaced in the new programs that were added. During the Kennedy administration, the Area Redevelopment Act offered private businesses financial incentives to help impoverished areas of the country. And the Johnson administration's Community Action agencies opened the door a bit wider to citizens through a requirement for "maximum feasible participation," which I'll say more about in chapter VIII.

There were also obstacles to a fledgling *with* strategy. In the federal programs, the citizenry wasn't treated as a body of actors and producers as they had been during World War II. In the Community Action programs, "the people" were individuals receiving the benefits of federal funding. The beneficiaries didn't organize themselves so much as activists took on the mantle of being their representatives. Activists put pressure on local officials. And that prompted these officials to complain that the Community Action programs were bypassing elected municipal officeholders. This wasn't what President Johnson had intended. He wanted greater cooperation with local and state administrators in what he touted as "creative federalism."[12]

A MOVEMENT THAT CHANGED
THE POLITICAL CLIMATE

Washington politics was not the only politics that came to dominate the 1960s and 1970s. The most significant was the Civil Rights—originally the Human Rights—Movement, which was briefly discussed earlier. I want to say more about the role of citizens in the Movement and the Movement's debt to what happened long before it became political news.

The standard story of the Movement starts in 1954 when the Supreme Court ruled that segregation was unconstitutional. When the ruling was applied to public schools, it sparked resistance, first in the South and later in the inner cities of the North. The response to the resistance led to the 1963 March on Washington and the passage of the 1964 Civil Rights Act.

The lesser-known story of the Movement goes back quite far, certainly to the 19th-century abolitionist movement and the antidiscrimination efforts of the early 20th century. Citizens were very much actors joining forces. Long before 1954, African American communities, with some outside allies, had worked steadily to build a foundation for changes that would come a half-century later.[13] Alabama historian Wayne Flynt tells that story well:

> Increasingly, we are beginning to understand that the story was not about Martin Luther King Jr, and this story was not about the March on Washington. This story was about a thousand places where millions of people fought this battle in nameless, anonymous relationship with their hearts and their minds. And in a sense, the real story of the Civil Rights Movement, from a historical perspective, is now not about the generals and the captains, but rather it is the story of the privates and the thousands of small battles for freedom and justice that were fought and are still being fought, not in Washington but here in the boondocks, in places like Tuskegee.[14]

RIGHTS TALK

The political success of the Civil Rights Movement in Washington wasn't lost on those advocating rights for other groups, such as women and people with disabilities. Their causes were assisted by the proliferation of well-organized interest groups, which had been used successfully before by businesses, banks, and labor unions. These special interest groups now formed in almost every area in which the government was a major player. HEW's multiple divisions of health, education, welfare, and the Social Security Administration were prime targets. Although government agencies were supposed to be staffed by impartial professionals, studies have shown that they often became closely aligned with the sectors they oversaw.[15]

Taking a leaf from the Civil Rights Movement, many of these interest groups started making their cases in moral terms. And using the language of the Bill of Rights, they developed a very effective political strategy based on what is described by several scholars as "rights talk."[16] Questions about rights have been central to American democracy since the ratification of the Bill of Rights. But there was a special edge to the rhetoric. I heard good people who were so convinced that what they advocated was a *right* that they attacked those who disagreed with them as not merely being mistaken but immoral. (Maybe this was one of the sources of today's hyper-divisiveness.) Fortunately, the Ford administration and others in Washington remained pragmatic, yet "rights talk" was becoming increasingly evident.

Rights talk didn't necessarily recognize the distinction legal scholars make between natural rights and legal rights.[17] Regardless of race, gender, age, or other differences, all human beings are said to have inherent natural rights— to life, liberty, and the pursuit of happiness. We don't have these rights because someone bestowed them on us; we come into the world with them. That isn't true of legal rights. Legal rights are no less important, but they have to be bestowed on us by legislative actions, court orders, or another external authority.[18]

The distinction between types of rights breaks down when questions come up about whether certain conditions have to be met in order to exercise natural rights. I have a right to life, but I can't afford to pay for health care. So does that give me a right to Medicaid? That is, does the means needed to exercise a natural right take on the same authority as the natural right itself? When that kind of question arises, political talk becomes even more moralized and open deliberation suffers as advocates use their claims to moral authority to silence potential opposition. People with different positions on an issue or who just want to explore different options don't want to be charged with being morally despicable.

Decision-making also becomes quite difficult when legal rights conflict. Natural rights are almost absolute. They can't be denied except in extreme circumstances. We are free to speak, but we can't cry "Fire!" when there isn't one in a crowded theater. Are legal rights also absolute?[19] It became politically effective to argue that they were. However, if everything is treated as a right to government funding or services, how can decisions be made to allocate finite resources? Not even the richest governments have unlimited resources.

This dilemma becomes even more difficult to deal with if moral claims are held to be universal and fit all conditions—as well as to serve a supposedly homogenous class of beneficiaries. Beneficiaries, however, aren't all the same, nor are conditions. Philosopher Jürgen Habermas criticized such moral claims in his discussion of law and democracy.[20] Human rights may not be given standing in the law, he argued, as though they were preexistent moral facts merely needing to be written into legislation without any regard for other considerations. If there is no need for other considerations, then there is no place for the exercise of judgment by deliberating. A *with* strategy needs both institutional and public deliberation to find ways everyone can move forward, reasonably together, when full agreement on the best course of action isn't possible.

I didn't come to the conclusion that democratic deliberation is more important than human rights but that the two are interdependent. In the case of social welfare policy, for instance, the *way* policy is made, not just the policy itself, is crucial. Open, inclusive, and thorough deliberation must occur to make sound decisions. This is true in all branches of government, even the executive and administrative, which legislate through regulations. Regulations tend to treat uniformly the variety of ways people live their lives. That results in unintended and sometimes negative consequences for the very people who are supposed to benefit. Given this tendency, Habermas insisted, "The appropriate interpretation of needs and criteria [must] be a matter of public debate."[21]

These problems notwithstanding, the success of rights talk in the political arena about issues such as those in health, education, and welfare quickly led interest groups to see the advantage of recasting the benefits that they wanted as inviolable rights. It protected the funding they wanted from budget cuts. While budgets could be legitimately curtailed if revenue wasn't available, funding for absolute rights could not.

THE INFLUENCE OF PRESIDENTS

The prospects for a *with* strategy were influenced not only by interest groups and bureaucracies, but also by the role presidents, particularly Ford and Carter, played in the 1970s. Because both had lived through World War II, they had some appreciation for the necessity of action by citizens. But their ability to act was constrained by what happened to the office after the fall of President Nixon.

In 1972, when Nixon was running for a second term, a break-in at Democratic Party offices in the Watergate Hotel and a subsequent cover-up implicated White House staff and the President himself. To avoid impeachment, Nixon resigned in 1974 and Vice President Gerald Ford became president. Obviously, the scandal diminished public confidence in the highest level of the federal government, confidence that had already been tested by the costly war in Vietnam.

Having worked with him in and after my time in government, I knew Jerry Ford, as he liked to be called, fairly well. My impression of him was of a decent, dedicated, knowledgeable president who had his ego well in check. He did what he thought was best for the country, popular or not (as demonstrated by his widely criticized pardon of Nixon). Ford was heir to a heightened loss of trust in government as well as a faltering economy and growing federal deficit. He worried about an inflation of prices that would harm everyone. The country also faced rising unemployment, which could have led to a recession.[22] Fighting inflation by controlling federal spending was one of the Ford administration's highest priorities, although this was not all that was on the agenda. One of the President's initiatives called on citizens to be actors in a version of a *with* strategy, which was probably inspired by the appeals to citizens during World War II.

Unless the People Pitch In

In a 1974 address to a joint session of Congress, President Ford spoke about combating the inflation that was reaching unprecedented levels and increasing

FIGURE 9. *A form that pledged to "enlist as an Inflation Fighter and Energy Saver" could be mailed to the President and the sender would receive a WIN button. (Photos of the WIN form and button courtesy of the Gerald R. Ford Presidential Museum.)*

the federal deficit. "Unless every able American pitches in, Congress and I cannot do the job. Winning our fight against inflation and waste involves total mobilization of America's greatest resources—the brains, the skills, and the willpower of the American people."[23]

When inflation didn't end, a journalist asked Ford whether his program, Whip Inflation Now (WIN), should be dismantled (*Figure 9*). He responded, "No. I said in the State of the Union and I said in my Monday night speech that you have to have governmental action but you also have to have nongovernmental action. The day that we can totally rely on what the Government does to solve these problems, I think, just does not exist. The one is complementary to the other. I think the American people are basically oriented toward voluntary action, and they have done some good things. I don't think it is helpful to disparage what people do in a voluntary way."[24] I don't recall any efforts in grassroots organizing for WIN, but there was a call for people to support businesses that agreed not to raise prices.[25]

The WIN program was, in the words of Ford speechwriter Robert Hartmann, "the last noble experiment at volunteerism on a national scale."[26] The campaign was certainly in the spirit of *with* the people but people in the role of volunteers. Unfortunately, inflationary pressures overwhelmed WIN and other countermeasures.

Without a mandate from an election to generate political clout, Ford encountered opposition even from within his own party, in addition to that from the Democrats in Congress who saw their certain rise to power in the next presidential election. As President, Ford had to rely on vetoes to get any traction in Congress.

Ford's successor, Jimmy Carter, also faced a lack of congressional support in his own party. One reason was Carter's reluctance to provide traditional favors or patronage for fellow party members in Congress. Adding to Carter's challenges, Thomas Sugrue wrote, "[He] became one of the most prominent voices to call into question some of the fundamental verities of liberalism. Liberal social programs, he maintained, emanated from big, unresponsive government too far removed from its constituents." Yet Sugrue also saw that the marriage of bureaucracy and expertise that had been central to reform politics since the Progressive Era was now subject to criticism as elitist and undemocratic.[27] Sugrue's insight was by no means shared by Washington. Maybe Carter paid the price for being ahead of his time.

Early on, he recognized the public's loss of confidence. When he said, "Our people are losing . . . faith, not only in government itself but in the ability as citizens to serve as the ultimate rulers and shapers of our democracy."[28] The remedy for the loss of confidence in government, Carter believed, was better government. "What you see too often in Washington," he continued, "is a system of government that seems incapable of action." He blamed "well-funded special interests" for preventing the compromises necessary to address difficult problems. He called for a return to "the path of common purpose and the restoration of American values."[29] Carter especially worried that Americans were losing confidence in their fellow citizens. He regarded the Office of Citizen the highest office in the land.

Despite belonging to opposing parties, the Ford and Carter presidencies had similarities. I had gotten to know Jimmy Carter when we worked together on the Southern Growth Policies Board. I took over responsibility for completing the Board's first report, *The Future of the South*, in 1974 and chaired the Commission that produced the 1980-1981 report. I thought well of Carter and his administration. Having worked with both presidents, I was pleased to see the two grow to be good friends. They became models of bipartisanship.

PROSPECTS FOR A *WITH* STRATEGY

The government clearly needed citizens to meet demands similar to those that they had had to meet during World War II. Still, any idea that citizens should be complementary producers with government was stifled as the public lost more and more confidence in the government, and the government lost confidence in the people. This situation naturally disposed the government to be defensive rather than collaborative. Nonetheless, a *with* strategy, while not recognized as such, was implicit in what some political leaders said. President Ford stands out by recognizing that the government cannot be totally self-sufficient.

What was less recognized in Washington was that citizens, as actors, could reinforce the government in doing its work. And the contention that there are some things *only* citizens could do, other than voting, was not, by any stretch of the imagination, the usual wisdom—even when a president was speaking.

IMPRESSIONS OF WASHINGTON

Not having lived in Washington, I was often surprised by what insiders saw as unexceptional business-as-usual. Some of the surprises were disconcerting. Yet, on the whole, I developed a deep respect for the people I met there and for the intent of the federal government's programs. I wish I could name all the people I was indebted to in DC, but the list would be too long.

"O wad some Pow'r the giftie gie us, To see oursels as others see us!"

This heading is a line from Scottish poet Robert Burns.[30] I never thought that I was sent to save Washington. I was an outsider, and I was happy to be seen as from "the provinces."[31] I thought that perspective could be put to good use. I wanted to share what I had seen with what I hoped would be new friends in the Capitol. I also wanted to understand Washington's way of seeing the country.

Despite my outsider status, I did have a connection with HEW that dated back to its creation in 1953 when I was 18. During that summer, I was one of about a hundred high school juniors given a week's stay in Washington by the American Legion. Those were the heydays of Senator Joseph McCarthy and his anti-Communist crusade. One of many briefings we heard was by a young Nelson Rockefeller, later to become President Ford's Vice President. He was then Undersecretary of the newly created Department of Health, Education, and Welfare. I am sorry to say that witnessing the birth of this new department didn't make as much of an impression as the hullabaloo surrounding Senator McCarthy. Ranting against people in government, he claimed they were subversives. His attacks didn't appeal to me. Had I known what I would be doing 22 years later, I would have paid more attention to Rockefeller's briefing at HEW.

My other experiences in Washington included a visit to the White House in 1974. I was asked to consider taking the position of director of the new Bicentennial Commission. That wasn't for me; I was deeply committed to what I was trying to do in my home state, Alabama. I did accept a place on the Commission. Later, I met President Ford in Washington when the University of Alabama was named the country's first Bicentennial university.

The reaction to my being nominated for HEW Secretary shows how Washington worked. Partisanship was robust. As I mentioned earlier, and as I told President Ford, I am a moderate independent. Today, most Republicans think I am a Democrat, and most Democrats think I am a Republican. That's fine with me.

When it was announced that the President had personally selected someone who was unknown in Washington, warning lights flashed on his right flank. Opposition to my appointment came from conservatives who wanted to keep the Department out of the hands of big-spending liberals. A publication called *Human Events* had run an article charging that I was a "trendy liberal."[32] Fortunately, the largely conservative House delegation from Alabama gave my nomination unqualified support. Still, other conservatives grumbled that the President was buying a pig in a poke and warned that a member of Rockefeller's staff, Jack Veneman, who had been a former Undersecretary of HEW under Nixon, would actually run the Department from the Domestic Council.[33] I may have met Veneman once, but I never had any sense that he was influencing either the Department or my relations with the White House.

Given the opposition from the Right, you might think that I would have had the support of the Left, but that wasn't the case. At our first meeting, Senator Jacob Javits, a liberal Republican from New York, told me that no one from Alabama had ever done anything for HEW. I wondered how he could have overlooked Senator Lister Hill from Alabama, who had authored a good deal of the federal legislation on education and health. In the eyes of some, I was from the same state as George Wallace, and that was probably all anyone needed to know. Even though Wallace and I had taken opposing positions on integration and freedom of speech at the University of Alabama, he had endorsed my nomination. I imagine that confirmed the liberals' worst fears.

Despite the partisan alignment in Washington, I had some advantages as a noncombatant; I hadn't picked up enemies in the wars on social policy. And most news organizations around the country gave me the benefit of the doubt. There were exceptions, however. A citizen from my state warned the President that he was making a great mistake because I had shown a gross lack of administrative leadership at the University. She was incensed because "perverts and a notorious porno queen" had been on campus.[34] Perhaps she was referring to an actress in a controversial movie whom students had invited to campus as part of a speaking tour.

Family, Friends, and Allies

Going to Washington was more than a political experience for me; it was a family affair. And we saw the way Washington worked from the point of view of a family. My wife, Mary, and I still recall with fondness the people we got to know—many of whom became lifelong friends. With our daughters, Lee Ann and Lucy, we left the University of Alabama after the August 1975 commencement and took up residence in a three-bedroom split-level house in McLean, Virginia. Our friends Paul and Mary Harmon Bryant, the University football coach and his wife, worried that Washington wasn't suitable for our girls and offered to keep them while I was on leave. We were touched by their gesture but declined.

Alabamians on both sides of the aisle in Washington welcomed us warmly, which influenced the way I saw the government. These included Doug and Libby Cater from the Johnson administration. Also, my cousin Dale Bumpers, Democratic governor of Arkansas recently elected to the Senate, was in town, and we had an opportunity to build closer ties with him and his wife, Betty.

Mary was particularly fond of Betty Ford, who talked about her own experience in moving to Washington and raising children when their father's work threatened to absorb every minute of every day. Betty was still undergoing chemotherapy for breast cancer at the time, which made her genial manner and concern for others all the more remarkable. We were also fortunate to find members of the Ford administration like Carla and Rod Hills who became good friends. They dispelled any reservations we might have had about the "Washington crowd."

Colleagues and Students

I was also very fortunate to have a number of faculty, staff, and students from the University of Alabama who were willing to join me at HEW. They, too, influenced how I saw Washington, some adding the perspective of a younger generation. The list of those who made the journey is far too long to put here, but I will mention one person who, sadly, died several years ago. He was Floyd Mann, a hero of the Civil Rights Movement (*Figure 10*). He rescued John Lewis, later a member of Congress, from a mob that attacked a group of Freedom Riders in Alabama. Floyd helped me with congressional relations.

I especially wanted to keep my ties with students. Nothing in academe had been more rewarding than teaching, both in the course I offered each fall and through an internship program that brought undergraduates into the University's administration. A number of these young people came to Washington in 1976 as interns in HEW.[35] Some I had gotten to know well when they participated in sit-ins in the University president's office. These students were very taken with the company they kept in DC—literally

FIGURE 10. *Col. Floyd Mann (right) speaks with a student at the University of Alabama. Mann is best known for his role in protecting Freedom Riders, including John Lewis, under attack at a bus station in Birmingham, AL, in 1961. Mann was Director of the Alabama Department of Public Safety at the time. He served as an Assistant at HEW during David Mathews' tenure as Secretary. (Photo courtesy of the University of Alabama Libraries Special Collection.)*

bumping into Henry Kissinger; seeing John Warner off to meet his wife, Elizabeth Taylor; and using the tickets to the President's box at the Kennedy Center. But it was watching a well-known member of Congress pick his teeth with a matchbox cover that seemed to give them the greatest sense of being "on the inside."

I also found allies in HEW. I will always be indebted to the departmental staff who came to the informal "brown bag" lunches to share their views on what the Department should be doing. Also, the real powers in Washington, as everybody knows, are the secretaries and administrative assistants; I was happy to have some very able ones (*Figure 11*). And I was particularly fortunate to have the support of Marjorie Lynch, whom I asked to be my

FIGURE 11. *Secretary with Special Assistants. Front Row: Alan Reich, Joffre Whisenton, Roger Egeberg, Robert McKenzie, Pat Harbour, Tom Lias. Back Row: Sandy Winston, Bill Jones, David Mathews, Jim Wilder, Mike Licata, David Roe, Stan Murphy, Larry Wyatt. (From David Mathews' photo collection at the Kettering Foundation. Date and photographer unknown.)*

Undersecretary. From the state of Washington, Marge had won five elections to the legislature, and she chaired her state's Committee on Higher Education.[36] She was the second-highest ranking female official in the Ford administration. (Carla Hills, Secretary of Housing and Urban Development, was the highest.)

A Mixed Welcome

Despite a warm personal reception from friends living in the capital, the arrival of "outsiders" prompted anxiety in Washington as it always does. Fewer than 60 days after my swearing-in, an article appeared in the *National Journal* describing the group I brought with me to HEW as "compromisers" (not such a good thing to be) rather than "activists" (what we were supposed to be).[37][38] The language was telling, especially the verbs. We were going to "loosen" the Department's regulatory structures and "ease" its enforcement authority. Social programs were going to be secondary to national defense priorities. Such policies, the article warned, "threatened" to create a high-level controversy. The Department "feared" the possibility of accommodation with state and local agencies. Organized lobbying groups had cause to "worry" that their established patterns of dealing with HEW would be disturbed. I was said to have "shunned" the bureaucracy by "surrounding" myself with others who had no previous experience with government. That was particularly interesting since I actually kept most of the senior officials as assistant secretaries. Curiously, it was also alleged that I was turning the Department over to these veterans. Those reactions are a good indication of what the political environment was like.

Making matters worse, according to the *Journal*, I had named Marge Lynch in a "surprise move," instead of elevating someone on the staff with a deep working knowledge of the Department, "the kind of person who usually occupied the post of undersecretary."

One of my strongest impressions from working in the federal government was the competence of the professionals in the bureaucracy and their dedication to doing what they thought was best for the country. When I was in Washington, I wish I had said more to be clear about that because I did question bureaucratic routines on democratic grounds. But I was talking about the system of government, not the people in it. My making that distinction clearer might have made it easier for officials to see the difference between friendly critics and hostile, antigovernment opponents. Even the bureaucrats in HEW were sometimes frustrated by the bureaucracy.

Cast in a Play Already Written

Anyone in the Department or in Congress who wasn't already concerned about the new HEW administration surely had reason to be after the *Journal* article appeared. It created a stereotype with characterizations that took on a life of their own. That was, and perhaps still is, very much the way Washington works. My friend Sheldon Hackney, who later headed the National

Endowment for the Humanities during the Clinton administration, explained what it was like to become "typecast" in Washington. He said watching himself being portrayed in the media was an out-of-body experience that only became less troubling when a former senator told him, "It is not about you."[39] In the capital, Sheldon's friend told him, there are any number of dramas being played out, and newcomers are brought into them to fit a particular story line, which had already been written. One of the dramas I saw immediately was a story of liberals fighting conservatives; the characters would be labeled "trendy" if they were liberals or "reactionary" if they were conservatives. Another favorite Washington narrative was about how the in-the-know insiders would wield power over the haplessly naïve and impractical idealists or "lightweights."

Although the *Journal* piece was based on the narrative about politics that had come to dominate Washington in the 1970s, it wasn't totally inaccurate. In fact, it gave a pretty good account of my agenda. My colleagues and I *were* "marching to the beat of a different drummer." We were certainly interested in change and wanted to reexamine basic assumptions about HEW's mission. Someone told the *Journal* that I was having agency heads sign their own letters rather than putting them out under my name. That was true. Congress and everyone else in the country knew that cabinet secretaries didn't really write all of their official letters—but no one knew who did. The article also reported, correctly, that I held the heads of the three main divisions—all seasoned insiders—accountable for the day-to-day details. The *Journal* went on to say that I was willing, even eager, to discuss issues that alienated the Department from outsiders. That was especially true.

Parts of the article threw me into other narratives common to Washington: stories of cabinet officers battling White House staff. Early on, I persuaded President Ford to reverse a decision to end health manpower grants to schools of medicine, dentistry, and osteopathy. I argued that the funding should be continued, provided the schools were willing to establish programs to increase the supply of health professionals in locations where they were badly needed—inner cities and rural areas.[40] The Domestic Council in the White House supported that position, and the President agreed not to phase out the grants.[41] There was no battle.

Palace Politics

I always considered fellow Alabamian Jim Cannon, head of the Domestic Council in the White House, a friend in court, but I was too independent to suit some of the veteran White House staff from the Nixon era. In fact, one insider leaked to the press that the staff there was unhappy because I was acting like I was "my own man." President Ford didn't seem to have any problem with that.

What is called "palace politics" in Washington wasn't my game. There were numerous policy issues like health manpower on the Department's agenda, and they were also typically framed as contests between categorically opposed policy positions, which overstated the differences. Controlling spending versus initiating new programs was another favorite theme. For example, when we continued the health manpower grants, it was interpreted as a signal that the Ford administration was willing to support initiatives that didn't require new taxes. That was true. Even though President Ford was opposed to increasing the deficit, I found him quite open to initiatives that fell reasonably close to existing spending levels.

My main focus was on the troubled relationship between the government and the people. And measures to respond usually didn't require new funding. Admittedly, what I was trying to do in Washington was difficult to get across. At best, I was characterized as "eccentric." Meg Greenfield, a *Newsweek* columnist, however, was willing to see the possibility that my colleagues and I weren't anarchists or antigovernment crusaders. A seasoned journalist, she reported what my critics in the White House, on the Hill, and in the interest groups were saying. But Meg also recognized that we were living in a time of growing public discontent with Washington and that trying to make HEW "more rational and humane" from the perspective of citizens might have some merit. She found a high-level HEW official (not named) who described me as "fascinating and infuriating" because my colleagues and I were constantly asking questions about the legitimacy of criticisms of the Department and the harm to intended beneficiaries that would result from acting on federal threats to cut off funds.[42] Meg was sure we would retreat from our "unorthodoxy" in a few months, but when we didn't, she was open to the idea that our efforts to serve as intermediaries between the public and the government might be useful at the end of an administration when there was no new money for new programs and the Congress and White House were at odds.

WHAT'S NEXT?

The next discussion in the book will move from this account of the way Washington worked to a closer look at HEW—its internal politics and the political influence of all the interest groups it affected. The Department gave me a front row seat to observe some of democracy's most formidable challenges. It was at HEW that I began to see the need for what would later be called a *with* strategy.

While troubled by some of what I saw in Washington, I certainly didn't come away with the feeling that the federal government was "bad." However, I saw that, in trying to solve one problem, the government often, and perhaps inescapably, exacerbates others. In serving one interest, it neglects another. In being fair to one group, it can be unfair to another. To me, these unintended consequences call for a broader and deeper relationship with the public than can come from responding to one pressure or crisis after another. That is one of the things a *with* strategy offers. How that strategy can fit into a department like HEW is a key question. Every department develops its own culture and way of working. That has to be taken into consideration in proposing a new strategy. I'll begin to do that in chapter VI.[43]

NOTES

1.   A Kettering Foundation memo by Laura Carlson, October 29, 2012, examined the use of this phrase by presidents. Carlson notes that it "has been a common refrain, with shifting meaning, among presidents and presidential candidates, Republicans, Democrats, and Independents alike." The earliest reference she found was by Woodrow Wilson in *The New Freedom: A Call for the Emancipation of the Generous Energies of a People* (New York: Doubleday, Page & Co., 1913). Along with Gerald Ford, Presidents Richard Nixon, Ronald Reagan, Jimmy Carter, Bill Clinton, and George W. Bush have also used the phrase, or variations of it.

2. Even though local levels of government might be more open to citizens, the *with* strategy being proposed here goes beyond accessibility. It recognizes the need for all levels of government to relate to citizens working *with* citizens.

3. Daniel J. Boorstin, *The Genius of American Politics* (Chicago: University of Chicago Press, 1953).

4. Alan Wolfe, *One Nation After All: What Middle-Class Americans Really Think about God, Country, Family, Racism, Welfare, Immigration, Homosexuality, Work, The Right, The Left, and Each Other* (New York: Viking Penguin, 1998).

5. Walter I. Trattner, *From Poor Law to Welfare State: A History of Social Welfare in America,* 6th ed. (New York: The Free Press, 1999), 273.

6. Roger K. Newman, *Hugo Black: A Biography* (New York: Pantheon Books, 1994), 154.

7. Trattner, *From Poor Law to Welfare State,* 289-290. Trattner states that the Social Security Act of 1935 "set up a federal-state system of Unemployment Insurance designed to encourage states to carry the administrative burden."

8. Robert Wiebe observed, "In the 19th century, democracy measured public policy against a universalist standard, an ideal of one . . . policy for all. . . . The model of the mid-20th century was the diametric opposite." Robert H. Wiebe, *Self-Rule: A Cultural History of American Democracy* (Chicago: University of Chicago Press, 1995), 207.

9. John Dewey, *The Public and Its Problems* (Athens, OH: Swallow Press, 1927/1954), 213.

10. Walter Lippmann, *The Phantom Public* (New York: Macmillan, 1927).

11. Gareth Davies, *See Government Grow: Education Politics from Johnson to Reagan* (Lawrence, KS: University Press of Kansas, 2007).

12. Lyndon B. Johnson, "Memorandum on the Need for 'Creative Federalism' through Cooperation with State and Local Officials," November 11, 1966. Online by Gerhard Peters and John T. Woolley, The American Presidency Project, https://www.presidency.ucsb.edu/documents/memorandum-the-need-for-creative-federalism-through-cooperation-with-state-and-local.

13. The role of women in this Movement has been emphasized recently in such works as Lynne Olson, *Freedom's Daughters: The Unsung Heroines of the Civil Rights Movement from 1830-1970* (New York: Scribner, 2001) and Martha S. Jones, *Vanguard: How Black Women Broke Barriers, Won the Vote, and Insisted on Equality for All* (New York: Basic Books, 2020).

14. Wayne Flynt, Speech at the 50th Anniversary of Tuskegee Public High School Integration, Tuskegee Human and Civil Rights Multicultural Center, Tuskegee, Alabama, August 24, 2013, https://www.c-span.org/video/?314498-1/50th-anniversary-tuskegee-public-high-school-integration. It is only recently that other historians have recognized that the foundation for the Movement was laid much earlier. One of these recent histories is aptly titled *Local People.* John Dittmer, *Local People:*

The Struggle for Civil Rights in Mississippi (Urbana, IL: University of Illinois Press, 1994). This book documents the work citizens did long before the national movement. I knew this history well thanks to my experiences in Tuskegee, Alabama, where I became familiar with Booker T. Washington's Tuskegee College, which was the epicenter for a Civil Rights Movement that began in the 1870s. See Robert J. Norrell, *Up from History: The Life of Booker T. Washington* (Cambridge, MA: Belknap Press, 2009). Also, Robert J. Norrell, *Reaping the Whirlwind: The Civil Rights Movement in Tuskegee* (New York: Alfred A. Knopf, 1985).

15. James Morone, *The Democratic Wish: Popular Participation and the Limits of American Government*, rev. ed. (New Haven, CT: Yale University Press, 1998), 132; Matthew A. Crenson and Benjamin Ginsberg, *Downsizing Democracy: How America Sidelined Its Citizens and Privatized Its Public* (Baltimore: Johns Hopkins University Press, 2002), 122-123.

16. Haskell, Thomas L., "The Curious Persistence of Rights Talk in the 'Age of Interpretation,'" *Journal of American History* 74, no. 3 (December 1987): 984-1012; Neal Milner, "The Denigration of Rights and the Persistence of Rights Talk: A Cultural Portrait," *Law & Social Inquiry* 14, no. 4 (Autumn 1989): 631-675; Mary Ann Glendon, *Rights Talk: The Impoverishment of Political Discourse* (New York: The Free Press, 1991).

17. Rights are discussed at length in learned texts like Jeremy Waldron, ed., *Theories of Rights* (Oxford: Oxford University Press, 1984).

18. When I was being confirmed by the Senate as HEW Secretary, I was asked why I thought of education as a right. Because people are learning beings, I could have said that there is a natural right to education. But the holder of the right to learn is not so much an individual as it is the public or "The People" collectively. The best response to the question would have been that a democratic government has an obligation to educate citizens because such a citizenry is essential to maintaining a democracy. The citizenry collectively holds this "right."

19. Scholars recognize this question as a problem in moral theory. L.W. Sumner, *The Moral Foundation of Rights* (Oxford: Clarendon Press, 1987).

20. Jürgen Habermas, "On the Internal Relation between the Rule of Law and Democracy," in *The Inclusion of the Other: Studies in Political Theory*, eds. Ciaran Cronin and Pablo De Greif (Cambridge, MA: MIT Press 1998), 260 (English translation in 1996).

21. Habermas, "On the Internal Relation," 263.

22. Franklin Tugwell, *The Energy Crisis and the American Political Economy: Politics and Markets in the Management of Natural Resources* (Stanford, CA: Stanford University Press, 1988), 97.

23. Gerald R. Ford: "Address to a Joint Session of the Congress on the Economy," October 8, 1974. Online by Gerhard Peters and John T. Woolley, The American

Presidency Project, https://www.presidency.ucsb.edu/documents/address-joint-session-the-congress-the-economy. As originally conceived, the Whip Inflation Now (WIN) program would allow companies or unions who agreed to hold prices and wages at current levels to advertise their status as certified inflation fighters. Ford hoped that citizens would then voluntarily choose to patronize businesses and buy goods that bore this label, thus limiting inflation through public action.

24. Gerald R. Ford, "Exchange of Remarks during a Briefing for Economic Writers," January 29, 1975. Online by Gerhard Peters and John T. Woolley, The American Presidency Project, https://www.presidency.ucsb.edu/documents/exchange-remarks-during-briefing-for-economic-writers. Also see Yanek Mieczkowski, *Gerald Ford and the Challenges of the 1970s* (Lexington: University Press of Kentucky, 2005), 141-142.

25. Ford's program was also reminiscent of the Blue Eagle campaign instituted by Franklin Roosevelt during the Great Depression.

26. Robert T. Hartmann, *Palace Politics: An Inside Account of the Ford Years* (New York: McGraw-Hill, 1980), 296.

27. Thomas Sugrue, "Carter's Urban Policy Crisis," in *The Carter Presidency: Policy Choices in the Post-New Deal Era*, ed. Gary Fink and Hugh Davis Graham (Lawrence: University Press of Kansas, 1998), 139.

28. Jimmy Carter, "Energy and National Goals: Address to the Nation," July 15, 1979, https://www.jimmycarterlibrary.gov/assets/documents/speeches/energy-crisis.phtml.

29. Steven H. Hochman, Assistant to President Carter and Director of Research, The Carter Center, e-mail message to author, June 18, 2019.

30. Robert Burns, "To a Louse, On Seeing One on a Lady's Bonnet at Church," 1786, https://www.scottishpoetrylibrary.org.uk/poem/louse-seeing-one-ladys-bonnet-church/. Translation available at http://www.robertburnsfederation.com/poems/translations/552.htm.

31. My identity as an outsider was evident in the list of the obvious candidates for the HEW job. I certainly didn't apply for it and had no intention of making a career in Washington. Before filling the HEW post, President Ford received a good deal of advice. In May of 1975, Charles Bartlett reviewed the likely choices in the *Washington Star*—Elliot Richardson, Melvin Laird, and Jack Veneman. They would have been good Secretaries. Charles Bartlett, "Finding the Right Chief for HEW," *Washington Star*, May 23, 1975.

32. "Have Conservatives OKed Liberal for HEW?" *Human Events* 35 (June 28, 1975): 3.

33. "Will Liberals Wrap Control of HEW?" *Human Events* 35 (July 5, 1975).

34. "Your Opinion," *Decatur Daily,* June 27, 1975.

35. The internship program had been established at the University's New College in 1974 under Dean Neal Berte and Assistant Dean Bernie Sloan. Those coming to

Washington included John Bivens, Steve Berryman, Johnny Johns, Ed O'Neil, John Plunk, John Saxon, and Dale Wallace Jr. They joined Sandy Sanford Gunter from Auburn who was already at HEW.

36. James Free, "Dr. Mathews's 'Right Hand' Thinks He's Tops," *Birmingham News* (n.d.), Sunday Notebook Section.

37. John K. Iglehart, "HEW Report, Mathews Envisions Department as Compromiser, Not Activist," *National Journal* (October 18, 1975): 1445-1449.

38. A somewhat different interpretation of the new Secretary appeared in the July 5, 1975, issue of the *National Observer* (Robert W. Merry, "New 'Snake Pit' Boss: Ford Reaches South, Picks a College President for HEW," 3). Such stories typecast me as a newcomer, and almost everything in the media thereafter is written with reference to the themes of the initial articles. In the *Observer* piece, youth, lack of experience in Washington, and a political orientation were counter-posed with a characterization of department bureaucrats as liberal, tough-minded, turf conscious, and all powerful. These "framings" usually controlled the narrative line of future stories.

39. Sheldon Hackney, *The Politics of Presidential Appointment: A Memoir of the Culture War* (Montgomery, AL: NewSouth Books, 2002), 126.

40. Nancy Hicks, "Mathews Saves Program of Aid to Medical Schools," *Birmingham Post-Herald*, October 7, 1975.

41. Iglehart, "HEW Report," 1445-1449.

42. Meg Greenfield, "Jerry Brown—East," *Newsweek*, January 19, 1976, 84.

43. For details on issues in HEW or partisan infighting over policies between Republicans and Democrats or liberals and conservatives, other books are better sources. For accounts of HEW history up to the 1980s, I suggest my successor, Joseph A. Califano Jr.'s, *Governing America: An Insider's Report from the White House and the Cabinet* (New York: Simon and Schuster, 1981); Elliot Richardson, *The Creative Balance: Government, Politics, and the Individual in America's Third Century* (New York: Holt, Rhinehart and Winston, 1976); and Rufus E. Miles, *The Department of Health, Education, and Welfare* (New York: Praeger Publishers, 1974).

CHAPTER VI

WELCOME TO THE UNITED STATES DEPARTMENT OF HEALTH, EDUCATION, AND WELFARE (HEW)

This chapter will look inside the workings of the federal government. A *with* strategy has to be carried out with a recognition of what goes on in large bureaucracies day to day, and it must find its fit within that reality. Why would governing institutions make the effort? I think it is because working *with* the people as complementary producers serves the self-interests of these institutions, and it can help their professionals become more effective. A *with* strategy can be helpful because it brings new, unique resources to support the work of institutions. It can also better align their work with the work of citizens, which can assist people in making the difference they want to make. A *with* strategy is based on reciprocity between an active citizenry and their governing institutions.

The focus here will be on where there have been opportunities for collaboration and the conditions that favor an alignment. When I say "conditions," I'm thinking about something like what meteorologists say—that conditions favor a break in the rain and the return of sunny days.

If there is to be a better alignment, it will have a great deal to do with the conditions or environment within an agency or cabinet department like HEW. That environment may or may not be conducive to collaboration *with* those outside a governing institution.

A TOUR OF HEW

When I worked at HEW, it was one of the largest of all the federal departments. Formed by President Eisenhower in 1953, this department saw its budget increase from $5.4 to $200 billion by 1980, while the staff expanded from 35,000 to more than 150,000—not to mention a million state and local government administrators, plus an army of private contractors employed with departmental funds.[1] All these people were needed because the Department, which originally housed 50 programs, had grown to more than 380. Nearly every American was affected by HEW.

Given the Department's impact, interest groups were everywhere around HEW and in Congress, where 40 committees and subcommittees had oversight.[2] In fact, pressure groups from various service professions had played a major role in creating the Department. Its separate divisions of health, education, and welfare were the result of interest groups demanding their own agencies.[3]

Because of its broad scope and the sensitivity of its work, disputes in HEW were routine. The Department was party to so many lawsuits that its legal staff dwarfed that of most law firms. HEW also had an extensive internal system of administrative courts for adjudicating a mountain of disputes. This created a litigious environment—the opposite of the collaborative environment needed for a *with* strategy.

I've already described my own views on the role of government in a democracy, which translated into the agenda I set as Secretary. That agenda was rooted in my respect for the Department yet was influenced by my conviction that the lack of public confidence in the government had to be recognized and addressed. I saw my job as representing the people of the country to the government, as well as representing the government to the people.[4]

The public's dissatisfaction with the government didn't have as much to do with the quality of the services the Department provided as it did with the *way* the government used its power. Americans liked most HEW programs, although there were concerns about their scope and intrusion into private life. Many of the complaints were about the processes the government used in its work and the way they affected people's lives. Critics charged the government with being insensitive to their realities and lacking in common sense, as well as being inflexible and often adversarial. If the Department were to administer humane programs, surely it had to do it humanely, or so I reasoned. I didn't buy into the operating assumption that the people "out there" were often up to no good, that they had to be coerced into doing what was right and then monitored closely to be sure they did what they should be doing.[5]

The way HEW used its power could also be at odds with democratic norms that called for the separation of power into executive, legislative, and judicial divisions. Rather than diffusing power, it was concentrated in the Department, which played executive, legislative, and judicial roles. Perhaps this combining of functions may be unavoidable, given the nature of the tasks the executive agencies had to perform. From the public's point of view, however, a department that acted as both judge and jury on its own activities was troubling.

HEW's Self-Image

The Department's image of itself in 1975 had been shaped by earlier eras of activist central government and social reform. Clearly, the challenges of the Great Depression and World War II impressed people with the need for a strong, federal government. HEW also was the governmental incarnation of the humane instincts of the American people. The power of these instincts was evident in reform movements dating back to the decades between 1830 and 1860 and, before then, in the social ideas of colonists like Roger Williams. Williams and other reformers were convinced that the lot of humankind could be improved by tapping into the energies of a free people. Much of that faith was in the perfectibility of social institutions. However, earlier reformers didn't turn first to government. Their primary strategy for change was to reach the hearts and minds of their fellow citizens.

In the 1970s, as noted, faith in government, particularly HEW, was eroding as citizens lost confidence in Washington. The Department became everyone's favorite whipping boy. Critics from the right like George Wallace were one thing. But Richard Nixon, who began with the hope that he could redirect the programs of the Great Society, soon became a much more formidable critic. President Ford, in contrast, never indicated that he shared this animosity and, while generally opposed to increases in spending, never gave me reason to believe he wanted to abolish the Department. Personally, I admired HEW's concern for our most vulnerable citizens.

Old Assumptions in a New Reality

Because HEW's self-image and underlying philosophy dictated both its mission and its practice, the assumptions in that philosophy were pivotal. I decided to concentrate on them because the political environment in which the Department had to operate in the 1970s was quite different from the one in which these assumptions originated (*Figure 12*). One of the most problematic was equating interest groups with the public. While the interest groups were powerful in Washington, they didn't represent the citizenry that was losing confidence in government. This loss of public trust was one of the overarching issues I believed the Department had to address. And addressing these issues is the first step to recognizing the value of a *with* strategy.

As HEW Secretary in the Johnson administration, John Gardner had "managed" HEW by posing overarching questions, so there was some precedent for what I would attempt to do. The challenge was that, although the Department's self-image influenced what it did, the assumptions on which that image was based were rarely discussed—only program details were. To get at these underlying assumptions, I wanted to dig into what was unstated or implied in the programs. Addressing these fundamental problems behind the more obvious symptoms of the problems appeared to departmental veterans as philosophical rather than practical. But my objective was better practice,

FIGURE 12. *In the 1970s, the headquarters of the Department of Health, Education, and Welfare moved to the Hubert H. Humphrey Building, designed by architect Marcel Breuer and located at the foot of Capitol Hill. (Photograph in the Carol M. Highsmith Archive, Library of Congress, Prints and Photographs Division.)*

not better philosophy. I found congenial company for this approach to the Department at the White House in informal, Saturday morning sessions that Bill Baroody organized for the President and cabinet members. These were occasions for thinking about basic issues in government.

Of all the assumptions undergirding the Department's programs, perhaps the most influential was a notion from Franklin Delano Roosevelt's era that the entire fiscal power of government, including the power of deficit financing, should be used to combat society's ills, particularly to protect citizens from the negative effects of a highly competitive economic system.[6] The Department's self-image was equally influenced by the Civil Rights Movement. HEW came to see itself, and to be seen by others, as a quasi Justice Department, at least as far as enforcing laws on discrimination was concerned. The image was no illusion. While HEW didn't have any responsibilities for desegregation in the 1960s, by the 1970s, it had hundreds of mandates.

Another formative influence shaping the Department originated in the consumer revolution, as evident in the tremendous growth of the Food and Drug Administration (FDA). That agency quadrupled in size in its first nine years and kept on growing.[7] This revolution did more, however, than affect the size of HEW. Perhaps unintentionally, it may have given some the impression that citizens were the customers rather than the owners of the government. Of course, customers are purchasers of goods, consumers, who sometimes need protection from the manufacturers of those goods. But citizens are more than just consumers.

As I've emphasized, the citizenry is sovereign in a democracy. And sovereigns exercise their powers by the things they do. Zeus, the king of the Greek gods, hurled bolts of lightning. In a democracy, citizens exercise power by producing public goods. Those are more useful than lightning bolts. While the Department had to protect people, I didn't think it should treat citizens just as consumers. This conviction would eventually lead me to consider the possibilities of treating citizens as complementary producers of health, education, and welfare. That understanding of citizenship became central to a *with* strategy.

The Department's concept of itself also drew heavily from its earlier incarnation as an agency of benevolence charged to take care of the "unfortunate." That, too, influenced how citizens were seen, which was more as beneficiaries than producers. Providing benefits was much of the work done by the immediate predecessor to HEW, the Federal Security Agency (FSA).[8] The Great Depression increased the number of those needing assistance, and the government responded by providing relief in the form of direct payments. Other federal programs were more "workfare" than welfare—the Civilian Conservation Corps (CCC) is an example. My father, who was a CCC official in Auburn, Alabama, would have been insulted by the suggestion that any of the young men working for him were on welfare.[9]

Manageability and Collaboration

A department providing "welfare," by whatever name, would have been challenged enough, but the modern HEW had to do much more. It had to protect people's health, support public education, defend consumers, and develop regulations to carry out a multitude of laws.[10] HEW wasn't alone. When it was necessary to deal with the misuse of funds or when antidiscrimination laws were violated, HEW relied on the US Department of Justice. But even when other departments helped, HEW had acquired so many responsibilities by the time of the Johnson administration that it raised a question of whether it was possible to manage such a vast and disparate array of programs.[11]

HEW Secretary John Gardner, on the other hand, saw opportunities where others saw chaos. He was quick to realize that the scope of the Department, while creating problems of manageability, opened up significant possibilities for collaboration within the Department.[12] And a spirit of collaboration is one of the conditions favorable to actual collaboration *with* the citizenry outside.

DAILY ROUTINES

The most frequent question I've gotten since I left office is, "What was it like day to day?" This seemingly mundane "busy work" provided intriguing insights. Naturally, the way I went about my work was influenced by my years as a university administrator. A federal department, with its separate and independent divisions, has some similarity to a large university, which has separate and independent colleges. Both institutions are filled with highly trained professionals and research scientists, making it necessary to evaluate expert advice from microbiologists, psychologists, accountants, physicians, sociologists, and so on. Yet experts seldom agree. So decision-making requires not only testing the reliability of the data but also examining the assumptions being made and, most of all, considering the intangibles that can't be determined by evidence—the things people consider most valuable. This experience began to open my eyes to the possibility that decision-making, from the public's perspective, might augment government decision-making, although, at this point, I hadn't yet recognized the difference between a deliberative citizenry and the public in general.[13]

Aligning Democratic Values with Bureaucratic Necessities

When I arrived, many of the disputes on HEW's agenda had been there for some time, not because past secretaries hadn't acted, but because there were long-term, ongoing conflicts like those in the relationship between the federal and state governments. Some of the intergovernmental disagreements were substantive, others less so. But even those that seemed mundane influenced the tenor of the relationships among levels of governments. I wanted to improve those relationships if I could, always with an eye on the interests of democracy and citizens.

I recall a federal-state dispute over the wording in announcements of entitlements under Title XX of the Social Security Act. The benefits, ranging from day care for children to social services for the elderly, were financed under a revenue-sharing program in which the federal government paid 75 percent of the cost and the states the remainder. In August 1975, the Department was about to enter a protracted court battle with state agencies over these notices, a battle that could have resulted in withholding millions of dollars from citizens. I thought this might be a situation where federal-state collaboration might be possible.

In one of those cases, under federal law, state agencies had to publish their plans for use of the Title XX funds and receive comments. HEW was only to monitor the process. The catch was that the legislation contained federal "statutory directions," which the states had to follow. The Department also had to ensure that there were no procedural errors. A dispute with California erupted in 1975 when the state objected to paying $65,000 to re-advertise its plan because of five technical defects.[14] One was a typographical error in the listing of program funds. Another was the absence of what the federal authorities considered sufficient detail in descriptions of homemaker services and the role of volunteers.

Although other governors had acquiesced to HEW's demand to re-publicize their plans, California's governor, Jerry Brown, refused. His state filed suit to stop the federal government from withholding benefits. In response, I asked Assistant Secretary Bill Morrill and Joe Maldonado in the Department's regional office to try to negotiate a mutually satisfactory settlement. They did. Rather than spending $65,000 on newspaper advertisements, California agreed to identify the defects in a press release and to send notices to interested parties.[15] This didn't prove to be an opportunity for federal-state collaboration, but it didn't end in a legal battle.

I tell that story here because it shows that governments do benefit from cooperation with other parties, although this case was with another level of government. While collaboration outside of government in the public sphere is a big leap, it only requires recognizing the citizenry as another part of our governing system.

The most difficult conflicts couldn't be resolved as easily as the one in California. These required aligning democratic imperatives with bureaucratic necessities. For example, the democratic right to privacy had to be balanced against HEW's need to determine eligibility for federal assistance. I had to deal with these conflicting imperatives when faced with the necessity of protecting taxpayers' dollars. I believed in personal privacy, but I added an Office of Inspector General to the staff to deal with fraud.

A *with* strategy flourishes when the government is open. Negotiating with other states showed a degree of openness, although it raised eyebrows in some quarters as we pushed ahead. To reduce future controversies, I asked the American Bar Association for advice on alternatives to litigation. With the assistance of lawyers like Douglas Arant of Birmingham, Stan Murphy at HEW formed a panel to recommend different procedures. The group suggested creating teams of intermediaries to work out problems. Later, negotiation and mediation would be accepted as reasonable ways of settling disputes. But at the time, settling disputes with states prompted the charge of "capitulation," a term implying that the federal and state governments were at war.

To prevent disputes and find opportunities for collaborations, we created a departmental task force on state relations, headed by Undersecretary Lynch. It opened doors into the Department using projects like state-federal staff exchanges. The Office of Education had an excellent exchange program that brought representatives of state and local education agencies to "shadow" their federal counterparts in the regions and in Washington. The Department had also sent staff members who wrote regulations for institutions like schools, colleges, and hospitals to work for a year in the institutions they proposed to regulate. Although not what I mean by *with*, the exchanges helped create a collaborative culture in the government.

Sometimes better aligning democratic imperatives with the inner workings of the Department required finding likely allies. One of these cases involved historically black colleges and universities (HBCUs), which had been at the forefront of efforts to bring African Americans into full democratic citizenship. The HBCU leadership was open to collaboration. These institutions were supported financially for three to five years under the federal Institutional Development Program, with the objective of making these institutions self-reliant. However, by 1976, it was clear that this goal was yet to be met.[16] (I know what difficulties these institutions faced because I had worked with and served on the board of one of them, Miles College in Birmingham.) Presidents of these institutions complained that three to five years to become financially self-sufficient was unrealistic and that the federal support wasn't sufficient to meet rising costs and declining revenue resulting from inflation pressure.[17] Frequent meetings with these educators were arranged by Joffre Whisenton, who had come with me from Alabama. New projects like the Strengthening Historically Black Colleges and Universities Program were created to ensure funding would continue. For their part, the institutions committed themselves to strengthening efforts—such as establishing endowments—to provide long-term financial stability.[18]

Addressing the continuing financial problems of these institutions made it possible to explore possibilities for collaboration in other areas. The HBCUs and HEW were both concerned about racial justice and the underserved in society. Those interests came together in an HEW initiative that reached out to the underrepresented young people in the college and university populations.

Collaboration in Higher Education

The most enjoyable days for me were those when innovation was possible. Some of these innovations had collaborative elements. For instance, regulations on desegregation called for adding more minorities to college and university faculties, and most institutions had submitted plans to do that, plans the Department had approved. The problem was that the total number of minority faculty to be added far exceeded the number available to take those positions. In 1973, only 976 African Americans had received PhDs, which was roughly 3 percent or less of all doctorates.[19]

The government already had some programs to encourage more minorities to go to college. Head Start (1965) was originally a summer program for academically struggling students designed to prepare them for the next school year. Upward Bound (1965) helped low-income high school students get into college.

However, these programs did not begin early enough to encourage young people to go to college. Beginning with students in the last years of high school or the first years of college was far too late to find enough candidates to pursue advanced degrees; the pool was just too small. So two of the people I brought to HEW, Whisenton and Patricia Harbour, helped establish a new federal grant program, the Graduate and Professional Opportunities Program (GPOP), that started with elementary schoolchildren.[20]

Encouraging and supporting young elementary students isn't something that governments and educational institutions can do alone. Families and community institutions like religious congregations and youth organizations can be as—if not more—helpful. There was good reason for all the parties to collaborate. I'm sure that happened in some cases, but I'm not sure what was documented. Nonetheless, the potential was there.

Many HBCUs had closer ties to their communities than other institutions did, and the communities would benefit when it was time for the third-graders who were part of GPOP to move from high school to college. That would result in a better-educated citizenry. (Later, when I came to the Kettering Foundation, Whisenton helped us create a collaborative research exchange with HBCU and tribal college faculty.)

Categorical Programs versus Block Grants

Other contentious issues at HEW had to do with federal categorical programs. These are federal programs that are precisely targeted to specific problems or populations and provide a specific benefit. This specificity worked against collaboration among levels of government and had implications for the nongovernmental organizations that served the targeted group.

The streams that swelled the flood of categorical programs ran deep. By the 1950s, professional specialization in health, education, and welfare had taken hold, and interest group politics reinforced compartmentalization. The result was a discrepancy between the way the country's problems were structured and the way the Department was organized to deal with them. Real life doesn't come in "H," "E," and "W" components. And HEW was only one of many departments with multiple categories of programs.

As Secretary, John Gardner had tried to combat this fragmentation by changing the unit of analysis in departmental planning from programs to the people who were affected by them. We followed his example and focused on the impact that various welfare programs would have on a single family.[21] Beneficiaries could become like patients being treated by several dozen physicians who never compared diagnoses or prescriptions. Another HEW Secretary, Elliot Richardson, described the difficulties that categorical programs create:

> The average middle-sized city has between four and five hundred service-providing agencies. Eligibility for their help is normally based on residence, but the applicable residential areas are not consistent. One agency accepts only the residents of a city, a second accepts only the residents of a district within the city, and a third accepts only the residents of a neighborhood within the district. A father is helped by one program at one location, his daughter by another elsewhere, and his elderly parents by still another program at still another location.[22]

After Marge Lynch came to the Department, I asked her to give her highest priority to addressing this fragmentation. She started with programs for children, and before leaving office, she had developed a plan that integrated maternal and child health care. It was a step toward collaboration. She urged President Carter to include her plan in his child welfare program, and the Carter administration did.

During Vice President Rockefeller's Domestic Policy Forums, held in late 1975, the call for social services to be consolidated was a consistent theme. With years of experience in Congress, President Ford understood the problems created by categorical programs.[23] He publicized HEW's efforts to grapple with fragmentation, pointing out in speeches that the Department and other agencies were looking for alternatives to the "hodge-podge" of services.[24]

As a remedy, some of the categorical programs were being consolidated into "blocks" and given to states with more latitude to administer the programs as local circumstances dictated. The emphasis on "local" helped open the Department a bit more to the citizenry, which is largely grounded locally. I was sympathetic to the consolidations and giving local communities as well as state administrative agencies greater latitude. Block grants were responsive to governors and municipal officials who complained about their inability to coordinate various federally assisted services at the point of delivery. That was an impediment to the most elementary forms of collaboration.

Block grants had a good political pedigree. They were also potential allies of *with* strategies. Scholars of public administration had proposed something like block grants as early as the 1940s, but support for them didn't really develop until the 1960s. By the 1970s, evidence of the failure of the categorical programs was impossible to ignore. There was, however, considerable opposition when block grants were used to reduce spending.[25]

Court Cases and a Collaborative Climate

Given the scope and controversial nature of the issues HEW dealt with, there were inevitable court orders that had to be implemented. Doing that was particularly challenging when funding was limited or when the orders were contradictory. This made relationships with litigants anything but collaborative. And the litigation sometimes pitted different groups of citizens against each other.

On October 15, 1975, the *New York Times* reported that the Dallas branch of the Office of Civil Rights (OCR) had refused to act on discrimination complaints relating to sex, national origin, or disability on the grounds that all their resources were directed toward complaints of racial discrimination and enforcement of the *Adams v. Weinberger* decision.[26] In that case, agreeing with the African American plaintiffs, Judge John H. Pratt had ruled that HEW "has a duty to commence prompt enforcement activity upon all complaints or other information of racial discrimination in violation of Title VI."[27]

A day later, HEW received a letter from Senator John V. Tunney, who "strongly objected" to HEW's apparent "freeze-out" of Mexican American communities in enforcing Title VI. Tunney insisted that the decision in *Adams* ordered HEW to enforce Title VI without a priority system of enforcement. Furthermore, he believed that, even if HEW were to set up a priority system based on race, it had to include Mexican Americans.[28]

The legal staff of OCR, however, held that the *Adams* decision did, in fact, require that priority be given to cases involving African Americans. Because the plaintiffs in *Adams* were African Americans, the issue of the applicability of the order to other minority groups was not litigated; therefore, the court order reached only those complaints filed by the citizens who alleged racial discrimination. It was proper for the Department, including its Dallas office, to regard a court order as having the highest administrative priority. That did not mean, however, that other responsibilities were disregarded. Individual complaints such as those concerning discrimination against Mexican Americans were not being given a "freeze-out." In fact, of the approximately 52 complaints relating to Mexican Americans that had been filed between 1973 and June 1975, 45 had been resolved.[29]

As might be expected, in 1976, the *Adams* suit was formally joined with separate suits by the Mexican American Legal Defense Fund and the Women's Equity Action League to ensure that their respective constituencies were included.[30] This, however, created conflicting claims on finite resources. That put HEW in an impossible situation until a subsequent amendment to Title IX regulations provided some relief.[31]

My purpose in including this case is to show how, even though each plaintiff is certainly justified in opposing discrimination, the litigiousness is infectious; it spreads and creates a climate that makes collaboration difficult.

With *Potential*

I don't want to give the impression that I had a *with* strategy in mind at HEW. And I don't recall anyone who did. That said, some things did happen in the Department that had something of a *with* spirit.

For example, controlling rising health-care costs was a serious problem (and still is), and HEW was testing two experiments, Professional Service Review Organizations (PSROs) and Health Systems Agencies (HSAs), to see whether they could help. Establishing PSROs was an attempt by the government to work *with* physicians and other health professionals to hold down costs.

HSAs, approved by President Ford in 1975, also had elements of a *with* strategy. These agencies were meant to bring citizens, providers, and government officials together at the community level. The purpose was to improve the health of people by increasing the accessibility, acceptability, continuity, and quality of health services while also restraining increases in cost and preventing unnecessary duplication of resources. The innovation was giving citizens, not professional providers, the majority of seats on the agency boards that were charged with encouraging local control in matters like health-care planning.

As is the case with all experiments, these programs didn't always work as intended. Still, they left valuable lessons. Numerous forces were driving up costs, and neither of the experiments was as effective as hoped in reducing expenditures. And HSAs tended to be dominated by professionals; citizens were seldom if ever recognized as producers. Consulting with citizens isn't the same as working *with* them. Furthermore, these programs weren't popular with the advocates who lobbied for greater economic competition in the health sector.

Another program with the potential for collaboration involved patients struggling with mental illness who failed to get better in state-supported hospitals, a failure that opened the way to more collaboration with communities.[32] Institutions like hospitals are designed to care for patients; that is, to provide the best medical science can offer. But health is more than a matter of good medicine. Some healing forces, like compassion and nurture, are outside institutions of medicine and in communities. They are resources that citizens can bring to collaborative projects. (I'll say more about that in chapter XV.)

When at HEW, I visited the Hell's Kitchen neighborhood in New York City and found a program for patients with mental illnesses who had been released from local hospitals. When they failed to get better, they still needed care, so former patients created a community facility, Fountain House, to make use of the healing force of a community. This is an excellent example of the importance of citizen initiatives in a *with* strategy.

Fountain House began as a result of citizens working together—in this case, former patients from Rockland State Hospital. In the mid-1940s, a group of them began meeting on the steps of the New York Public Library and formed a club called WANA (We Are Not Alone). The "members" of this club raised money and, in 1948, bought a brownstone on Manhattan's West 47th Street and established Fountain House.

The club helped its members transition into employment. Work opportunities were found, and members filled the positions. These jobs gave people a sense of being needed; the jobs were real, and expectations were not lowered for them. Often members began with part-time or temporary jobs and worked their way to full-time, permanent positions. Research showed that ex-patients who were members of Fountain House spent less time in isolation than the average ex-patient and they experienced better community adjustment.

The members were not cared for by a staff; instead, they were trained to care for themselves and others. Fountain House was an example of what can happen when institutions and communities work *with* one another. It's also an example of the kind of complementary production that shows how citizens can make a difference. And when institutions make use of what citizens produce, it helps rebuild public confidence.

I found another example of how HEW could work *with* citizens, not just for them, when I visited the PRHCA Day Care Center in New York's Lower East Side. It served children of Puerto Rican, African American, and Irish families. Because of the involvement of the parents and the interest of the surrounding community, the center helped more than the children. It became a focal point of the community, a place where parents and children learned from one another. HEW helped fund a nutrition program for the center. Other resources came from local businesses and the state. In short, the community, through the center, formed its own helping network based on multiple levels of collaboration.

WHAT'S NEXT?

These examples show when there was potential for developing a *with* strategy. What would it take for this potential to be realized more often? There was no obvious answer. But I believe the way forward requires a better fit between the way the bureaucracies in governing institutions do their work and the work of a democratic citizenry. And that requires a closer look at why bureaucracies work as they do—and, in some cases, must work as they do.

NOTES

1. Joseph A. Califano Jr., *Governing America: An Insider's Report from the White House and the Cabinet* (New York: Simon and Schuster, 1981), 19-24.
2. Califano Jr., *Governing America*, 23.
3. Rufus E. Miles, *The Department of Health, Education, and Welfare* (New York: Praeger Publishers, 1974), 27.
4. In reflecting on my time at HEW, I couldn't always distinguish what I was thinking then from what I was thinking when working on this manuscript. Sometimes I would read an interpretation of the 1970s that would fit my experience so perfectly I would think, "That was it." Whether it was, in fact, what I had had in mind—or only later wished I had been thinking—is sometimes unclear. I want to acknowledge that.
5. These views were expressed in interviews with Meg Greenfield from *Newsweek*. Meg Greenfield, "Jerry Brown—East," *Newsweek*, January 19, 1976, 84.
6. Miles, *The Department of Health, Education, and Welfare*, 10-17.
7. Miles, *The Department of Health, Education, and Welfare*, 3.
8. "Welfare" didn't appear in the Department's title until FSA became part of HEW in 1953—and then only by chance. The name was to have been Health, Education, and Social Security until someone noticed that the initials would spell HESS, Hitler's deputy. So "HEW" it was, and the Department embraced its role as the representative of America's social conscience.
9. The young men included such independent and resourceful people as Peter Turnham, who became the "dean" of the Alabama House of Representatives. For information on the CCC, see Miles, *The Department of Health, Education, and Welfare*, 18-19.
10. Anthony Celebrezze, Secretary during the time the Department grew the fastest, worried that this federal gargantuan had developed an appetite that exceeded its capacity to act effectively. Under President Johnson's Great Society legislation, the Department, which had been a provider of services, became the great provider; and as a regulator, it became the great regulator. In a matter of months, the 88th and 89th Congresses added 60 new programs. In 1965 alone, HEW acquired new authority in elementary and secondary education, higher education, health care, and drug abuse control—in addition to its recently acquired responsibilities for civil rights. Miles, *The Department of Health, Education, and Welfare*, 45-46.

11. Pursuing all these worthy but ambitious goals in the Department inevitably sparked controversies, which opened the manageability issue. The first Secretary, Oveta Culp Hobby, had scarcely taken the oath of office when she was drawn into a clash with the agricultural interests over the cleanliness of wheat. Hobby brought in James Bradshaw Mintener from Minnesota as an assistant secretary to help with the crisis. In his history of HEW, Rufus Miles gives Mintener high marks for his work with the FDA. (I mention this because, by coincidence, Brad Mintener's grandson, Kip Heegaard, married our younger daughter, Lucy.) I had the pleasure of swapping stories with Brad before he died; he was a true civil servant and an example of the kind of public administrator I came to admire.

12. Miles, *The Department of Health, Education, and Welfare*, 46-52, 59-61.

13. I also learned that it's useful to get other perspectives by going outside one field and listening to the reactions from professionals in other related specialties. That is why I put all of the leadership from the different agencies in the Department around a common table to review the critical issues before HEW. We met regularly, and the sessions helped identify possible conflicts in policies as well as opportunities for internal collaboration.

    Externally, I found it useful to get out of the Department office and into the American mainstream to confer with people outside the government. By July in 1976, I had made 50 out-of-town trips, visited 20 states, and addressed more than 23,000 people in 48 national and local forums. Those trips were also part of the daily routine. I recall a two-day trip that involved going from Washington, DC, to Dayton, Ohio, back to Washington (to talk with the President), and then on to Lincoln, Nebraska, the same day. The next day, I flew overnight to Charleston, South Carolina, to give a speech and hold a press conference and was back in Washington by the afternoon. What is government like? Busy. But the benefit of all this travel was seeing that how citizens saw policies was often quite different from the way government officials saw them. I would later begin thinking about bringing these differences to the attention of the government because they were an obstacle to collaboration.

14. Special to the *New York Times*, "California Facing a Welfare Court," *New York Times*, August 15, 1975. David Lissy, memorandum to Sarah C. Massengale, August 29, 1975. This document can be found in the David Mathews collection, Kettering Foundation archives. For more information, contact archives @kettering.org.

15. Lissy, memorandum to Massengale.

16. Luther Hilton Foster, letter to David Mathews, July 31, 1976. This document can be found in the David Mathews collection, Kettering Foundation archives. For more information, contact archives@kettering.org.

17. Luther Hilton Foster, letter to David Mathews, August 2, 1976. This document can

be found in the David Mathews collection, Kettering Foundation archives. For more information, contact archives@kettering.org.

18. David Mathews, memorandum to the President of National Association for Equal Opportunities in Higher Education, Charles A. Lyons, January 19, 1977. This document can be found in the David Mathews collection, Kettering Foundation archives. For more information, contact archives@kettering.org.

19. Commission on Human Resources of the National Research Council, *Minority Groups among United States Doctorate-Level Scientists, Engineers, and Scholars, 1973* (Washington, DC: National Academy of Sciences, 1974), 8.

20. GPOP provided young people with some of the same experiences that children from professional, middle-class families enjoyed—experiences that would allow them to see the possibilities of careers that their circumstances otherwise obscured. It brought elementary schoolchildren to campuses where they could observe what engineers, lawyers, and health professionals did and where they might imagine themselves doing the same things. The program then followed these children from elementary school to entering college. By the end of GPOP's first year, approximately 30 institutions were receiving grants with fellowships going to 300 students—a good beginning. We were pleased that the Carter and succeeding administrations continued to fund the program. It lasted until 1995.

21. Miles, *The Department of Health, Education, and Welfare*, 46-52, 59-61.

22. Elliot Richardson, *The Creative Balance: Government, Politics, and the Individual in America's Third Century* (New York: Holt, Rinehart and Winston, 1976), 179.

23. In 1976, President Ford pressed Congress to group health, child care, and community services programs under his Financial Assistance for Community Services Act. The President advocated combining $2.5 billion in grants for day care, family planning, foster care, special services for the aged, and alcohol and drug addiction programs, along with homemaker and home health aid programs. The President didn't call for a reduction in federal spending for these services. Every state would receive at least as much money as it had been receiving and also be relieved of the requirement to match every three federal dollars with one of its own. There would still be some federal guidelines; for instance, 75 percent of the funds were to go to individuals with incomes below the poverty line or to those who received other benefits. The administration also favored allowing states to set their own standards for staff-to-child ratios. This policy was supported by the states and voluntary organizations that had asked Congress for authority to set their own priorities. These changes would have been helpful in carrying out a *with* strategy.

Congress, however, had its own community services plan. Consequently, members clashed with the administration, specifically over day care. Even though the administration favored federal assistance for this service, Ford vetoed a bill based on Congress' preferences because it would have perpetuated federal standards and increased day care matching rates for states. His veto was sustained, which forced Congress to come back and pass a compromise bill that allowed states to set their own standards, as the President wanted, and also added $200 million in new funds. That is the way government compromise worked in the mid-1970s.

24. Gerald R. Ford Library and Museum, "Social Programs," *President Ford '76 Fact Book,* March 24, 1998, https://www.fordlibrarymuseum.gov/library/document/factbook/social.htm.

25. Timothy Conlan, *From Federalism to Devolution: Twenty-Five Years of Inter-governmental Reform* (Washington, DC: Brookings Institution Press, 1998), 23.

26. Nancy Hicks, "Inquiry into Bias Curbed by H.E.W.: Dallas Office Says It Lacks Means to Check Complaints—Desegregation Blamed," *New York Times,* October 15, 1975.

27. *Adams v. Weinberger,* 391 F. Supp. 269 (D.D.C. 1975).

28. John V. Tunney, letter to David Mathews, October 16, 1975. This document can be found in the David Mathews collection, Kettering Foundation archives. For more information, contact archives@kettering.org.

29. David Mathews, letter to John V. Tunney, December 2, 1975. This document can be found in the David Mathews collection, Kettering Foundation archives. For more information, contact archives@kettering.org.

30. Jeremy Rabkin, "Office for Civil Rights," in *The Politics of Regulation,* ed. James Q. Wilson (New York: Basic Books, 1980), 349. Rabkin cites *Adams v. Mathews,* 536 F. 2nd 417 (DC Circ. 1976); *Adams v. Mathews,* No. 3095 (D.C.D.C. March 30, 1976). In 1977, people with disabilities were also added, *Adams v. Califano,* No. 3095-70 (D.C.D.C. December 29, 1977).

31. Rabkin, "Office for Civil Rights," 350-351.

32. I've mentioned that I was already familiar with these hospitals and their patients because Bryce, Alabama's hospital for those with mental illness, adjoined the University.

CHAPTER VII

ADMINISTERING THE PUBLIC'S BUSINESS

You have seen that I believe a *with* strategy might help bridge the divide that now separates much of the public from governing institutions. I've also said from the beginning that a *with* strategy is not a set of practices to adopt but a mind-set about what the relationship between citizens and all institutions should be like in a democracy.

In this chapter, I will move from a focus primarily on HEW to elaborate further on the need for a *with* strategy in all governing institutions. Most are staffed by administrators and other professionals. The way they do their jobs is critical for the future of democracy.

Administrators, particularly those in government, are often called "bureaucrats." Earlier, I acknowledged that I was once a bureaucrat myself. Although "bureaucrat" sometimes has a negative connotation, my experience in their ranks left me with the strong impression that the problems associated with public administrators are not usually clashes between something good and something bad but rather clashes of good versus good. That is, public servants are charged with serving the public good, although the public often has a different understanding of what is good. I am not talking about bureaucrats as individuals but about a "bureaucratic" mind-set or what has been called "seeing like a state."[1] This way of seeing and thinking appears to grow out of an understandable need in both nongovernmental and governmental institutions for order, structure, and uniform rules to inform and guide actions.

I believe that a *with* strategy can provide opportunities to strengthen governing institutions through complementary efforts taken *with* citizens. An example: Nongovernmental, or track-two, diplomacy that is carried on by people not in government, yet in cooperation with diplomats, can benefit what officials do. The Kettering Foundation has studied this kind of diplomacy since the 1960s. The oldest of this research goes back to the time a US spy plane was shot down over the Soviet Union, beginning the Cold War. President Eisenhower told publisher Norman Cousins, a Kettering trustee, that the US government couldn't talk to the Soviets but that someone needed to. That led to the creation of the Dartmouth Conference, a still ongoing joint venture between American and Russian citizens. Kettering has also had these exchanges with the Chinese for nearly 50 years and with Cubans for 25 years.[2]

While governments at all levels have bureaucracies (as do most nongovernmental institutions), the federal bureaucracy is the largest and most studied. So, this and the next seven chapters use bureaucracies in our national government to show how they work, while acknowledging that public administrators in local governments may differ somewhat in their work. The cases I will cite show how a bureaucracy responds, or fails to respond, to opportunities for collaboration with the citizenry and why that happens.

BUREAUCRACIES IN HISTORY

Because some readers may not be familiar with the history of bureaucracies, I'll start by covering some ground well known to public administrators and scholars. Here is a brief overview of the origins of bureaucracies, their historical roles in the United States, and the changes in these roles that have occurred as our form of government has evolved.

Bureaucracies are found worldwide and have been around for a long time. Their origins go back as far as the founding of ancient cities in Mesopotamia and Egypt.[3] Bureaucracies collected tributes, kept records, and enforced the decrees of rulers.

In the US, the role of bureaucracies has been controversial, beginning with the colonists' hostility to the king's ministers. In the 19th century, the US bureaucracy was small and limited, reflecting the view that the least government was the best government. The exceptions were projects of internal improvements (like roads and canals) to facilitate economic growth. Then, the Civil War began to change the government. It grew as the federal budget increased to more than a billion dollars in 1865.[4] This increase required more bureaucrats.

Also in the mid-19th century, some social reformers had turned to the federal and state governments for assistance. However, neither noted figures like Henry David Thoreau nor most of his fellow reformers thought using government policy would be their primary instrument for change. As I said earlier, their favorite strategy was to reach into the hearts of the people with a compelling message. Still, at both the state and national levels, governments funded hospitals, schools, and social welfare agencies to carry out reformers' objectives.

Instrumental or Constitutive?

Nationally, our Constitution created a government with ministers, called secretaries, and they became a cabinet for the President. But what was their role to be? Two very different concepts of the federal bureaucracy emerged. From one perspective, cabinet members and their staffs would only carry out the will of an elected President. This has been called the "instrumental" concept of the bureaucracy.[5] The other, a "constitutive" concept, would give cabinet officers and their bureaucracies the power to determine what the objectives or purposes of government should be, rather than being restricted to devising means for carrying out directives from elected officials.[6] The rationale for the constitutive concept is that law-making by elected representatives moves too slowly to be the source of authority for all that government has to do. There has to be a bureaucracy to respond to events not anticipated in legislation.

This means that the impact of the government on society will often extend beyond what is sanctioned by law. The bureaucracy, from this perspective, plays a semi-independent role.[7]

I lean toward the instrumental theory because it reflects democratic values. Nonetheless, I recognize that the constitutive theory has been dominant, particularly since the 20th century. My own experience was with a bureaucracy that saw its role as constitutive. I recognize, too, that responding to people's fear of the government's power to coerce and their antipathy toward today's version of the king's ministers has to be balanced against 21st-century reality, which requires a large, central government to carry out an ever-growing number of duties.

Bureaucrats Become Experts

Our concept of government changed significantly when the 19th century gave way to the 20th. Lester Frank Ward, a bureaucrat in the United States Geological Survey and later the chair of Brown University's sociology department, saw the federal government as an underused agent for social progress. He argued for more, not less, government. And he believed in the power of science to guide the government in progressive endeavors. I think I first heard about Ward from historian Henry Steele Commager, when he stayed with my family on a visit to the University of Alabama. Commager paid close attention to Ward in his 1950 book, *The American Mind*, and later called him the "father of the modern welfare state."[8] Anthropologist Margaret Mead, whom I came to know when I was at HEW, was also very familiar with Ward. We talked about his influence on the capital.[9]

President Theodore Roosevelt was, in many ways, the embodiment of Ward's philosophy. They were contemporaries, and when Roosevelt became president in 1901, he greatly expanded executive power. He believed that he had the right to act for the public welfare "whenever and in whatever manner was necessary, unless prevented by direct constitutional or legislative prohibition."[10] And he did just that by such means as executive orders, which he used more than a thousand times.[11] Contrasting his concept of the presidency with the conventional "Unless I can, I can't," Roosevelt believed, "Unless I can't, I will."[12] He busted economic monopolies, promoted the construction of the Panama Canal, and quadrupled the amount of land set aside for the national parks.

Not only was the role of government being changed, so was the nature of the bureaucracy. "To the victor belongs the spoils" had been the accepted rule for appointing bureaucrats as newly elected officials brought their supporters with them to office. This spoils system was susceptible to political favoritism. However, it wasn't until 1883, when President Garfield was assassinated by a deranged office seeker, that Congress created the Civil Service Commission. Competency and merit, not partisan loyalty, were to be the new standard for appointments.

Wilson's Tension

A young scholar, later to become President, Woodrow Wilson, shared similar progressive convictions with Ward. They were articulate advocates for a more assertive federal government as well as devotees of a growing faith in the power of the social sciences to lead the way to collective well-being. Although Wilson favored Populist reforms like referendums, he is best known for putting government in the hands of professionally trained administrators, who, of course, were unelected. After Wilson, the growth of expert administration and faith in the social sciences was irreversible.[13]

Wilson wasn't unaware of the tension between scientific professionalism and the norms of a democracy. He noted that, while it is fairly easy for a bureaucracy to carry out the commands of a single monarch, serving a sovereign public is more difficult. How could administrators respond to a ruler who couldn't be found at any specific location and whose opinions might vary from time to time or issue to issue? Wilson tried to solve the problem by restricting bureaucracies to an administrative sphere outside of politics. He insisted that administration was not political at all, but rather a neutral, objective instrument that had to be protected from political interference, even from the public. Wilson, however, went on to recognize that it really wasn't possible to make the distinction in practice that he favored in theory. In the final analysis, he concluded, government administration had to be an instrument serving objectives established in law.[14]

Centralization

As the US grew and its economy was transformed by the expansion of industry and business, greater centralization in government was inevitable. And the role that the bureaucracy played grew.

By the 1930s, the bureaucracy was moving to the center of the political system and was given considerable power when President Franklin Delano Roosevelt used federal agencies to insulate his programs from political parties. He expanded the rights that government protected to include the right to economic security. Protecting rights imposed a responsibility on government to act, to be assertive. Once again, the role of the bureaucracy was being reshaped by changes in the role of government.

THE MODERN BUREAUCRACY

In the modern era, bureaucracies came to be staffed by professionals who could claim superior knowledge based on their scientific expertise. They would operate, not just under the law, but also through their interpretations of laws, known as regulations. Regulations are expansive in that they apply to general classes of behavior rather than being limited to specific instances.

An Argument That Hamilton Won

Initially, the belief that the government that governed least governed best was reflected in the small size of the bureaucracy and its limited role. Thomas Jefferson has been used as the symbol for the view that the US is best served by keeping the central government restricted and relying on small, self-governing institutions in communities, such as school boards. Alexander Hamilton has been the political leader most identified with the counterargument for a powerful central government under the leadership of a strong executive.

Hamilton would be pleased today. The size of the federal bureaucracy exploded in the mid-20th century. It crossed the million-employee mark in the lead-up to World War II and has rarely dipped below two million since then.[15] Despite this growth, however, opinions have continued to clash over how centralized the governing system should be.

Sovereignty Divided

To guard against concentrating authority, our system divides power into different levels of government and also acknowledges sovereignty within sovereignty—as in the case of recognizing Native American nations. While Congress would have the supreme law-making power in specified areas, all other matters not so specified in the Constitution were to be handled by state governments. And as one historian added, "The people reserved sovereignty in still other matters, refusing to entrust it to government at any level."[16] That helped make it possible for nongovernmental institutions to be part of the governing system.

A Reconfiguration: The Bulge in the Middle

Modern US government has not only grown in size, it has changed its shape. Paul Light's research shows that what was once a hierarchical pyramid has become a trapezoid, which is evolving into an oval. The growth has been in mid-level bureaucrats. He particularly noted a tendency for bureaucracies to add control on top of control. He writes, "The federal government has never had more layers of leaders or more leaders per layer." Light found 64 discrete titles at the top of the federal government and almost 2,600 titleholders, up from 51. Although some of the growth was the result of the "war on terror,"

Light reported that every department expanded.[17] This tendency to grow in size is also found in nongovernmental bureaucracies.

FROM THE PUBLIC'S PERSPECTIVE

As the role of government increased and bureaucracies changed in size and function, public concerns have multiplied, even as many people have enjoyed the benefits of a more assertive federal establishment.

Tyranny without a Tyrant

As the federal government took on a more centralized role, it did not follow that the bureaucracy became a single, unified force in government. There are many bureaucracies, and they aren't always coordinated. In fact, they seldom are. The left hand doesn't necessarily know what the right is doing. To the extent that the bureaucracy functions like a tyrant, the tyranny lacks coherence. That has been called "tyranny without a tyrant."[18]

Today, the bureaucracy might be less subject to public criticism if it were coherent and predictable. People would know what the rules were and could count on getting a definitive answer when they had questions. However, there are a great many bureaucracies, and they exist throughout different levels of government from local to national. Having to deal with multiple bureaucracies that may have conflicting rules can be maddening. That is why it is said that multiple authorities without a coherent focus create a tyranny of confusion even when there is no actual tyrant.

Citizens and even presidents have complained about this tyranny. While circumstances have varied from administration to administration, getting control of the bureaucratic system has continued to be an issue for our chief executives, who have wanted—to various degrees and for various reasons—to curb what they have seen as interference by the federal bureaucracy.[19] Richard Nixon, for example, is said to have reacted to the bureaucracy's growing power by using the White House staff to direct the day-to-day operations of the cabinet departments and other agencies. Scholars noticed the change. According to a report by a panel from the National Academy of Public Administration, Nixon allowed the White House's National Security and Domestic Council to bypass "departments and agencies in the areas of their assigned responsibilities."[20]

Jimmy Carter dealt with what he felt was a lack of support from subordinates by reorganizing his administration. Through the Civil Service Reform Act of 1978, he abolished the Civil Service Commission and replaced it with the Office of Personnel Management. His actions, which were augmented by both Ronald Reagan and Bill Clinton, began to restore a good measure of presidential control after the Watergate scandal weakened the presidency.[21]

Apparently though, the bureaucratic encumbrances didn't go away. Tommy Thompson, Secretary of Health and Human Services in the George W. Bush administration, was nostalgic about his power as Governor of Wisconsin. There he had a staff that could act on a new idea in a matter of hours. In Washington, Thompson said he encountered a troubling inertia. First, he had to sell his ideas to his own department. Then, he had to battle the Office of Management and Budget in the White House. (Bureaucracies can battle bureaucracies.) If his proposal were ever to reach the President and get to Congress, he feared it would be time to retire.[22]

There have been times when a bureaucracy of experts has had public approval. These have been rare and under extreme circumstances, but this support should be noted.

A Lack of Common Sense?

Many of the public's current concerns about the bureaucracy have to do with what people consider its lack of common sense. What the bureaucracy does can appear to ignore everyday realities.

Americans sometimes feel about the government as though King George III were still in power. There are serious concerns about whether the bureaucracy is sufficiently aware of what happens in people's lives, particularly when there are qualitative issues and idiosyncratic local conditions. The federal government, because of its size and distance from citizens and their communities, may not be able to see clearly the actual effect of a program on recipients or the ability of citizens to act on their own behalf. How a social worker influences a person receiving assistance or how a teacher encourages a child with special needs is a critical factor in determining program effectiveness. A massive and distant government, however, has limited instruments for reading such intangibles and, consequently, difficulty in considering those intangibles in decision-making.

Because distant realities are hard to measure, government agencies use proxies. They count hospital beds or students in a class as indicators of what officials really want to know. But the numbers don't reflect people's day-to-day experiences. The result is that big government seems blind or insensitive to citizens who are acutely aware of the realities that the national government stumbles over. (In the next chapter, I'll say more about how this problem might be used for constructive purposes.)

Seeing Like the State Does?

Why do bureaucracies appear to miss the obvious and fail to use common sense? There may be a reason, which I've mentioned. While the administrators who staff bureaucracies are no less perceptive than citizens in general and are usually quite intelligent, they are also as susceptible to fellow feelings and benevolent intentions. Yet working in bureaucracies requires them to look at the human condition from a distinctive perspective. I've used a phrase originated by James Scott, bureaucrats are prone to "see like a state," or from the perspective of the government.[23] While that perspective is helpful in detecting the kinds of things that are important in the administration of the government's business, it can obscure the things citizens consider important. This can lead to what people consider an absence of common sense. What follows is an example of how seeing like a state influenced the enforcement of rules and regulations.

Grandmother and the 14-Day Rule

This HEW case involved a grandmother who was told that she had to return to a nursing home on Christmas Eve rather than stay with her family. Why would any regulation not allow this woman to spend Christmas with her loved ones? Well, as you may know, there are two types of nursing homes: immediate care and intensive care. In immediate care nursing homes, patients need some assistance, though not round-the-clock medical attention. They are free to come and go. The costs for this kind of facility are far less than what the government pays for an intensive care nursing home. Intensive care facilities have a full-time nurse and a doctor on hand. The government pays a great deal for their services. Naturally, the government has to be sure that, if it is paying for intensive care, those patients truly need it. The government makes that determination on the assumption that, if patients can be away from the nursing home for more than 14 days, they don't need intensive care.

By Christmas Eve, this particular grandmother, who had been with her family since Thanksgiving, would have used up her 14 days. If she was not back in the nursing home, she would lose her eligibility for intensive care. The family's argument was that her infirmities were episodic. She might feel fine one week but have serious problems the next. The government, however, would find it difficult to make a uniform policy that took into account all possible fluctuations in every person's health.

Confronted with making a decision on this appeal, and expecting sympathy for the grandmother, I asked the advice of my colleagues in the Department. Instead, I learned a lesson in how a bureaucracy sees like a state. The assumption in this case was that, like the blindfolded statue of Justice, departmental decisions had to be made blind to an individual's circumstances. Rules and regulations had to be enforced uniformly. The Department could not make a policy that would say, "When your grandmother is well, she can go into immediate care; when she is not well, she can go into intensive care." That is the reason the bureaucracy has rules like the 14-day limit.

In this case, when the decision finally came down to me as HEW Secretary, I ruled in favor of the grandmother. I hope she had a wonderful Christmas.

THE INTEREST GROUP STATE

Another force bearing on what were supposed to be independent, objective, professional bureaucracies was the increasingly effective pressure from special interest groups. Bureaucracies don't work alone.

Creating the Iron Triangles

My own experiences in Washington included encounters with what has been called an "iron triangle" of special interest influence. The term was coined in 1964 by my friend Douglass Cater from Alabama, who served in the Lyndon Johnson administration. An iron triangle is formed by collusion. Staff members from an interest group move into a federal agency and also into the congressional body that regulates the agency. From these three locations, it is relatively easy to carry out an interest group's agenda.[24] The result is a formidable political force outside the control of the executive branch. Interest groups are well organized, have resources, and are easily mobilized. They are skilled in lobbying, which is augmented by campaign contributions. Interest groups also provide information to congressional committees and government agencies that is useful, although biased in favor of their objectives.

Despite their power, however, interest groups are not always successful. As a new Congressman from Michigan, Gerald Ford shared President Eisenhower's concern that interest groups representing military contractors were influencing the defense bureaucracy. Ford, just returning from his service in the Navy, reacted negatively to making national policy that would benefit self-serving interests. True to his convictions, Congressman Ford refused to support a plan that would have located a military base in his district, even though it would have brought grateful voters to his side.[25]

Even though the power of special interest groups was quite evident when I was in Washington as Secretary, I never felt I was without influence or held captive to these outside forces. However, after the presidency was weakened by the scandal in the Nixon administration, a good deal of political power shifted to a much enlarged and diversified body of interest groups in the

1970s. Theda Skocpol reported that "between 1960 and 1990, the total number of national associations [including public interest groups] grew from some 6,000 to 23,000."[26]

The Real Public?

The large number of interest groups and the span of the interests they represented encouraged them to claim to be the true public. However, citizens don't seem to buy this argument, even though a large number of people support various groups. The reason may be that, as individuals, we synthesize, integrate, and moderate our positions on the various issues that concern us. This creates an internal coherence, which is what actually represents us. We are a composite of many interests. That is not what interest groups represent. Each group represents only one particular interest. Even all the groups combined don't have the internal coherence people have.[27] In fact, as Theda Skocpol observed, the mushrooming of special interest groups may have contributed to reduced opportunities for "large numbers of Americans to work together for broadly shared values and interests."[28]

I think Skocpol is right about this threat to democracy. Still, I wouldn't ignore the constructive influence interest groups have had in such cases as advocating for Americans who need federal assistance. This constructive influence is evident, for example, in the long history of groups championing veterans and people with disabilities.[29] That said, I'll cite a case shortly where, in advocating for a good cause, interest groups formed an iron triangle that bypassed both congressional and public deliberation.[30]

I found very insightful Brian Cook's report on how interest groups came to master the political system. He pointed out, "When civil service and progressive reforms sufficiently disengaged the political parties from control of administration, many of these [interest] groups moved in to fill the vacuum." The result was "making interest groups one of the new masters of administration. This . . . influence was to involve agencies in policy making in a way that flew in the face of the dominant ideology and the rhetoric of instrumental, subordinate administration."[31] As Cook noted, this influence was at odds with the precept that professional public administration is to be objective and neutral.

The hope was that the bureaucracy would protect the broader public interests from narrower interests because administrators weren't answerable to political parties. That, however, doesn't appear to be what happened. Hugh Heclo has described our current system as government "of the activists, by the activists, and for the activists." They can affect government "without really engaging the general public in a decisive argument about the choices."[32]

Ironically, this failure to engage the public has occasionally created a crisis for an interest group. For instance, in 1988, when AARP and other associations supported a bill to provide coverage for catastrophic health costs, they soon had to back down when senior citizens, who hadn't been consulted, rose up in protest over the costs to them. Except in situations like this one, most of what interest groups want is done. The issues are so complex that only the well-organized and professionally staffed groups can have any significant influence on policymaking.[33] Consequently, according to scholars, this is why well-organized special interest groups tend to enjoy benefits while larger but unorganized groups of citizens bear the burdens.[34]

In this account of how the iron triangle works, something should be mentioned about the judiciary. This is not the place to go into detail, but the federal judiciary can also be affected by the triangle. Robert Katzmann described how this occurs: "Congress creates a statutory right, but then withdraws. An interest group then files suit in court, seeking enforcement of the right. The judiciary interprets these rights expansively and requires the executive to implement them—regardless of the president's policy preferences."[35]

Managers of Virtue

To fully understand a bureaucracy, it is important to take into account the influence of over-moralized politics or "rights talk," which I touched on in chapter V. It gave professionals a claim to moral authority to go with their claim of scientific expertise. The two claims have reinforced bureaucracies in interpreting their role as countering popular sovereignty and the potential despotism of an ideological majority.

To the extent that a bureaucracy came to consider itself an agent of the moral interests of the country, it assumed the authority to restructure power relations in the name of social justice. As Karen Tani found, "Federal administrators did not use rights language to mobilize rights-holders, to demand resources from the state, or to press rights claims in court. . . . Rather, they used that language as an administrative tool, a substitute for more formal mechanisms of influencing the myriad administrative decisions occurring on the ground."[36]

The American reform tradition includes a caution about the good intentions in morally based politics that should be noted here. Roger Williams, the 18th-century minister and social reformer, contended that true progress required understanding not only of the powers of evil but also the limits of goodness. Historian Perry Miller said of him, "Williams' greatest insight [was] into the corrosive effects not of sin but of virtue."[37] This tough-mindedness was characteristic of Williams, who was a founding father of social reform in the United States.

THE BUREAUCRACY'S ULTIMATE CHALLENGE: LOST TRUST

Even though I've given just a quick account of the forces shaping today's bureaucracies, I believe that some grounding in this history is essential to understanding why bureaucracies act as they do. They are what they are, both for good and ill. They will continue to defend rights, be influenced by special interests, remain large with a "middle-aged" spread, uphold professional standards, and believe in scientific expertise. The issue I want to dig into is the role that the bureaucracy plays in response to its greatest challenge: the avalanche of falling public trust that could evolve into a loss of legitimacy, which would be fatal. This steady decline has been halted from time to time by threats to national safety, such as the 9/11 terrorist attack, but these have just been pauses in a decades-long trend.

The extent of this loss is already staggering, and I won't repeat the account of it that I gave earlier. I'll share a story about public administrators acknowledging the challenge. It didn't come from Washington. When I left office in 1977, HEW transition teams for the new Carter administration received memos from HEW staff in regional offices. One of these described the impact of declining confidence on employee morale: "In recent years the 'bureaucrat' has come under increasing criticism for governmental problems and inefficiencies. The nature of HEW administered programs has thrust its employees into positions of prominent criticism more often than other agencies. HEW employees have been required to administer numerous controversial and often defective laws and regulations. Lack of public trust has had a corrosive effect on employee morale."[38] This memo shows that the loss of public confidence was beginning to have an effect, and the recognition was coming from the bottom up, where public administrators had more direct contact with everyday people.

As might be expected, criticisms of the government have prompted strong criticisms of the citizenry. I've already cited Bachner and Ginsberg's *What Washington Gets Wrong*. The authors documented the misperceptions and negative attitudes that some unelected officials hold about the public. This study opens with a description of a dinner party conversation with an official in the Department of Health and Human Services, HEW's successor: "According to [an] experienced public servant, 'everyone knew' that Washington officialdom did not think much of the American people. After a pause she added, 'Many of the people are quite stupid, aren't they?'"[39]

IN DEFENSE OF THE BUREAUCRACY

The loss of public confidence has been countered by a vigorous defense of the bureaucracy. In *The Case for Bureaucracy*, Charles Goodsell argues, "American administrative agencies of government function surprisingly well. In other words, the bureaucracy is not nearly as 'bureaucratic,' in the pejorative sense, as commonly thought."[40] Yet, Goodsell says, in the popular media, the bureaucracy is maligned, using horror stories of incompetence. He suggests that one of the key reasons the bureaucracy has become a "hate object" is because people have unrealistic expectations. But a bureaucracy "cannot be everything to everybody." Goodsell cites survey data showing that the performance of bureaucracies is acceptable or satisfactory in the majority of cases. He goes on to refute the fear that bureaucracies will grow and become too powerful, saying that bureaucracies check each other and are subject to external restrictions.

Another more recent study suggests that the confidence problem doesn't have to do with the professional competence of public administrators. Despite the perception that federal workers are not as qualified as those in the private sector, 75 percent of the people who actually interacted with federal employees reported a positive experience. And younger people are "more likely to give federal civil servants a positive review."[41]

The assumption that the criticisms are about incompetent administrators may miss the mark. Many of the negative comments are about the bureaucratic system, not so much the people in it. Bill Muse, a former university president whose field is management, has written, but not published, an account of why federal bureaucracies are mismanaged. He based his conclusions on what he observed when he was brought into the Office of Education from 1977 to 1978 in the Presidential Executive Exchange Program.[42]

In his defense of the bureaucracy in the *Public Administration Review,* Kenneth Meier blames the electoral system for not encouraging enough deliberation to resolve conflicts and promote good policy.[43] Bureaucracies, he argues, have greater expertise than elective bodies and are reasonably responsive. He believes that they will be effective if given clear goals, have adequate resources, and are allowed the autonomy to apply their expertise to problems. The basic problem, Meier concludes, is that the political system "has swung too far in the direction of democracy. [People] now demand not just that the bureaucracy be responsive to electoral institutions, but that it be hyperresponsive." Meier's subtitle says it all: "The Case for More Bureaucracy and Less Democracy."

Paul Verkuil is even more blunt in making the case for professional government: "Bureaucracy is a reality in democratic as well as oppressive societies because it is the most efficient way of organizing public and private sector institutions. What it takes to run government well is the same thing it takes to run private firms well: professional managers who have appropriate levels of competence and dedication. These professionals are bureaucrats inevitably, and they must be valued."[44]

My field isn't public administration, which I may have just proven. However, these books make a very consistent argument over a span of 20 years. That argument in defense of bureaucracies seems to be that an ever-more-complex, multilayer government must have professional civil servants who know what is going on and how to make the political system work.

But without denying that bureaucracies are here to stay, I have heard arguments recently that this defense ignores a tremendous challenge in the first decades of the 21st century. I like the way Tina Nabatchi, professor of public administration and international affairs at Syracuse University, described this challenge in remarks made during a Kettering Foundation research meeting in 2019.[45] She is alarmed by talk about the "deconstruction of the administrative state." She fears a "growing democratic rollback" and calls for new thinking in public administration. However, she finds the field "reluctant (perhaps incapable) of responding in a meaningful way." Her evidence includes the failure of the accrediting agency for public administration (Network of Schools of Public Policy, Affairs, and Administration, or NASPAA) to even mention democracy in its standards.

WHAT'S NEXT?

I don't think it would be useful now to say whether the defenders of bureaucracy have made a better case than the critics. I want to move on to look at how the citizenry responds to efforts the bureaucracy has made to engage the public and demonstrate its accountability. In doing that, I'll continue to use democratic precepts as the standards for assessing whether the efforts made by the bureaucracy go far enough.

NOTES

1. James C. Scott, *Seeing Like a State: How Certain Schemes to Improve the Human Condition Have Failed* (New Haven, CT: Yale University Press, 1998).

2. Harold Saunders and Philip Stewart, "The Dartmouth Conference: A Simple but Grand Idea with World Peace Hanging in the Balance," *Connections* (2015): 59-64; *China-United States Sustained Dialogue: Celebrating 25 Years* (Kettering Foundation, 2011), 5; Paloma Dallas, "A Comparative Study of Coastal Communities in Cuba and the United States," *Connections* (2016): 44-52; Philip D. Stewart, *Breaking Barriers in United States-Russia Relations: The Power and Promise of Citizen Diplomacy* (Dayton, OH: Kettering Foundation Press, 2020); Maxine Thomas and Zhao Mei, *China-United States Sustained Dialogue, 1986-2001* (Dayton, OH: Kettering Foundation Press, 2001).

3. Christopher Seddon, *Humans: From the Beginning* (Glanville Publications, 2015), 336-337, 345.

4. Eric Foner, *A Short History of Reconstruction* (New York: Harper & Row, 1990), 10.

5. Brian J. Cook, *Bureaucracy and Self-Government: Reconsidering the Role of Public Administration in American Politics* (Baltimore, MD: Johns Hopkins University Press, 1996), 4–5.

6. Cook, *Bureaucracy and Self-Government*, 5.

7. Cook, *Bureaucracy and Self-Government*, 176.

8. Henry Steele Commager, ed., *Lester Ward and the Welfare State* (Indianapolis, IN: Bobbs-Merrill, 1967).

9. My first meeting with Margaret Mead is described in Wilton S. Dillon, "Margaret Mead and Government," *American Anthropologist* 82 (1980): 318-339.

10. Theodore Roosevelt, *An Autobiography* (New York: Charles Scribner's Sons, 1920), 357.

11. Lorraine Boissoneault, "The Debate over Executive Orders Began with Teddy Roosevelt's Mad Passion for Conservation," Smithsonianmag.com, April 17, 2017, https://www.smithsonianmag.com/history/how-theodore-roosevelts-executive-orders-reshaped-countryand-presidency-180962908/.

12. Boissoneault, "The Debate over Executive Orders."

13. Larry Walker, "Woodrow Wilson, Progressive Reform, and Public Administration," *Political Science Quarterly* 104, no. 3 (Autumn 1989): 509–525.

14. Some scholars have argued that the Progressive Era is not the foundation of public administration. See Larry S. Luton, "The Tale That Wagged the Dog: Is the Progressive Era the Foundation of American Public Administration?" *Administrative Theory & Praxis* 24, no. 3 (September 2002): 439–456.

15. It has been argued that the size of the federal civilian workforce hasn't changed much since the early 1960s. However, contractors have been added to provide needed staffing. Contractors now exceed the number of federal workers. See Paul Verkuil, "The Case for Bureaucracy," *New York Times,* October 3, 2016.

16. Forrest McDonald, *States' Rights and the Union: Imperium in Imperio, 1776-1876* (Lawrence, KS: University Press of Kansas, 2000), 4.

17. Paul C. Light, *A Government Ill Executed: The Decline of the Federal Service and How to Reverse It* (Cambridge, MA: Harvard University Press, 2008). I can't improve on Light's description of the change in the shape of government, so I'll just quote him: "Demography and history come together to reshape the federal hierarchy—employees grow older, missions expand and contract, personnel policies shift, new technologies emerge, and jobs evolve. The changes are easy to track with the number of technical, administrative, clerical, and blue-collar positions at any given point in history. In 1940, the federal hierarchy looked like a standard bureaucratic pyramid, with most employees at the bottom and a small number of supervisors, managers, and presidential appointees sorted in decreasing numbers above. By 1960, the federal hierarchy still looked like a pyramid, but the distance between the bottom and top was starting to increase as new layers of professional and technical employees arrive. By 1980, the federal hierarchy was changing from a pyramid to four-sided trapezoid, with roughly equal numbers of federal employees working at the bottom, middle, and top of the hierarchy. By 2000, the federal hierarchy looked like a pentagon, with more federal employees working at the middle and top than at the bottom. By 2040, the federal hierarchy could evolve into an oval if current trends continue." Paul C. Light, *The True Size of Government: Tracking Washington's Blended Workforce, 1984–2015* (New York: The Volcker Alliance, 2017), 18; http://www.volcker alliance.org/true-size-government.

18. Hannah Arendt, *On Violence* (Orlando, FL: Harcourt, 1970), 81.

19. John E. Schwarz, *America's Hidden Success: A Reassessment of Public Policy from Kennedy to Reagan,* 2nd ed. (New York: W. W. Norton, 1988).

20. Frederick C. Mosher et al., "Watergate: Implications for Responsible Government," in *Classics of Public Administration,* eds. Jay M. Shafritz and Albert C. Hyde, 2nd ed. (Chicago: Dorsey Press, 1987): 488–495.

21. Christopher Kelley, "The Unitary Executive and the Presidential Signing Statement" (PhD dissertation, Miami University, 2003), 84.

22. Louis Jacobson, "Tommy Thompson, Calling the Shots," *World Traveler* (November 2003): 45-67.

23. Scott, *Seeing Like a State.*

24. For more information, see Larry E. Sullivan, ed., *The SAGE Glossary of the Social and Behavioral Sciences* (Thousand Oaks, CA: SAGE Publications, 2009), 272.

25. James Cannon, *Time and Chance: Gerald Ford's Appointment with History* (New York: HarperCollins, 1994), 62.

26. Theda Skocpol, "The Narrowing of Civic Life," *The American Prospect* (May 17, 2004), http://prospect.org/article/narrowing-civic-life.

27. As Ted Lowi pointed out, the assumption that everyone belongs to a group isn't valid. All interests aren't formally organized, and the people in organized groups don't necessarily have homogenous concerns. Lowi charged that interest group politics contributes to "the atrophy of institutions of popular control" and shuts the unorganized citizenry out of the most critical phase in policymaking, "where the problem is first defined." Theodore J. Lowi, *The End of Liberalism: The Second Republic of the United States*, 2nd ed. (New York: W.W. Norton, 1979), 51-59.

28. Skocpol, "The Narrowing of Civic Life."

29. Richard K. Scotch, *From Good Will to Civil Rights: Transforming Federal Disability Policy* (Philadelphia: Temple University Press, 1984), 86.

30. My predecessor at HEW, Caspar Weinberger, had a lot to say about the influence of the iron triangle, and I saw the validity of his observation that, "virtually the only people that the Congress hears from and the only people who attempt to influence the executive branch are those who are united in wanting programs continued. Lobbyists, staffs of Congressional committees which oversee the programs, and those permanent employees of the government who administer them—these three groups have been appropriately called 'the iron triangle'. . . [and] are far more powerful than occasional lonely voices raised against either individual programs, or the trend caused by the predominance of the iron triangle." Caspar Weinberger, "Creativity and Collaboration in Government—The Budget Process," *The Frontiers of Knowledge*, The Frank Nelson Doubleday Lectures (Garden City, NY: Doubleday and Co, 1975), 263-264.

31. Cook, *Bureaucracy and Self-Government*, 95-96.

32. Cook, citing Heclo, *Bureaucracy and Self-Government*, 128. City managers do have a code prohibiting participation in electoral politics.

33. Cook, citing Lowi, *Bureaucracy and Self-Government*, 136.

34. Cook citing Lowi, *Bureaucracy and Self-Government*, 136. In addition, Jonathan Rauch writes, "The fact is that all groups, without exception, claim to be serving some larger good, and almost all believe it. And all groups, without exception, are lobbying for more of whatever it is that their members want, generally at some expense to nonmembers. By the same token, every single law, regulation, subsidy, and program creates losers as well as winners, and whether you think justice is served depends on who pays when the bill arrives." Jonathan Rauch, *Demosclerosis: The Silent Killer of American Government* (New York: Times Books, 1994), 47.

35. Robert A. Katzmann, *Institutional Disability: The Saga of Transportation Policy for the Disabled* (Washington, DC: The Brookings Institution, 1986), 14.

36. Karen M. Tani, "Welfare and Rights Before the Movement: Rights as a Language of the State," *Yale Law Journal* 122, no. 2 (November 2012): 322.

37. Perry Miller, *Roger Williams: His Contribution to the American Tradition* (Indianapolis: Bobbs-Merrill, 1953) 242-243.

38. Bernard E. Kelly, HEW Regional Director, memorandum to the HEW Under Secretary, December 3, 1976. This document can be found in the David Mathews collection, Kettering Foundation archives. For more information, contact archives@ kettering.org.

39. Jennifer Bachner and Benjamin Ginsberg, *What Washington Gets Wrong: The Unelected Officials Who Actually Run the Government and Their Misconceptions about the American People* (Amherst, NY: Prometheus Books, 2016), 9.

40. Charles T. Goodsell, *The Case for Bureaucracy: A Public Administration Polemic* (Chatham, NJ: Chatham House Publishers, 2003).

41. Lisa Rein and Ed O'Keefe, "New Post Poll Finds Negativity toward Federal Workers," *Washington Post*, October 19, 2010, https://madison.com/ct/news/new-poll-finds-negativity-toward-federal-workers/article_d4e06ce2-dacb-11df-b360-001cc4c03286.html.

42. William V. Muse, "Improving Management Operations in OE: In Pursuit of the Impossible Dream" (unpublished paper, August 1978).

43. Kenneth J. Meier, "Bureaucracy and Democracy: The Case for More Bureaucracy and Less Democracy," *Public Administration Review* 57, no. 3 (May/June 1997): 193-199.

44. Paul R. Verkuil, *Valuing Bureaucracy: The Case for Professional Government*, 2nd ed. (New York: Cambridge University Press, 2017), 92-93.

45. Tina Nabatchi, address to the joint staff and partners meeting at the Kettering Foundation, September 18, 2019.

CHAPTER VIII

PROBLEMS WITH POSITIVE POTENTIAL

In explaining why bureaucracies act as they do and how they lost public confidence, the last chapter noted the tension created by bureaucratic norms clashing with democratic norms. Now, I want to talk about the potential for creating a more positive relationship between the people of the United States and their governing institutions.

Although a *with* strategy can benefit nongovernmental institutions, which also have bureaucracies, in this chapter I'll concentrate again largely on government bureaucracies.

POSSIBILITIES FOR CHANGE

Several areas stand out immediately in the bureaucracy-public relationship where greater attention might help reduce the loss of confidence. One is in the way bureaucracies understand democracy.

Giving More Attention to Democratic Standards

Woodrow Wilson was right about the inherent tension between a professional administration and democratic norms. But taking certain democratic standards more into account in bureaucratic rule-making could be useful in improving the relationship. For instance, consider the importance of deliberation in decision-making, both by citizens and officials. According to Tina Nabatchi et al., deliberating might encourage more flexibility in the bureaucracy because democracy is grounded not in strict procedures but in deliberative decision-making.[1]

Are there administrators who might consider deliberating in their agency and with citizens? I think so. I met a group of professionals at HEW called "access professionals," who didn't see the bureaucracy's problem as too much democracy but rather too little. I admired what they were doing and, after leaving HEW, I assisted those who were forming their own associations, the American Society of Access Professionals and the International Association for Public Participation.

HEW created the Task Force on Citizen Participation to encourage holding timely public hearings that would gather relevant information from diverse groups of people, not just interest groups.[2] While not universal, there was, and still is, some support inside the bureaucracy for democratic reform.

The Standard

The democratic reliance on open decision-making is described in *Utopia*, a 16th-century book by Sir Thomas More. Whether or not More was truly a democrat, he gives an account of how an ideal state (city) called Utopia makes decisions in a legislative council, which consisted of senators along with a few representatives from something like a house of commons. The decisions in Utopia had to be made openly to prevent a small group of politicians from conspiring to impose a tyrant on the city. The standard for the governing council was, in Old English: *"Nothinge touchinge the common wealthe shal be confirmed and ratified, onlesse it have bene reasoned of and debated thre daies in the counsell, before it be decreed.*"[3] Note the three-day rule. It gave the citizens of Utopia time to reflect on what was happening in their government.

A good many Americans continue to believe that open deliberation is the proper measure for government decision-making. When decisions are made behind closed doors, people are quite likely to be upset. Furthermore, carrying out a *with* strategy in collaboration with the citizenry would be difficult, if not impossible, were decisions about either laws or regulations not made openly.

Of course, every detail of what a bureaucracy does can't be debated in public; that would be impossible to manage. Nonetheless, when it comes to promulgating regulations, it is difficult for me to see why Thomas More's standard for deliberation carried out for a reasonable length of time isn't applicable. I understand that More was talking about only a legislative body, but I believe the standard is even more broadly applicable today. In chapter IX, which deals with regulations, I'll describe some ways that this standard can be applied, which might help to restore at least some of the public's confidence.

Seeing through More Than One Lens

Government institutions are state institutions, and they have to see like a state, but they don't have to be one-eyed. One of Kettering's most striking insights, thanks to the NIF deliberations, is that often people see issues in a way that is different from the government's way of seeing them. Citizens see issues from the perspective of their experiences, which are evaluated by what they consider valuable. The government's view is shaped by professional expertise and partisan political concerns. For example, when people think about health policy, they recall the time they've spent trying to navigate a maddeningly complex system. Government officials tend to be more focused on constantly rising costs that defy all efforts at control. Neither concern is "wrong," but they aren't the same. Looking at such issues using two lenses shouldn't be that difficult.

Democracy is seen from many perspectives because it has many dimensions—a quest for justice, a love of freedom, a hostility to tyranny. Which of these is most valuable to citizens in a given situation, however, may not be what is most valuable to professionals, especially if they have a different understanding of democracy. What's more, different branches of government can have diverging views on how democracy applies to them. For instance, what democracy means in the legislative branch isn't always the same for the executive branch, where most of the bureaucracy is found. If the executive branch is not thought to have legislative power, an easy assumption is that the standard of openness doesn't apply to the promulgation of regulations, even though those rules have the force of law. (I recall that when I was at HEW, the number of regulations was approximately twice the number of laws that Congress passed.)

MAKING MORE USE OF COMMON SENSE

A strategy based on *not* always "seeing like a state" would allow governments to collaborate with nongovernmental institutions like nursing homes, which could draw on the caring qualities of families, friends, and neighbors. The people in government understand the power of this human compassion, but, as bureaucrats, they can't see or measure it. Rules stand in the way. An exception in one case might lead to more exceptions; soon the rules would no longer hold.

But must rules be unbending?[4] If they can't bend, why do we have judges and juries to take circumstances into consideration and to exercise judgment? In *The Death of Common Sense*, Philip Howard, a lawyer and the founder of Common Good, an organization that advocates simplifying government, laments the eclipse of common sense, which he sees as the triumph of legalism over practicality.[5] Laws and regulations can be insensitive to context because no rule can cover every eventuality. When there is a morass of conflicting restrictions and prescriptions, Howard argues, the results are inaction, which feeds people's frustration.

BREAKING PATTERNS

Allowing for the exercise of judgment in the service of common sense, taking a broader view than just that of the state, and giving more consideration to democratic standards would make using a *with* strategy more likely. Taken together, these measures could begin to change bureaucratic culture. However, such change may encounter more than the usual resistance if, as some research shows, bureaucracies are trapped by patterns in their behavior that resist change. Ironically, some of these traps may be in the very efforts that officials make to listen to citizens.

Changing Counterproductive Outreach

Despite the many engagement programs, public confidence has continued to fall, even as participation and accountability initiatives have grown. Few suspected—I certainly didn't while at HEW—that these efforts to engage citizens could be, at best, too little, and, at worst, counterproductive.

By 1996, doubtful that the federal bureaucracy was "carrying out the will of the Nation,"[6] numerous controls had been placed on agencies to make them more responsive to the citizenry. Ironically, according to scholars like Brian Cook, some of these measures have had the opposite effect. Cook found that accountability measures, for example, have "created an arrangement of administrative controls and political relationships that is nearly incomprehensible and inaccessible to average citizens."[7] Cook saw that these controls had grown quite elaborate and the political interactions they set in motion had become extremely complicated.[8] They had become serious obstacles, not just to realizing democratic norms, but also to the bureaucratic effectiveness that administrative agencies prized. Cook concluded: "An increasingly vicious circle has emerged in which anxiety about control and accountability of public administration has led to more extensive, more complex controls, which in turn have increased the bureaucratic distance between administrators and the public they are expected to serve."[9]

Of course, we all want accountability in our institutions. Albert Dzur, the author of *Democratic Professionalism*, points out, "There's real value to accountability—meaning, roughly, that our schools, courts, hospitals, etc., are doing what they say they are doing *and what the public has decided they should do* [emphasis added]."[10] However, like Cook, Dzur fears this isn't happening. In fact, he sees signs that institutions are moving in the opposite direction by developing even more expert and technical processes in hopes of restoring lost public legitimacy or creating better defenses. He calls this movement "super professionalism." As an alternative, Cook proposes that "public administrators engage in deliberation and debate," not only among themselves and elected officials, but with substantial segments of the public at large.[11] The subjects on the table should be the goals and larger ends of the polity.[12]

RETHINKING ACCOUNTABILITY

Not only have accountability demonstrations proven problematic, the subject itself is ripe for reassessment. The most common strategy that both governmental and nongovernmental institutions have used to demonstrate that they aren't unaccountable is to provide hard data showing they produced good results and are, therefore, truly worthy of the public's trust. These performance measures have been based on various benchmarks, such as the standardized test scores of students in secondary and elementary schools.[13]

Despite being done in the name of restoring public confidence, many accountability projects have actually been defensive measures to protect institutions from what their officials consider unwarranted criticisms and intrusions into their work. That's an understandable reaction, although not one likely to restore confidence.

What exactly is accountability? And is what the government sees as being accountable the same thing that citizens want? After I left government, I came to realize that citizens differ significantly with institutional leaders over what being accountable means. While institutional leaders typically have in mind providing data and other information, citizens are more concerned about the kind of *relationship* they have with institutions. That is true of all institutions, governmental and nongovernmental.[14]

School officials, for example, may think that they are models of accountability when they cite voluminous test score data. They believe these performance measures are in line with the public's demand for higher standards. Citizens, on the other hand, although wanting higher standards and appreciating the information on test performance, may still not be convinced that the schools are doing the job they want them to do. People may think that test scores are only one indication of school performance.[15] They want to be informed yet may feel overwhelmed by what they consider meaningless numbers. Skeptical of metrics, they worry that they are being manipulated by the way statistics are used.

Whether citizens are talking about officeholders in governments, colleges and universities, or hospitals, the expectations are similar. People look for a frank, open, morally grounded exchange. And they want relationships that provide opportunities for public influence. Citizens who have these kinds of relationships with institutions tend to be more productively engaged with them. John Gaventa and Gregory Barrett found that in mutually beneficial relationships, people became more knowledgeable and had a greater sense of their own political efficacy. And the institutions were considered to be more responsive and accountable.[16]

THICKENING CIVIC ENGAGEMENT

The government's efforts to engage the citizenry often began with laudable, democratic intentions. However, these efforts have changed form over time, becoming, in many cases, "thinner."

In the Beginning—Maximum Feasible Participation

Officials in the Kennedy and Johnson administrations attempted a major shift in the government's relationship with the public by calling for "maximum feasible participation." The phrase soon became a banner for civic engagement in all federal programs in the 1970s and beyond. The intent was to give poor people representation on the boards that controlled local agencies. However, the poor came to be represented not so much by those who were living in poverty as by advocates who attempted to speak for them. And "feasible" came to mean exactly 30 percent of the membership on boards.[17] Few, if any, reformers thought that the poor themselves would actually control the boards or run the programs. Participation was more *for* certain citizens rather than *with* the citizenry. And there doesn't appear to have been much recognition of what the people benefiting from the federal assistance might contribute themselves. Research has found that the federal action programs failed to develop beneficiaries' capacity to combine with other citizens to solve community problems.[18]

A 2018 study by Thomas Bryer and Sofia Prysmakova-Rivera looked into what was actually happening to people in poverty, using the criterion of "Nothing about us without us is for us."[19] Their analysis showed that poor people were better judges of the value of proposed solutions to their problems because of their direct, personal experience. The authors also analyzed the counterargument that citizens aren't the best judges because they are lacking in reason, can be overly emotional, and may be prone to "temporary delusions." That will always be true of some individuals but less likely true of the entire population.

These criticisms led to the conclusion that important decisions should be left to advocates representing the poor because the advocates were informed and objective. Even if these advocates were self-appointed and not accountable to those they represented, they would be the best guardians of those in poverty. They were skilled in influencing the political system and the poor weren't. Working *with* the poor was impossible.

Bryer and Prysmakova-Rivera found this pattern so pervasive that the government's requirement for maximum participation actually became "maximum feasible manipulation" by well-intended advocates. However, not convinced by the case being made by advocates, these scholars wanted the government to increase its responsiveness to the people it served, a responsiveness that they called "entrepreneurial and collaborative."[20]

Thinning Out

Unfortunately, as time passed, what had begun as efforts to involve more citizens ran into even more difficulties. Locally elected officials were concerned about their loss of power. Just as damaging, the language of participation became imprecise. Words that came to mean everything eventually came to mean nothing. So policies with this language could be difficult to implement and led to conflicting expectations. One critic was provoked enough by what was happening that he wanted the term "civic engagement" to be put in the dustbin because it meant so many different things to so many different people.[21] Similar terms, including "public participation," became susceptible to the same reaction.

Thicker Engagement?

The good news from a *with* or democratic perspective is that, in 2018, scholars found some evidence of "thicker" forms of participation developing.[22] What I think of as thick participation involves more direct interaction with citizens and features public deliberation in joint planning and policy formation. I contrast that with the typical or "thinner" participation, which is characterized by hearing concerns and providing information. Maybe there will eventually be a better understanding of the role of citizens that does not assume their role has to be the same as the role of technically savvy professionals.

CONSULTATIVE DEMOCRACY?

Despite reports in the 1970s on the public's declining confidence, most of the federal government's bureaucracies were wedded to the idea that they were the best guardians of the true public interest and that the role of the citizenry should be limited to voting and being consulted—to the maximum extent possible (as determined by government officials). Citizens were thought of as consumers or clients, not as actors working in collaboration with the government. This led to the growth of a limited kind of democracy called "consultative."[23]

"Nonsultation"

Whatever the merits of consultative democracy, it has serious limitations. In fact, just being consulted can make some people quite angry. A journalist at the UK *Telegraph* described consultation as actually "nonsultation," by which he meant "a cynical technique used by governments, local authorities and some businesses [in England] to provide spurious legitimacy or fake PR cover for a pre-determined decision." He continued, "All major decisions, and many minor ones . . . must now, by law, be consulted on. . . . The purpose . . . is almost never to act on the public's views. It is to manage, manipulate, or suppress them."[24] This conclusion may be too harsh, but the public's pushback can be severe.

CITIZENS' RESPONSIBILITIES
FOR BRIDGING THE DIVIDE

I have already written about the power citizens can have. Here, I want to emphasize their responsibility. Although I have been concentrating on the bureaucracy, I don't want to give the impression that civil servants bear all the responsibility for improving relationships with the public. They don't and can't. I don't know of many bilateral relationships that have been improved through efforts of just one of the parties. Improvements usually require reciprocity and collaboration by all. A *with* strategy certainly does. As I've said, there are some things the citizenry can—and must—do on its side in order for the collaboration to be effective. However, in saying that, I am not suggesting that the reservations that bureaucracies have about what the public can do can be cursorily dismissed.

To cross the divide separating the people from the government, citizens can't just go to officials and ask for support or demand the government act in certain ways. There isn't anything wrong with doing either. Nonetheless, if these are the only things citizens do, it is inevitable that the government will see them more as supplicants, clients, or consumers rather than what they must be in a democracy—producers.

I would emphasize again that a citizen's approach to government should be based, whenever possible, on civic initiatives that are begun in a collaborative spirit. I gave an example of an offer to collaborate in chapter II: "Here is what we as citizens working together are doing to solve this problem; what can you in government do to complement our efforts?" That one sentence captures the essence of a *with* initiative.

Our Political DNA

As you have read, the conviction that citizens can move beyond only asking for or demanding things from the government is rooted in our country's history. Our laws have always recognized and encouraged the nongovernmental organizations that play similar roles to those of the government. Religious institutions provide social services, libraries educate, and voluntary groups offer emergency relief. Our tax policy is tacit recognition of the necessity of working *with* the citizenry.

Using Civic Democracy to Strengthen Institutional Democracy

While institutional democracy is in serious trouble, local organic, civic democracy, which underpins institutional democracy, is healthier. The task ahead is to better connect the two, which is the objective of a *with* strategy. Furthermore, all of the civic groups able to do their part in carrying out a *with* strategy aren't limited to formal, nongovernmental institutions. The strategy can make use of the often informal grassroots associations that citizens use to do their work. These are found in what might be thought of as the political wetlands.[25]

Like nature's wetlands, the political wetlands are teeming with life—in this case, civic life. The small cells of civic life are made up of people working *with* people to solve common problems. They turn frustration and anger into constructive energy for their work together. These civic relationships are based on reciprocity—receiving and giving in return. They develop, for example, when citizens take the initiatives to construct houses for the homeless or come together with police to keep young people safe.

Recall chapter IV's report on a study by sociologist Patrick Sharkey that showed the significant role "ordinary" citizens have played in reducing crime.[26] Sharkey didn't claim that these citizen initiatives alone caused the nationwide decline in crime, but he did point out that their contributions, although significant, have been largely ignored. These citizens weren't just providing better parks or more support for parents, they were demonstrating the ability of citizens to make a difference by working together. That is a good example of the civic initiative that is essential to a *with* strategy.

Unfortunately, some of our institutions may not recognize these civic cells because they are invisible when only "seeing like a state." They have few of the characteristics of organizations with political power. Most of the cells have little money and little political authority. They may not even have a street address. They seldom have offices and a staff. But what they do have is the power of civic energy and a human touch.

WHAT'S NEXT?

Recognizing and making use of the potential in what citizens can do is not without risk for administrators. They are responsible for what their institutions do. Nonetheless, there may be low-risk opportunities to make better use of what the citizenry can do, provided they aren't precluded by regulations. The next chapter is about this rulemaking and how it might become more compatible with democracy.

NOTES

1. Tina Nabatchi, Holly T. Goerdel, and Shelly Peffer, "Public Administration in Dark Times: Some Questions for the Future of the Field," *Journal of Public Administration Research and Theory* 21, issue suppl_1 (January 2011): i37, https://doi.org/10.1093/jopart/muq068.

2. US Department of Health, Education, and Welfare, HEW News Press Release, November 10, 1976. This document can be found in the David Mathews collection, Kettering Foundation archives. For more information, contact archives@kettering.org.

3. Thomas More, *Utopia* (London: J. M. Dent and Company, 1906), 66.

4. Robert K. Merton in "Bureaucratic Structure and Personality," points out, "(1) An effective bureaucracy demands reliability of response and strict devotion to regulations. (2) Such devotion to the rules leads to their transformation into absolutes; they are no longer conceived as relative to a given set of purposes. (3) This interferes with ready adaptation under special conditions not clearly envisioned by those who drew up the general rules. (4) Thus, the very elements which conduce toward efficiency in general produce inefficiency in specific instances" (564). Robert K. Merton, "Bureaucratic Structure and Personality," *Social Forces* 18, no. 4 (May 1940): 560-568.

5. Philip K. Howard, *The Death of Common Sense: How Law Is Suffocating America* (New York: Random House, 1994).

6. The President's Committee on Administrative Management, *Administrative Management in the United States* (Washington, DC: US Government Printing Office, 1937), 3, at https://babel.hathitrust.org/cgi /pt?id=mdp.39015030482726&view=1up&seq=3.

7. Brian J. Cook, *Bureaucracy and Self-Government: Reconsidering the Role of Public Administration in American Politics* (Baltimore, MD: Johns Hopkins University Press, 1996), 137.

8. Cook, *Bureaucracy and Self-Government*, 137.

9. Cook, *Bureaucracy and Self-Government*, 134.

10. Albert Dzur, memorandum to Kettering Foundation, November 27, 2012. This document can be found in the David Mathews collection, Kettering Foundation archives. For more information, contact archives@kettering.org.

11. Cook, *Bureaucracy and Self-Government*, 149.

12. Cook, *Bureaucracy and Self-Government*, 145.

13. Jean Johnson, *"Will It Be on the Test?" A Closer Look at How Leaders and Parents Think about Accountability in the Public Schools* (New York and Dayton: Public Agenda and Kettering Foundation, 2013), 15-16, 21-22.

14. Johnson, *"Will It Be on the Test?,"* 24.

15. Johnson, *"Will It Be on the Test?,"* 15-16, 21-22, 24; and Sheila A. Arens, *Examining the Meaning of Accountability: Reframing the Construct, a Report on the Perceptions of Accountability* (Aurora, CO: Mid-continent Research for Education and Learning, July 2005).

16. John Gaventa and Gregory Barrett, *So What Difference Does It Make? Mapping the Outcomes of Citizen Engagement* (working paper, Institute of Development Studies, October 2010), 27–32, 36, 41.

17. The Economic Opportunity Act of 1964 required "maximum feasible participation" of the residents of the places and members of groups served by Community Action Programs that were funded by the federal government. A 1967 amendment to the act specified the exact composition of the board of a Community Action Agency: "a maximum of one-third from the public sector and a minimum of one-third from the poor community." Lillian B. Rubin, "Maximum Feasible Participation: The Origins, Implications, and Present Status," *The Annals of the American Academy of Political and Social Science* 385, no. 1 (1969): 14-29.

18. Theodore J. Lowi, *The End of Liberalism: The Second Republic of the United States,* 2nd ed. (New York: W. W. Norton & Company, 1979), 212.

19. Thomas Bryer and Sofia Prysmakova-Rivera, *Poor Participation: Fighting the Wars on Poverty and Impoverished Citizenship* (Lanham, MD: Lexington Books, 2018), 41-56.

20. Bryer and Prysmakova-Rivera, *Poor Participation,* 41–56.

21. Ben Berger, "Political Theory, Political Science and the End of Civic Engagement," *Perspectives on Politics* 7, no. 2 (2009): 335-350.

22. Larkin Dudley, Kathryn E. Webb Farley, and Noel Gniady Banford, "Looking Back to Look Forward: Federal Officials' Perceptions of Public Engagement," *Administration and Society* 50, no. 5 (2018): 684-685; and Larkin Dudley, Noel Gniady-Banford, and Kathryn Webb Farley, *Public Participation in Five Federal Agencies: An Examination of Public Officials' Perceptions* (Dayton, OH: Report to the Kettering Foundation, September 30, 2016), 17.

23. For an account of consultative democracy in China, see Liu Jianfei, *Democracy and China* (Beijing: New World Press, 2011).

24. Andrew Gilligan, "A Government Ruse That's Nothing Short of an Insultation," *Telegraph,* August 20, 2010, http://www.telegraph.co.uk/news/politics/7955561 /A-Government-ruse-thats-nothing-short-of-an-insultation.html.

25. David Mathews, *The Ecology of Democracy: Finding Ways to Have a Stronger Hand in Shaping Our Future* (Dayton, OH: Kettering Foundation Press, 2014), 24-28.

26. Patrick Sharkey, *Uneasy Peace: The Great Crime Decline, the Renewal of City Life, and the Next War on Violence* (New York: W. W. Norton, 2018).

CHAPTER IX

DOWN WITH REGULATIONS?

The government works largely by the legislative branch passing laws and then the departments in the executive branch applying those laws to people, communities, and institutions through regulations. These regulations and the way they are formulated sometimes make people quite angry about the government's intrusion into their lives, which diminishes their control. The intrusion seems worse when it comes from officials who aren't elected by the people.[1] These feelings aren't quite the same as the loss of confidence. But they reinforce it.

So much was being regulated by the 1970s and so many people were angry that it sparked a widespread call for deregulation—a call that was directed primarily at the government's bureaucracies. According to Philip Howard, "Between 1969 and 1979 the *Federal Register* nearly quadrupled in length, expanding not just the scope of regulation, but the granularity of its mandates. Forest rangers used to have guidelines in a pocket pamphlet. Now they had volumes of rules."[2] A 1973 Harris survey found that more than 80 percent of those polled agreed with the statement, "Elected officials have lost control of the bureaucrats who really run things."[3] This perception contributed to the falling confidence in the government. And the rigidity in regulations made working *with* the government in more flexible ways less likely.

The number of people calling for less regulation in the 1970s grew rapidly in the 1980s. Eventually, even staunch advocates of strong government, like Senator Edward Kennedy, supported certain types of deregulation. Deregulation is still a perennial political issue, although opinions vary on who and what should be regulated.[4] For example, although concerned about excessive regulation, people have favored environmental regulations aimed at toxic spills, nuclear waste, and other contaminants.[5]

This chapter goes into some detail on the process of formulating regulations, including attempts at deregulation and the reduction of paperwork. A few of these reforms opened the regulating process to more of the people who would be affected as well as to the general public. This openness is critical to a *with* strategy.

The larger objective here is to better understand the troubled relationship between the public and the government. I will build on the earlier discussions about the nature of the federal bureaucracy and its effect on the relationship between the public and the government. The question is how a strategy of working *with* the people can be useful when administrators are carrying out their responsibilities for formulating government regulations.

Earlier, I wrote about the nature of bureaucracies, which influences the regulatory process. Please keep in mind Philip Howard's observation that laws and regulations have difficulty taking context into consideration.[6] Also note Robert Merton's observation that rules, which is what regulations are, lead to absolutes that don't adapt well to conditions different from those when the rules were made.[7]

In this chapter, I'll continue to be candid about obstacles to a *with* strategy, though I hope without being unfair to either the legislative or the regulatory process. The government working *for* the public presents few problems for public administrators, who already see themselves as public servants. The government working *with* the citizenry, however, is another matter. It raises questions about the competence of citizens, and it also threatens bureaucracies with loss of control. Perhaps the public's relationship with bureaucracies was bound to become an issue as governments came to play an increasingly greater role in people's everyday lives.

DEREGULATION AND THE FORD ADMINISTRATION

First, a little context is needed as background for discussing regulation reform in the mid-1970s. Return for a minute to the earlier discussion of the political environment at the time. Congress had become fragmented by subcommittees that were championing very specific causes. The presidency had been weakened by the Watergate scandal, and the White House and Congress were locked in a bitter dispute over fiscal policy. Party rivalry, although not at current levels, was intense for the time because the Democrats were convinced they had a good chance of routing the Republicans in the 1976 election. Gerald Ford, although well respected on both sides of the aisle in Congress, was not able to overcome the partisan battles. As an appointed president, he had no electoral mandate to convert into political leverage on the Hill.

Given this environment, opportunities to enact new legislation were rare. In addition, federal expenditures outstripped revenues, and the Ford administration faced the dual threats of high inflation and high unemployment. By 1975, the country was in a major recession. Convinced that short-term measures would exacerbate the economic downturn, President Ford opposed any additional federal spending. The 1975 deficit had climbed sharply and was on its way to climbing even higher by year's end, reaching World War II levels. Ford responded by using veto after veto in disputes with Congress.

He was particularly concerned about the inflationary impact of federal regulations.[8] In October 1975, he asked Congress to establish a national commission to promote deregulation. He explained the reasons in his autobiography, citing numerous instances of costly, counterproductive, or just foolish rules. One that caught his eye was issued by the Occupational Safety and Health Administration (OSHA) in the Labor Department. Ford wrote, "Presumably, the Occupational Safety and Health Administration was concerned about the presence of 22,000 different toxic substances used in American industry. Yet, since its creation in 1972, it had issued regulations governing workers' exposure to fewer than 20 of them. At the same time, however, it had devoted countless hours to the proper construction of portable wooden ladders and had published 12 pages of regulations about them."[9]

While concerned with overregulation, President Ford didn't reject the use of the government's regulatory powers. For instance, he relied on that authority when his food stamp reforms stalled in Congress. He had the Department of Agriculture create rules to carry out the changes he wanted to make. Even though critical in specific instances, as in the OSHA case, Ford was by no means anti-Washington, nor were those of us in the cabinet.

Critics charged that the real reason for reducing regulations was to favor business interests. However, I don't recall HEW reducing its oversight of the industries in its purview. It is true that the Council of Economic Advisors urged the Department to deregulate the Food and Drug Administration (FDA). The Department reviewed the regulatory practices of the agency, but finding no compelling cases of abuse, we didn't do as the council urged.

President Ford also made the point that "obsolete and unnecessary regulations" were not the result of "perversity on the part of some regulatory body or government official." Instead, the problem was the *very nature* of the regulatory process itself, which Ford said was "inherently static." In 1975, Ford remarked, "Regulations do not automatically expire when they have outlived their usefulness. There is no systematic pattern of review, and even when it is acknowledged that changes are warranted, procedural delays often result in obsolete rules remaining in force for years. In short, while the intention of regulation is to protect consumers, it sometimes does just the opposite."[10] This is an example of what has been called "government ill executed," and that does affect public confidence.[11]

REGULATING AS TAKING

Is the solution to the problems caused by regulations simply deregulation? In the case of out-of-date rules, perhaps it is. But my own position on HEW regulations had to do with the way the government exercises its "taking powers." Everyone who pays taxes knows that governments have the power to "take" from citizens. Most all of us accept that as legitimate—under certain conditions. Government legitimacy rests on deliberative processes being used in making judicial and legislative determinations. The standard also applies, I believe, when the executive branch "takes" through regulating.

Taking, when it appears to be unfair, reduces more than confidence in government. It arouses ancient feelings like those when monarchs seized farmers' grain and other possessions to enrich themselves. That is the reason US courts have long ruled that there are limits to taking powers. In 1922, Justice Oliver Wendell Holmes, writing the majority opinion in *Pennsylvania Coal Company v. Mahon*, ruled that state regulation had crossed the line into uncompensated taking. Where that line is precisely has been disputed, but the disputes reaffirm that there are indeed limits. Regulating without being subject to public deliberations tests these limits.

The bureaucracy began to exercise more of the taking powers of the state after the Great Depression of the 1930s and World War II. President Roosevelt's Committee on Administrative Management laid out a concept of democracy that has influenced government operations ever since. It was that the federal government has to be efficient and effective in order to be an "instrument for carrying out the will of the Nation."[12] Some Roosevelt New Dealers went even one step further and argued that the federal government had become truly the people's agent, so citizens no longer needed protection from their own ministers and bureaucrats.

There is no denying that "We the People" benefit when the government uses our taxes to pay for building our roads and schools, as well as a multitude of other services. We also benefit from regulations that make these services effective and efficient. Yet, from a democratic perspective, the taking and regulating have to meet democratic criteria, even if done by *our* ministers. How these ministers carry out their duties affects public confidence.

Who Is and Isn't Regulated?

Taking is coercive, even in the best of cases when it is necessary for the good of all. In some cases, the taking that regulations can do is unavoidable. In other cases, I don't think it is. For instance, I thought it was possible to give greater consideration to the impact of regulations on the professionals (such as teachers and social workers) who provide services to the beneficiaries of laws. Regulations can take away the latitude service-providing professionals have to act and constrain them. That is likely to happen if administrators have no discretion to do what they think is best because regulations are based on inflexible legal requirements. When the government overuses its coercive powers, it can also forego the essential complementary production that only citizens can provide, as well as diminish public confidence.

By the 1970s, the federal bureaucracy had become empowered to take a great deal, not just from private individuals and businesses, but from state and local levels of government through mandatory requirements to use their funds to match and receive federal money. Controversies sparked by disputes with those "taken from" heighten antagonistic feelings toward the federal establishment.

REGULATING AS LAWMAKING

While regulations can move power away from service-providing professionals, they also give power to the bureaucracy. The most problematic effect of combining powers in a department of the executive branch is that regulations become de facto laws, which only the legislative branch is supposed to enact. This heightens the tension between the norms for democracy and those for efficient public administration. A democracy looks to its citizens to determine what is in their best interest, while a bureaucracy looks to its expertise to determine those interests. There is a shift in authority. I recognize that this shift is compatible with the prevailing constitutive theory of the bureaucracy, yet, as I said in the last chapter, I believe more recognition of democratic standards is needed in this age of declining public confidence.

Regulation writing had become a major industry by the 1970s. HEW alone wrote volumes of regulations, which had the force of law. This meant that HEW had de facto legislative powers. Early in 1976, in an address to the HEW staff about dealing with the problem of governing by regulations, I said, "The public sees the Department as . . . a legislature. . . . Therefore, . . . [citizens] . . . want to be assured that we play by the rules that society has adopted for legislating. . . . They particularly want to be assured that we, who have been the champions of due process, are also 'due' in our own process."[13]

One way this can happen is by government agencies being more open to public deliberation. Recall what More's *Utopia* said on this subject: "Nothing touching the commonwealth . . . shall be confirmed and ratified unless it has been reasoned and debated three days in the council."[14]

In fairness to the regulation writers, they weren't trying to violate More's standard. However, many professionals in administrative posts believed that Congress should confine itself to instituting laws that set policy and then leave it to administrators to add the details needed for carrying out those laws in their regulations. That argument has merit. Nonetheless, because the norms for democratic lawmaking are so critical to political legitimacy, I believed that HEW had to revise its rulemaking procedures.

A MATTER OF INTERPRETATION

Deregulation would not necessarily give the government back to the people. That could be done only by giving more citizens greater opportunities to influence rulemaking. And it would require citizens to do more as producers in civil society. With that in mind, I thought HEW could do more to open its rulemaking to the general public.

First, efforts were made to change the way rules were written. Agencies frequently waited until they had decided what they wanted to do internally before notifying the public. Staff members often had different opinions, and an agency was under understandable pressure to reconcile these differences before publishing a draft regulation. Consequently, an informal agreement on the nature of a regulation was sometimes reached before the citizenry was aware of it. That was particularly true for people who were not involved in special interest groups. Because of close ties between officials in the bureaucracy and representatives of these groups, a regulation could be shaped by conversations outside the official channels. These conversations allowed staff members to test ideas and see what was acceptable to the interest groups. But Thomas More would be appalled by such "consultations outside the council."

Another barrier to the public's ability to influence the regulators was the terminology used in draft regulations. Regulation writers used technical and legal language because they considered their audiences to be professionals. Citizens, on the other hand, who were ultimately the ones affected by the regulations, often failed to see any connection between the things they valued and the professional/bureaucratic policy language.[15]

The Title IX Case

Even if the power of the legislative branch is recognized and administrators are only to implement the laws, they still have to determine, in some detail, how a law is to be applied. In HEW, that required interpreting the will of Congress, which could be obscure. Government agencies have an incentive to use broad interpretations because that gives them great latitude and influence. However, this can result in serious conflicts with Congress. For example, this happened when one of HEW's regional offices interpreted a regulation in a way that sent shock waves across the political spectrum. The case had to do with a broad interpretation of a statute protecting women's rights—Title IX of the Educational Amendments of 1972. The interpretation was that father-son, mother-daughter events were illegal. In Washington, HEW's Office for Civil Rights (OCR) had assured a regional office of the Department that its broad interpretation of Title IX was consistent with the law and the regulations. But as soon as I heard about it, I overruled the decision. President Ford also objected. Hearing the outrage, Congress denounced OCR's assurance as a gross misinterpretation of what it intended and quickly passed a law expressly authorizing father-son, mother-daughter events.

This incident illustrates why OCR had a reputation as a "hot bed of regulatory zealots obsessed with vast social engineering schemes," which had "little relation to . . . actual statutory mandates."[16] My successor in the Carter administration and a veteran of Lyndon Johnson's term in office,

Joseph (Joe) Califano Jr., wrote: "OCR also had a penchant for getting involved at very detailed levels, a propensity that undermined our credibility in pursuing the central task of assuring equal opportunity." He added, "At times it seemed as though OCR sought in its forms and bureaucratic cant refuge from the extraordinary subtleties the second generation of civil rights issues presented."[17]

Other critics leveled just the opposite criticism, calling OCR "timid, half-hearted, and ineffectual," charges whose validity is discussed in Jeremy Rabkin's study of the Office for Civil Rights.[18] In OCR's defense, in the case of Title IX, Rabkin noted that Congress gave "an extremely broad mandate in a very sensitive area, with a legislative history affording virtually no . . . guidance."[19] These circumstances favored those in the bureaucracy who wanted an activist government.

OCR was easy to criticize when things went "wrong." Rabkin observed, perceptively I think, that "buck-passing must be particularly tempting in . . . an emotionally charged political environment, where policy decisions usually turn not on questions of instrumental effectiveness . . . but on abstract notions of fairness." Under these conditions, it is tempting for politicians to blame the bureaucracy.[20]

The environment surrounding rulemaking was usually very emotionally charged because advocates of regulations on matters of discrimination made their case in moral terms, which discouraged questioning the rules. Rabkin also found that institutions that had to comply with OCR's rules were reluctant to ask Congress to modify regulations because they didn't want to "pit their historic claims to independence against the moralistic rhetoric of OCR's constituents."[21]

The Title IX regulations had been approved in 1975, before I arrived, so my job was interpreting them. Although not willing to ban parents from attending banquets, I was favorably disposed to the intent of the law, in part because I remembered my mother saying how much she had enjoyed sports in high school.[22] And I thought there were some immediate and practical things that could be done to make the interpretations and actual application of all regulations more effective. (Title IX dealt with more than sports.)

Regulating the Regulators

Waiting until regulations were being interpreted made meaningful democratic reform difficult. So, I wrote an op-ed for the *New York Times* in 1976 announcing that HEW was going to regulate its regulators. [23] The Department would post a notice of its intention to issue a regulation before a draft was written. And HEW would place the notice in more widely read publications than the *Federal Register*. Regional offices were also to hold regular public meetings in order to reach a wider audience. And what citizens said in response was to be shared with the public. Bureaucratic terms were to be replaced by standard English whenever possible. When there were unresolved issues in the Department over what should be in a regulation, those issues would be acknowledged and people would be invited to weigh in. The *Federal Register* was to list all the options being considered so citizens could participate in the deliberations going on inside agencies. This allowed people to comment on the proposed options or offer their own options. Finally, the Department would set deadlines for itself for evaluating the effects of new regulation and reporting on any changes that were made.

Another reform allowed draft regulations to be made public before final Secretarial action. HEW officials were authorized to put proposals out with their own signatures rather than using the name of the Secretary. This made previously nameless authors of drafts visible and accountable. The Department would also extend the period for commenting on proposed rules from 30 to 45 days. Then, when posting a final regulation, agencies were required to report the comments they received throughout the rulemaking process, along with their reasons for accepting or rejecting them.

I didn't think that these measures would solve all the problems associated with regulations. I did believe they could be helpful.

Even though these measures required more work, some professionals in HEW rallied behind them. These were primarily the staff (I mentioned them earlier) responsible for increasing public access under various open government statutes. We brought these professionals together in a department-wide task force to help implement the regulatory reforms, which included creating

a central monitoring office. That office coordinated and, when possible, consolidated regulations. The staff also had to watch for conflicting directives,
which were likely to occur because so many different agencies in HEW wrote
regulations.

In addition to these reforms, agencies throughout HEW were encouraged
to come up with their own ways of reaching out to a broader cross-section of
citizens. The agencies' responsiveness was heartening. And the staff that participated in making these changes were often the ones who later formed their
own association of access professionals.[24]

It is a truism that changing organizational behavior never comes easily,
and regulation reform required substantial modifications of bureaucratic
practice. When stories and editorials picked up on declining public confidence, it encouraged the reformers in HEW. The attention also encouraged
other people inside the government who wanted reform. One editorial writer
described what Americans were saying about the federal bureaucracy in
coffee shops and on street corners: "Over the years the public has become
increasingly put out over the petty rules and red tape that entangle it in a
morass of frustrations, aggravations and unanswered complaints. In dealing
with the federal government, the buck never seems to stop, it just passes from
one bureaucrat to another until the citizen finally surrenders to the system."[25]
This same editorial went on to note HEW's efforts to listen more carefully
and review old regulations to see whether their effects were consistent with
their intents. This journalist understood that more was at stake than bureaucratic efficiency.

WHAT'S NEXT?

A half-dozen cases of lawmaking and regulation writing are used in the next
section of the book to show the complexities that a *with* strategy will have
to face in order to use citizen-made "goods" to complement what the government does. Two of the cases have to do with serving Americans with
disabilities, certainly a proper role for government. These cases deal with
the relationship between lawmaking and regulation writing. If Congress

was to determine *what* should be done but leave to professional administrators the task of deciding *how* the law should be applied, legislators had to be clear about the intent of the law in order for it to be interpreted properly. Determining how a broad statute should be applied is difficult enough, but it is almost impossible if there is a limited record of what the lawmakers intended.

NOTES

1. However, when Congress has written detailed laws, they amount to legislated regulations. And that creates other problems.
2. Philip K. Howard, *The Rule of Nobody: Saving America from Dead Laws and Broken Government* (New York, NY: W.W. Norton & Co., 2014), 107.
3. Benjamin I. Page and Robert Y. Shapiro, *The Rational Public: Fifty Years of Trends in Americans' Policy Preferences* (Chicago: University of Chicago Press, 1992), 157.
4. See the Pew Research Center for People and the Press, "Auto Bailout Now Backed, Stimulus Divisive: Mixed Views of Regulation, Support for Keystone Pipeline," February 23, 2012, http://www.people-press.org/2012/02/23/auto-bailout-now-backed-stimulus-divisive/. The report found that, in general, more Americans say that government regulation of business is harmful than say it is necessary to protect the public. At the same time, when asked about regulations in specific areas, such as food safety and environmental protection, there is broad support for strengthening regulations or keeping current regulations as they are now rather than reducing regulations. The public also thinks that in many sectors there is too little rather than too much regulation. Pluralities think there is too little regulation of large corporations, banks and financial institutions, and the oil and gas industry. But when it comes to small businesses, far more say there is too much rather than too little regulation.
5. Page and Shapiro, *The Rational Public*, 159.
6. Howard writes, "Law that aspires to completeness doesn't leave room for questions of priority and practicality. For the legal mandarins who write laws and regulations, the litmus test is, as one critic described it, whether law has successfully 'eliminate[d] the human element in decision making.'" Howard, *The Rule of Nobody*, 33.
7. Robert K. Merton, "Bureaucratic Structure and Personality," *Social Forces* 18, no. 4 (May 1940): 564.
8. James E. Anderson, "The Struggle to Reform Regulatory Procedures, 1978-1998," *Policy Studies Journal* 26, no. 3 (1998): 482–498. In an April 1975 speech to the US Chamber of Commerce, the President distinguished between two broad kinds of

government regulation: (1) regulation designed to deal with competitive performance (e.g., trucking, airlines, utilities, banking); and (2) regulation concerned with social issues (e.g., occupational safety, consumer product safety, and the environment). Ford remarked that while the latter kind of regulation is "generally of more recent origin," it is "becoming more critical every day." He argued that this type of regulation needed to be evaluated to see the costs and benefits. The President said, "The question is not whether we want to do something about noise or safety, but whether in making changes in our regulations they would make more sense in terms of costs added and benefits gained." President Gerald R. Ford's Remarks at the Annual Meeting of the Chamber of Commerce of the United States, April 28, 1975, https://www.fordlibrarymuseum.gov/library/speeches/750220.htm.

9. Gerald R. Ford, *A Time to Heal* (New York: Harper and Row, 1979), 271-273.

10. Gerald R. Ford, "President Gerald R. Ford's Remarks at the Annual Meeting of the Chamber of Commerce of the United States, April 28, 1975," Containing the Public Messages, Speeches, and Statements of the President, Book 1—January 1 to July 17, 1975 (Washington, DC: United States Government Printing Office, 1977), 601.

11. Paul C. Light, *A Government Ill Executed: The Decline of the Federal Service and How to Reverse It* (Cambridge, MA: Harvard University Press, 2008).

12. The President's Committee on Administrative Management, *Administrative Management in the United States* (Washington, DC: US Government Printing Office, 1937), 3.

13. David Mathews, "Perspective and Perceptions," in *Directions for H.E.W.: In the Interest of the People: Major Speeches, 1975-76 by David Mathews, Secretary of Health, Education, and Welfare*, vol. II (remarks before departmental meeting, HEW Auditorium, Washington, DC, February 27, 1976).

14. Sir Thomas More, *Utopia,* The Second Book, Vol. XXXVI, Part 3, The Harvard Classics (New York: P.F. Collier & Son, 1909-1914), Bartleby.com, 2001, www.bartleby.com/36/3/.

15. David Mathews, "De-Obfuscationism," *New York Times*, December 10, 1976. This document can be found in the David Mathews collection, Kettering Foundation archives.

16. Jeremy Rabkin, "Office for Civil Rights," in *The Politics of Regulation,* ed. James Q. Wilson (New York: Basic Books, 1980), 304.

17. Joseph A. Califano Jr., *Governing America: An Insider's Report from the White House and the Cabinet* (New York: Simon and Schuster, 1981), 224, 226.

18. Rabkin, "Office for Civil Rights," 304.

19. Rabkin, "Office for Civil Rights," 315.

20. Rabkin, "Office for Civil Rights," 335.

21. Rabkin, "Office for Civil Rights," 337.

22. I promoted adding women's sports to the athletic department at the University of Alabama when I returned there after HEW. At the University, I had to implement the Title IX regulations that I had worked on in Washington. The institution had begun a women's sports program in the Office of Student Affairs, not in the Athletic Department, whose director was Paul Bryant. He was also head football coach with national championship teams to his credit. When I explained Title IX to him, I was surprised by his reaction because he guarded his department's budget as seriously as President Ford guarded the federal budget. But Coach Bryant also believed in winning teams, and he immediately said he would assume responsibility for women's sports—and pay for it. That meant taking the expenses out of the revenue generated by the men's football team. The women athletes were welcomed, supported, and not resented. They went on to win their own national championships.

23. Mathews, "De-Obfuscationism."

24. David Mathews, "A Key to Federal Effectiveness: Access Management" (remarks to the American Society of Access Professionals, Washington, DC: Charles F. Kettering Foundation, January 8, 1981). This document can be found in the David Mathews collection, Kettering Foundation archives. For more information, contact archives@kettering.org.

25. "Strange Words from HEW," *Montgomery Advertiser*, July 28, 1976. This document can be found in the David Mathews collection, Kettering Foundation archives. For more information, contact archives@kettering.org.

CHAPTER X

WORKING *WITH* AMERICANS WITH DISABILITIES

Despite its title, this chapter isn't only about disability policy, even though that policy is important. It is just and right that citizens with disabilities have access to the same opportunities and facilities that people without disabilities enjoy. Some of these people became disabled while serving in our armed forces. I met of few of these veterans when I served for eight years in the Army Reserves. Still wearing the brown shoes issued during World War II, which they had tried to dye into the new regulation black, the veterans who had been wounded but returned to service impressed me with their survival skills. As in this case, people with disabilities have abilities that are needed for the good of all.

This chapter is primarily about the relevance of a *with* strategy in federal programs for people with all types of disabilities. Disability policymaking provides an actual case that sheds a light on what can go wrong even if the cause is worthy and the efforts to serve it are carried on with the best of intentions. To explain the challenges, I have to go into considerable detail about how the federal government actually works. My apologies. The inner dynamics of the executive branch are especially complex, and that complexity is even greater when taking into consideration the roles that interest groups, Congress, and the courts play.

First of all, writing regulations for disability policy that uses a *with* strategy is nearly impossible if the lawmaking that authorizes those regulations isn't done openly. Unfortunately, that is often the case. That inhibits using a strategy to encourage more collaboration among all the relevant parties—from those with disabilities to those who care for them.

EDUCATING CHILDREN WITH DISABILITIES

Here is a case showing that good intentions don't necessarily result in good lawmaking. Look at Public Law 94-142 of 1975, also known as the Education for All Handicapped Children Act (EAHCA). Its purpose was to integrate children with disabilities into mainstream classes. The law required public schools to provide these children a free and "appropriate" public education in the least restrictive environment. In signing the legislation into law, President Ford warned Congress of the problems that might develop when the federal government was too prescriptive on a matter so sensitive to the individual's circumstances. The HEW staff, however, considered this law an unqualified victory. It was a dramatic step forward in long-standing federal efforts to assist people with disabilities. Having been familiar with and very supportive of better education for young people with disabilities during my time at the University of Alabama, I was happy to see their cause getting attention. Nonetheless, I had grave concerns about the way the new law was enacted and what that would mean for writing regulations.

Students with Disabilities at the University of Alabama

I had some experience with what PL 94-142 was intended to do. As I mentioned before, shortly after I became president at the University of Alabama, Alabama's governor, Albert Brewer, helped us establish a center on campus to serve young people with disabilities who had difficulty in a regular school but did not need institutional care. The objective was to offset these difficulties by preparing students for regular classes. This was called "inclusion" or "mainstreaming." The University began recruiting students with disabilities and, by 1971, had the largest enrollment of any institution in the Southeast.[1]

One of the young people admitted to the University's experimental inclusion program, Nathan Ballard, was born with severe cerebral palsy and needed a wheelchair. The program prepared him to pass college-level courses even though he didn't have a high school diploma. Students like Nathan did well in regular classrooms, demonstrating that mainstreaming could work.[2] He went on to take a job counseling freshmen who weren't attending classes. Later, he toured Japan to promote better treatment for people with disabilities and wrote a book about his experiences.[3] I should also mention that his ambition was to skydive into the University football stadium, which he eventually did. Even though not able in some ways, he proved that he was quite able in others.

Another lesson I learned from these programs at the University and from people like Nathan was how important it is for all the people and institutions serving these students to collaborate and reinforce each other's efforts. This requires a cooperative environment that fosters mutual assistance among students, parents, professional staff, educators, funders, and agency officials.

Potential Problems with PL 94-142

Given what happened at the University, I pointed out some potential problems to President Ford before he signed the EAHCA bill into law in November 1975. I thought a veto would prompt Congress to improve the legislation. Some parts were fine; others weren't. The federal government was being unnecessarily prescriptive, and I joined those in HEW who feared that the prescriptiveness would make it difficult for the affected parties to collaborate. Legal battles seemed certain to erupt, and they did.

EAHCA has been cited as "the most prescriptive education" law ever passed by Congress at that time.[4] The legislation required local school officials to take specific actions and spelled out in detail the services to be provided, some of which were medical and not offered by schools. These services were to be paid from school, not federal, funds, which placed an added financial burden on schools. Educators were to formulate individualized education programs (IEPs) that had to be developed with the participation of the parents and could not be changed without their permission. That was one of the better parts of the law.

Implementing this law also raised problems other than funding. What was an "appropriate" education? Putting children with disabilities in regular classes raised even more questions that couldn't be answered definitively. The law made no allowances for constructive adjustments.

Writing the Regulations

After the 1975 law was signed, HEW and the Justice Department drafted regulations attempting to define what constituted "appropriate education." However, professionals disagreed on both what a disability was and on what the proper placement of children for treatment should be. The legislation also stipulated that the draft regulations be sent to Congress, which was done. Both houses responded and expanded on what they intended.

The Department opened all facets of these issues to comment in public hearings and went to unprecedented lengths to listen to anyone who wanted to weigh in. Proposed regulations were put in the *Federal Register* on December 30, 1976, and the public was given 60 days to comment. During this time, hearings were held in cities across the nation. It soon became apparent in these hearings that federal regulations would conflict with not only school policies but also state laws.[5] The requirements of the federal law had far-reaching implications, which no one could assess. As a result of public comments, the rules had to be revised and reissued. HEW decided to publish the most basic and essential regulations and then amend them as experience warranted.

Final regulations were issued in August 1977, when Joe Califano was Secretary. As he should have, he took time to thoroughly review what we had done. Joe's conclusion wasn't too different from mine. He started with

Lyndon Johnson's premise, which was that responsibility for and control of education had to remain with local communities and the federal government shouldn't weaken that. I had operated on the same premise.

Influenced by interest groups, Congress could have its cake and eat it too by putting the financial burden on state and local governments with largely unfunded mandates. While recognizing the laudable objectives of the programs created by interest group politics, Joe pointed out that needs were outpacing resources.[6] The law said that the financial impact couldn't be considered, yet school officials were still going to have to reduce funding for other needed programs.

These concerns about the regulations weren't imaginary. Despite its accomplishments in reaching more children and expanding the field of special education, a number of problems became apparent. That is the subject of a book by John Merrow, who covered the programs for 25 years. He criticized "phony 'inclusion,' a bloated bureaucracy, questionable classifications, an appalling dropout rate, and a near-total lack of accountability."[7] Merrow's greatest concern was that while greater access was certainly important, it didn't necessarily result in academic achievement. Some schools even kept students with disabilities out of their reports on standardized tests, fearing they would pull down the average.[8] A government study in 2010 found that only 16 percent of children with learning disabilities had moved into regular classes and that barely half of students receiving special education services graduated.[9]

I remember one of the thorniest problems had to do with medical treatment. Could catheterization or tracheotomies be regarded as falling within a school's "educational" responsibilities? Other questions were also quite difficult to answer. Under what circumstances, and by whom, could a disruptive child, who also may have had disabilities, be suspended from school?[10] Hearings on these issues at the local level could be legalistic and adversarial.[11] [12] Because a program had to be devised for each student, it fell to federal judges to rule case by case on disputes.[13] The threat of a loss of funds, HEW's means of securing compliance, was so unrealistic that it wasn't a believable threat. A court decree, on the other hand, was.

The prospect of litigation and the adversarial relationship it would foster between educators and parents were troubling even though the legislation made it inevitable that the courts had to be used.[14] The 1975 EAHCA legislation raised a multitude of ethical and political questions. However, framing the issues as contests between inept school officials and deserving children did not encourage sound decisions.

Missed Opportunities for Collaboration

The purpose in presenting this case is not to fully cover all aspects of EAHCA. Fortunately, many of the problems associated with that legislation were later addressed in its 1990 successor, the Individuals with Disabilities Education Act (IDEA). My intent certainly isn't to demonize the 1975 law. Nonetheless, regulations couldn't solve all of the problems created by an overly prescriptive law. In this case, the law should have been clearer about its intent and relied on HEW to craft realistic regulations.

In the presence of such conflict, confusion, and frustration, both citizens and service providers can develop extremely negative attitudes about the federal government. These attitudes dim the prospects for a *with* strategy, which promotes and depends on collaboration. There was probably some *with*-like cooperation that occurred before 1990, irrespective of the disincentives. However, intentionally employing a *with* strategy could have had a constructive effect in fostering more collaboration. All the parties involved need to see themselves on the same side and not as adversaries.

SECTION 504

In the case of 94-142, the law was passed in the usual way, but adding Section 504 to the Rehabilitation Act of 1973 was different. The way this legislation was amended made it very unlikely, if not impossible, for citizens to work *with* the government. In this case, the intent of the legislation was so uncertain that HEW had great difficulty in developing realistic regulations. Section 504 has been the subject of several in-depth studies, and I have drawn on them as well as my own memories.[15] The studies show more forces in Washington politics that aren't favorable to a *with* strategy.

The Rehabilitation Act of 1973 protects people with disabilities from discrimination. It was another of a long series of legislative efforts that can be traced back at least to the 1920 Smith-Fess Act, which provided vocational rehabilitation services.[16] This series of laws continued in 1990 with the passage of the Americans with Disabilities Act (ADA) along with IDEA. Today, Section 504, IDEA, and ADA have resulted in significant improvement in the lives of Americans with disabilities, especially children.

How the Government Worked

The way Section 504 came into existence was not ideal for fostering cooperation among all the people and institutions serving people with disabilities. (Fortunately, some collaboration or at least consultation does occur now.) In the process of passing the 504 legislation in the 1970s, opportunities for complementary efforts were lost. But before saying more about this problem, I want to emphasize again, this chapter is not about the statute itself, and certainly not about its intentions. It is about the way 504 was enacted and what can be learned from the process that could make a *with* strategy a reality in the future.

Legislative Entrepreneurship

In his history of the legislation, Richard Scotch noted, "Section 504 . . . came to be a central objective for the disability rights movement, but it was not itself a product of that movement."[17] He meant that "[it] was not developed at the urging of representatives of disabled people."[18] The Section was the creation of a small group of congressional staff, including some who had been at HEW. They wanted to throw down a gauntlet in the contest for power between Congress and the executive branch, which became intense during the Nixon administration. The group's attitude was to "get those sons of bitches [referring to the administration] . . . we're going to really stick it to them."[19] This antagonism didn't mean that the staff members didn't want to help those they considered in need: "disabled people, minorities, poor people, you name it." They did.

Robert Katzmann sees the 504 case as an example of "legislative entrepreneurship." He describes the objectives of members of Congress like Representative Charles Vanik as wanting to extend civil rights to people with disabilities. After hearing from constituents who had encountered discrimination, his staff set about looking for a legislative fix for the problem.[20]

Then, HEW's staff in the Office for Civil Rights entered the picture in league with the congressional staff. Katzmann found that, unbeknownst to then-Secretary of HEW Caspar (Cap) Weinberger, they formed an alliance with the staff on the Hill to shape the legislation in ways that served the interest of OCR. This group was encouraged by special interest organizations advocating for people with disabilities. Although this type of collaboration often goes on behind closed doors, there isn't anything illegal about it. However, Katzmann notes that the staff bureaucracy can easily go around presidentially appointed cabinet officials, even a political veteran like Weinberger. This was a case of the iron triangle at its most effective.

Benefits as Rights

Section 504 was never in the spotlight in the legislative process, yet it opened a new chapter in disability policy. It consisted of just a few words that were taken directly from the civil rights legislation. It read: "No otherwise qualified handicapped individual in the United States . . . shall, solely by reason of his handicap, be excluded from the participation in, be denied the benefits of, or be subjected to discrimination under any program or activity receiving Federal financial assistance."[21]

No one could object to that declaration. But the implications of the Section went far beyond this laudable declaration of intent. The assistance and protections became rights. And if rights are absolute, there can be no morally justifiable opposition to them. That ends any deliberations. Furthermore, the costs associated with rights were not to be considered valid impediments, nor were the added responsibilities of those who provided benefits and services. Also, schools and colleges would have to pay to make their facilities accessible. Transportation agencies would have to modify their trains and buses. These measures would be reasonable if the federal government paid the cost of the improvements or shifted funding from another program.[22] It didn't.

How large these costs would be depended on how broadly the legislation was interpreted. Would it apply to every public building in the country and every single vehicle used in public transportation? Or would it be interpreted more narrowly to ensure that people with disabilities would have effective access, for example, to every academic program though not every facility on a campus? Those in the iron triangle wanted the broadest possible interpretation.

Despite the legislative victories, there were consequences for relying on moralized politics. As discussed earlier, if all rights are equal, there are no criteria for determining which one gets attention from the government. OCR, for example, was often faulted for being attentive to one group and neglecting another. That wasn't necessarily the case, but that didn't protect OCR and often led to lawsuits that made effective administration even more difficult.

Lack of Discernible Intent

Legislation that makes a significant change in policy, as Section 504 did, has to be applied to such everyday realities as operating schools, constructing buildings, and transporting people. However, with 504, there were only a few words to go on to determine what the law did or didn't intend. Unfortunately, the Section was never subject to an open congressional debate that could have shown this intent. Section 504 was added in a committee by the staff. Not advised of its far-reaching implications, members of Congress who saw 504 considered the wording "little more than a platitude."[23] [24]

When the legislation went to HEW to be interpreted in regulations, this lack of discernible intent was its Achilles' heel. Secretary Weinberger asked Congress what it expected from the regulations but got little response other than the obvious—HEW was to administer the law. The Senate's Labor and Public Welfare Committee did add that it wanted to continue to be involved in the implementation and enforcement of Section 504.[25] (Later, I would take note of that insistence on being consulted when the Department completed its final draft of the regulations.) In his evaluation of how well Congress did its job, Robert Katzmann gave the reputedly greatest deliberative body in our democracy a failing grade for 504.[26]

The Executive Branch

After President Nixon signed the Rehabilitation Act in September of 1973, responsibility for implementing it fell to his successor, President Ford. Despite Ford's reservations about regulations in general, he went ahead to authorize them for the Act. That included regulations for Section 504.

During the time that the White House and HEW were working on implementation, people with disabilities didn't have to wait before they could benefit from the law. In November 1975, I found that HEW was already working with the White House on an Executive Order to provide for consistent implementation throughout the government.[27] And by the early part of 1976, that Order was ready for the President's signature, which required implementing the Rehabilitation Act in all federal departments. Signed in April, the Order authorized HEW to assist other federal agencies as well as coordinate the total federal effort. By May of 1976, the Department was handling complaints of violations case by case.[28] All of this was happening while HEW was completing its own regulations. During this time of steady progress, I did not hear anything in HEW or from the White House about delaying regulations or finding a safe way to avoid the inevitable controversies.

The Office for Civil Rights

At the time President Ford was still considering his Executive Order, the Office for Civil Rights had already written the regulations for HEW. OCR's regulations had built up considerable internal approval, as well as intense interest group support. In fact, by 1975, the "draft" had attracted so much support that Richard Scotch recognized that it "had already become institutionalized to such an extent that those opposed to it were hard-pressed to change the regulation in major ways."[29]

The exception was HEW's Rehabilitative Services Administration, the agency most familiar with disability policy and a logical choice to have been the lead agency in HEW, an assignment that OCR had won instead. The Commissioner, Andrew Adams, favored incentives for more voluntary affirmative action and less reliance on regulations. He also urged a time-phased implementation, fearing a backlash against people with disabilities.[30]

Originally, Section 504 had not called for regulations. That requirement came in a 1974 congressional committee report. The report, despite the complexities, called for the regulations to be issued quickly, by the end of the year. And, as Katzmann found, "The report in effect ratified a role for HEW that the OCR had hoped to assume."[31] When successful, OCR used such assignments to argue for expanding its size eightfold.[32] That is how bureaucratic politics works. Territory and growth are incentives; they increase the power of an agency.

I found the lawyers in OCR quite conscientious and able. But their institutional mind-set was obvious. Katzmann explained, "A rights ethos governed the unit. Staff attorneys believed that disabled persons, like blacks and other minorities, had been deprived of their rights and had suffered discrimination and segregation. . . . They saw funding constraints as irrelevant: rights are absolute and cannot be compromised by fiscal considerations."[33] OCR's approach, Katzmann continued, would affect "about 16,000 school systems, 7,000 hospitals, 6,700 nursing homes and home health agencies, 2,600 institutions of higher education, and hundreds of libraries and day care centers."[34] However, the OCR "did not consider factors affecting recipients such as costs, inconvenience, and disrupting existing programs to be legitimate reasons for failing to meet requirements of nondiscrimination."[35] These factors had been cited in arguments opposing school desegregation, and OCR had routinely dismissed them.[36] As might be expected, the Office favored the most expansive interpretation of Section 504.

OCR was determined to carry out a forceful regulatory agenda, using the very broad language of the Section. Those institutions that would have to comply with the regulations, however, were largely unaware of all that would be required of them. The broad language gave OCR great latitude, and given the absence of clear legislative intent, there was little available to anyone who wanted to object to the regulations on the grounds that HEW had misrepresented Congress. Although Congress needed to be ambiguous in order to get enough votes to pass a piece of legislation, the executive branch had to be unambiguous in writing a regulation. The devil is always in the details, so the Department was always in the line of fire. Anyone serving in HEW realized that from day one. There was no point in looking for an escape—there wasn't one.

Bureaucratic Zeal

What happened with Section 504 is cited as an example of bureaucratic zeal, another phenomenon in the way government works. To show the effects of this zeal, I'll use another case that I encountered as Secretary.

Stanley J. (Stan) Murphy, one of my deputies from Alabama, dealt with a case in 1976 in which proposed legislation and its regulations would have been virtually impossible to interpret and enforce. It concerned a very serious problem: child abuse. The federal government already required states to have laws that met HEW standards for addressing abuse, and Congress was about to give more statutory authority to the Department. Stan discovered that departmental and congressional staffs, perhaps influenced by interest groups, were about to expand the definition of abuse to include "spiritual neglect" in a model Child Protective Services bill. Every state legislature would have to adopt this model or lose federal funds.

While these advocates were genuinely concerned about children, "spiritual neglect" could have meant almost anything. And responding to all cases that might be considered this sort of neglect would have diluted the states' ability to deal with situations in which there was clearly abuse.

Journalist Peter Schrag cited this legislation in a book warning against surveillance by the "benevolent eyes" of the government. He contended that service and therapy, which were very important to the Department's professional staff, had combined to create unwanted impositions on private life. Under the proposed act, all professionals who dealt with children—teachers, pediatricians, and day-care workers—would have been required not only to monitor spiritual neglect but also to report suspicions of "mental injury" evidenced by any "failure to thrive." Again, the language was vague. Schrag reported that intrusive federal requirements came "within a hair" of being put into place in the model legislation in 1976. He credited Stan with keeping the proposal from getting the Department's approval.[37]

Interest Group Politics

A host of groups advocating assistance for people with disabilities were already well organized and very influential in Washington before Section 504 was passed.[38] And Section 504 encouraged more of these groups to form; they had a new and potent argument to use: disability rights came under the mantle of the civil rights legislation. Making this connection was a stroke of political genius and, as noted, many other groups began making the same claim. A *with* strategy, in comparison, had no such interest groups calling for support.

DECISION TIME

Deciding how to apply Section 504 was particularly difficult because securing the rights of those with disabilities is not, as the legislation implied, the same as protecting people from racial discrimination. Recognizing the rights of minorities means ensuring that everyone is treated the same. Securing rights for Americans with disabilities requires more. While most agree that people with disabilities have an equal right to use such facilities as school buildings, this right is meaningless unless the buildings have ramps and elevators. People with disabilities require special, not simply equal, facilities. These facilities create the conditions necessary to exercise their rights. Even staunch champions of Section 504 in OCR recognized this distinction and pointed it out in drafting the notice that appeared in the *Federal Register* in May 1976:

> Section 504 . . . differs conceptually from both titles VI and IX. The premise of both title VI and title IX is that there are no inherent differences or inequalities between the general public and the persons protected by these statutes and, therefore, there should be no differential treatment in the administration of Federal programs. The concept of section 504 . . . is far more complex. Handicapped persons may require different treatment in order to be afforded equal access to federally assisted programs and activities, and identical treatment may, in fact, constitute discrimination.[39]

Adding to the complexities surrounding the 504 regulations, OCR's definition of "handicapped" (the term was later changed to "disability") was not the same as that used in other divisions of HEW. So, deciding who was to be protected raised a host of thorny questions. What about people who were addicted to drugs or alcohol? Did they have a "disability"? And what constitutes a barrier? Are barriers simply physical, like steps, or can they be attitudes of the people in the institutions who would have to do what 504 required?

Another danger to be avoided was writing a regulation so stringent that it would discredit the effort to protect people with disabilities—as happened in the attempt to ban father-son, mother-daughter events. Jeremy Rabkin noted that HEW might have taken the requirement that an "'otherwise qualified' individual not be discriminated against 'solely by reason of his handicap'" literally. To make this point, Rabkin used an absurd example. Someone who was blind could be entitled to employment as a bus driver, provided he or she was "otherwise qualified."[40] Fortunately, the 504 regulations did not take the law that literally.[41]

Furthermore, because regulation writers had to establish rules in advance and for all possible circumstances, they were put in the difficult position of having to make all decisions at once. It would have been better to be able to adjust rules over time as experience dictated.

Before my arrival, the Office for Civil Rights had tested various provisions in the draft regulation with both congressional staff and with agencies within the Department. As I mentioned, the proposal had also locked in considerable institutional backing. So it wasn't literally a "draft." However, OCR had done little to hear from people outside the government, other than the interest groups representing people with disabilities.

"Drafts" that aren't really drafts give citizens the impression they are being manipulated. And that fuels a downward spiral in confidence. Certainly, OCR had to be responsive to these interest groups because they were the ones who would take the agency to court for failure to enforce the regulations.[42]

One of the first things that had to be done before rules could take effect was pointed out by Martin Gerry, an OCR veteran whom I appointed to head the agency. An Executive Order required an analysis of the possible inflationary impact of regulations costing more than $100 million to implement. Section 504 rules would cost a great deal more, yet OCR argued that the costs would be balanced by financial benefits such as providing access in employment and elementary and secondary education.[43] Because of the magnitude of the expenditures, I thought that an additional assessment independent of OCR was in order. That was completed in February of 1976. This evaluation showed that the collective impact of all the provisions in the regulation could go as high as $2.3 billion dollars, not $100 million. Expenditures at that level would have significant impact on the institutions that had to modify their facilities.[44]

Protecting the Providers

I've said that one of my concerns with the draft 504 regulations was that the institutions having to comply wouldn't have time to respond to what was a de facto final ruling. These institutions needed an opportunity to do their own analysis, which was the only way they would have anything even close to equal standing with the interest groups that had already worked closely with OCR for months. To open the regulation process, HEW reforms, which I described earlier, mandated an early announcement of the *intent* to regulate.[45] Such an alert neither repudiated nor privileged the March 504 draft; it simply helped level the playing field.

Such a notice was put in the *Federal Register* in May.[46] The Department anticipated issuing the full draft regulation (revised if necessary) in July, which would have been a little less than a year after I saw the first draft.[47] The responses did show that changes were needed. Revised regulations were then posted on schedule in the *Federal Register* on July 16, 1976.[48]

The reactions in the comment period prompted some second thoughts within HEW, so the Department undertook two additional rounds of public hearings. The first were held in June 1976 in 10 regional centers, largely with client groups. Then, I asked for more town meetings to be held in 22 sites across the country in order to reach the general public. The meetings began on August 3, 1976. Open to all citizens, these were the Department's most aggressive efforts to hear from those who would have to implement the regulations as well as the public at large. OCR also continued to stay in close touch with the advocacy groups. These meetings resulted in more changes in the regulations, which some Department officials later acknowledged were improvements, even though they had questioned the need for the second, more open, round of hearings.[49]

Meeting Advocacy Groups' Objections

Advocacy groups objected to the extensive public hearings and labeled them delaying tactics intended to undermine the law. Advocates were not sympathetic to the need for a more democratic way of rulemaking. And they were probably annoyed by my insistence on reaching out to a broader cross-section of the country. The network of advocacy organizations rallied their forces and passed their criticisms of what I was doing on to Congress. According to one activist, OCR staff members in HEW even encouraged a demonstration in my office during the process of meeting the public participation requirements. Having been through many heated campus demonstrations, I was not overwhelmed. Later, I decided to take the initiative and meet with these critics.

Despite the resistance, the public meetings demonstrated that a more open process was necessary. An OCR observer at these meetings reported, "No one thought a lot about handicapped issues, and so it was somewhat new and it didn't make a lot of sense to people who hadn't thought a lot about it."[50]

"The Buck Stops Here"

As the Department proceeded with airing its draft regulations, so many groups wanted to be heard that HEW had to extend the deadline for responses to mid-October 1976. The staff then worked until the end of November to analyze more than 850 written comments. These surfaced four major issues that were referred to me for decisions.[51] First, should the regulations protect people addicted to alcohol or drugs? That was a tough call. President-elect Carter had opposed including them, and I had reservations myself. I was persuaded, however, by the medical argument that research showed these addictions were, in fact, diseases. Still, our regulations did not protect people in this category in all circumstances. The regulations didn't apply to those whose current abuse of drugs or alcohol prevented them from performing the job in question or would be a threat to the safety or property of others.

The second issue to be decided was how far institutions had to go to make old buildings accessible. I thought it reasonable to require access to every program though not every facility. For example, some, but not all, dormitories had to have accessible rooms.

Third, did workers with disabilities have to be paid the minimum wage regardless of the work they were able to do? Such a requirement might have made it financially impossible to maintain many of the highly successful programs of sheltered work. So, I favored fair compensation yet not necessarily the legal minimum.

Fourth, should state agencies have to inform local agencies of their obligations under Section 504 and monitor their compliance? My decision? Yes.

THE COURTS

In June, while the Department was reviewing responses from the initial notice in the *Federal Register,* one interest group, the Action League for Physically Handicapped Adults, filed a suit in a federal court, *Cherry et al. v. Mathews,* to force me to sign the draft regulations immediately, even before the public hearings were completed. Ruling in July 1976, the judge, noting that I had already issued proposed regulations, affirmed that final regulations had to be issued yet did not set a deadline. I then met with my critics in the interest groups, not expecting to convert them but in a spirit of openness.

While disability advocate groups developed a hard and fast position, the organizations on the other side, representing institutions that would be regulated, didn't try to derail the rulemaking, attempt to have the law repealed, or question the importance of equal opportunity for people with disabilities.[52] They did, however, ask for flexibility in order to make appropriate responses to particular cases and to develop innovative means to solve problems.[53]

BACK TO CONGRESS

On January 10, 1977, OCR gave me a final regulation that addressed these concerns. I was satisfied that the Department had done the best it could. One issue remained: the relationship with Congress, which had insisted on continuing to be involved with Section 504.[54] Congress had also taken the position that it had the right of "legislative vetoes" on sensitive regulations— and this was certainly one. Given Congress' insistence on being involved and the history of Section 504, I thought I should send the draft I had approved to the Hill and ask whether the draft was consistent with congressional intentions.[55] In my January 18, 1977, letter to Congress, I wrote, "Again, let me stress that I have completed my work on this regulation and have made all of the decisions necessary to its implementation."

I added, "There was some question about whether I could sign the regulation. I am quite willing for my signature to go on the document as an

indication of its completeness. Yet I was advised that legally I would be concluding this matter at the very point I say I am trying to open the regulation
to the Congress."[56] That, I thought, would be a significant and serious contradiction.[57] So I didn't sign.

Joe Califano was my successor, and I regretted leaving him with this
problem. Despite the protests, he did what he had done before. He took time
to review the draft regulation carefully and agreed with virtually all of its provisions. The final regulations were published in the *Federal Register* on May 4,
1977.

POSTSCRIPT: THE SUPREME COURT
HAS THE FINAL SAY

In 1979, in *Southeastern Community College v. Davis*, a woman who was deaf
sued a community college after being rejected for admission to a nursing program. The Supreme Court unanimously rejected OCR's defense of her rights
based on its broad interpretation of Section 504.[58] Katzmann wrote that this
"decision was a significant defeat for the disability organizations, bureaucrats, legislators, and committee staffers who hoped that Section 504 would
be viewed as more than a nondiscrimination statute. The unanimous court
had determined that section 504 . . . could not impose 'undue financial and
administrative burdens upon a state.'"[59] It is worth noting, however, that the
courts were not the prime forces driving this rights movement. They were not
as involved as either the Congress or the bureaucracy.[60]

REFLECTIONS ON *WITH*

Details of the 504 case, which I know can be tedious, are necessary to understanding how the government really works and the challenges a strategy of
working *with* the people faces. In one sense, the 504 case is a prime example of
what would preclude a *with* strategy. How could those responsible for serving
people with disabilities work *with* the government when they didn't know

what the government was doing? That would be impossible. There were no thoughtful congressional deliberations on Section 504 and none in the public arena. There were no debates to watch on the nightly news, no arguments to provoke editorials, nothing to alert people to the far-reaching implications of the legislation.

The way the government works when dealing with issues framed as moral absolutes or rights also has a definite bearing on the possibilities for employing *with* strategies. Recall that Jürgen Habermas warned that when governments act on what they consider "moral facts," they are likely to overlook important considerations in the application of laws based on these "facts."[61] That is significant for *with* strategies because they have to do with the way laws are applied. Jeremy Rabkin recognized this dilemma in the case of 504, noting that the "special mystique" of civil rights inhibited "political bargaining over the proper scope or direction of OCR's activity."[62] Rabkin's conclusion was that a "'rights' ideology is not a very useful guide for establishing an effective enforcement program."[63]

A Matter of Tone

Making government the arbiter and agent of morals also gives its actions an ideological cast, and that affects the tenor of its relationship with the public. The relationship can easily become adversarial. Cloaked in moral authority, the government becomes the absolute authority, and it must bring those it deals with "in line." I am not saying that the 504 case went to this extreme. Yet there was a troubling implication in the Section that those serving people with disabilities had to be watched, directed, and, if necessary, constrained. And there was no recognition that family and friends are essential complementary producers providing some of the assistance needed by those with disabilities.

This implicit assumption that citizens aren't producers who provide care defines their relationship with the government. That relationship can become distant and adversarial, not collaborative. I don't mean that there are no situations where the government should be a legal agent enforcing a law. On the other hand, I don't believe that should always be the government's defining role.

Missed Opportunities

Along the way in the history of Section 504, there were opportunities to foster collaboration that weren't realized. Most obvious, the legislative process could have been open to the public and followed the democratic standards for making laws. There was a related opportunity—to involve the institutions and professionals providing support and services early on rather than at the end of the regulation-writing cycle. And rather than giving sole jurisdiction to the Office for Civil Rights, HEW's Rehabilitative Services Administration could have had shared responsibility from the beginning. That could have helped change both the substance and tenor of the government's approach. There are ways that a *with* strategy could have been employed. But I don't know anyone who was thinking in those terms in the 1970s. I certainly wasn't. The furthest I had gotten was opening the regulating process a bit more to the public.

WHAT'S NEXT?

School desegregation in the 1970s is a case in which citizens in some communities did help produce something by working together across racial divides—peaceful integration. This complicated case takes the next two chapters to cover all the actors and what did and didn't happen.

NOTES

1. When I came to HEW, I asked one of the faculty in special education, H. William (Bill) Heller, to advise me.
2. The University's admissions office had no basis for enrolling a student like Nathan, but sympathetic faculty members took him into their classes to see whether he could pass them. He did pass and, after getting a GED certificate in 1979, was admitted to the University's New College. Nathan has gone on to coauthor a book with Michael Rogers, *Nathan: He Would Be Somebody . . . It Was Just a Matter of Time* (Elk Grove, CA: RBC Publishing, 2000).
3. Ballard and Rogers, *Nathan.*

4. R. Shep Melnick, *Between the Lines: Interpreting Welfare Rights* (Washington, DC: The Brookings Institution, 1994), 137.

5. By March 1, 1977, the Bureau of Education for the Handicapped (BEH) had received more than 16,000 written comments. Ervin L. Levine and Elizabeth Wexler, *PL 94-142: An Act of Congress* (New York: Macmillan, 1981), 114-122.

6. Joseph A. Califano Jr., *Governing America: An Insider's Report from the White House and the Cabinet* (New York: Simon and Schuster, 1981), 314-316. Levine and Wexler in *PL 94-142* discuss the rulemaking process in chapter 5. The proposed regulations appear in "Education of Handicapped Children and Incentive Grants Program; Assistance to States," 41 Fed. Reg. 56966 (December 30, 1976), pp. 56966-56967; and the final regulations in "Education of Handicapped Children; Implementation of Part B of the Education of the Handicapped Act," 42 Fed. Reg. 42474 (August 23, 1977), pp. 42474-42475. There are no major differences between the proposal and final regulations.

7. John Merrow, *Choosing Excellence: "Good Enough" Schools Are Not Good Enough* (Lanham, MD: Scarecrow Press, 2001), 159.

8. Merrow, *Choosing Excellence*, 163.

9. Institute of Education Sciences, National Center for Education Statistics, "Table 131: Number of 14- through 21-year-old students served under Individuals with Disabilities Education Act, Part B, who exited school, by exit reason, age and type of disability: 2008-2009 and 2009-2010." http://nces.ed.gov/programs/digest/d12/tables/dt12_131.asp.

10. Gareth Davies, *See Government Grow: Education Politics from Johnson to Reagan* (Lawrence, KS: University Press of Kansas, 2007), 167.

11. Melnick, *Between the Lines*, 156.

12. Adversarial relationships were likely since the interest group pressing for the legislation had spent years in legal battle and distrusted local school officials. Melnick, *Between the Lines*, 158. Continued legal wrangling was probably inevitable. Yet defensive measures to avoid the lawsuits that had grown up around the legislation took time from instruction, as did the paperwork. Legal fees, which tripled in states such as Connecticut in only three years, also cut into financial resources. Merrow, *Choosing Excellence*, 163-164.

13. Court cases arose around nearly every word in the act. Does the obligation of schools to provide assistance include assistance after the school year is over? (The courts said, "Yes.") Do related services include medical assistance provided by a school nurse? ("Yes.") Melnick, *Between the Lines*, 164-168. Despite all of these detailed decisions, hopes that the judiciary would be able to set clear and consistent standards proved hard to realize. In the face of this contentiousness, it is all the more remarkable that schools have been able to manage a program that has grown significantly since its inception.

14. Scholars like Shep Melnick see PL 94-142 as a prime example of the power of rights-based policy and its consequences, principally an unshakable legacy of formal procedures, "rules of law rather than issues of substance" (a criticism of parents), legal and administrative costs, and adversarial relationships (criticisms of schools). This observation is balanced by another, which is that "disabled students, their parents, and special education professionals have benefited enormously." Melnick asks, Why hasn't Congress addressed these complaints? His answer is that Congress considers its constituency the beneficiaries of the act and not school board members and school administrators. And he blames Congress for accepting the credit for the act but not paying the bills. Melnick, *Between the Lines,* 176-177.

    Congress also has not responded to findings such as those reported by David Schwartz. "It has become clear," he reports, "that the physical integration mandated by PL 94-142, The Education for All Handicapped Children Act, has not been sufficient to bring about social integration, as was expected by its framers. The social isolation of students in special education classrooms within schools, in fact, can parallel the isolation of residents of group homes noted earlier." David B. Schwartz, *Crossing the River: Creating a Conceptual Revolution in Community and Disability* (Cambridge, MA: Brookline Books, 1992), 120.

15. My sources for this chapter include Robert A. Katzmann, *Institutional Disability: The Saga of Transportation Policy for the Disabled* (Washington, DC: The Brookings Institution, 1986); Jeremy Rabkin, "Office for Civil Rights," in *The Politics of Regulation,* ed. James Q. Wilson (New York: Basic Books, 1980), 335-337; and Richard K. Scotch, *From Good Will to Civil Rights: Transforming Federal Disability Policy* (Philadelphia: Temple University Press, 1984). Of course, I drew on my papers along with my memories. But memories fade, and my collection of papers is limited. So I am grateful for the diligent research of scholars to bring back to mind my time at HEW.

16. The 1973 law wasn't the first or only federal legislation to benefit people with disabilities. Other statutes were already in force. In fact, the new law was one in a series of actions taken on behalf of people formerly referred to as "handicapped." In 1920, the Smith-Fess Act had provided vocational rehabilitation services through state departments of education. Then, the Communication Act of 1934 required equipment and services to be available to people with disabilities. A year later, the Social Security Act authorized more funds for vocational services, which was followed by legislation in the 1940s, 1950s, and 1960s, expanding the programs and extending eligibility. The Architectural Barriers Act of 1968 was particularly significant because it mandated that new federally funded buildings be accessible.

17. Scotch, *From Good Will,* 40.

18. Scotch, *From Good Will,* 57.

19. Scotch, *From Good Will,* 48. On page 48, Scotch quotes Nik Edes, a staff member for

Representative Harrison Williams, who said: "I'll tell you the frame of mind we all had. We had lived for three years under Richard Nixon and under being told no, no, no, no, no by an executive branch which was totally unresponsive to the programs of the sixties. . . . It was an important thread running through everything that was done at those times. It was: I'll get those sons of bitches, they don't want to show any positive inclination toward doing things at all, then we're going to really stick it to them."

20. Katzmann, *Institutional Disability*, 46.

21. US Department of Labor, Office of the Assistant Secretary for Administration and Management, Section 504 of the Rehabilitation Act of 1973, https://eeoc.gov/rehabilitation-act-1973-original-text.

22. Scotch, *From Good Will*, 90.

23. Scotch, *From Good Will*, 54.

24. After the fact in 1974, in adding amendments to the 1973 act, staffers from the Senate Labor and Public Welfare Committee tried to create a legislative intent that had not been articulated during the 1973 enactment. The amendment explained that 504 had been modeled on the Civil Rights Act of 1964, stating that while "Section 504 does not specifically require the issuance of regulations or expressly provide for enforcement procedures, . . . it is clearly mandatory in form, and such regulations and enforcement were intended by this Committee and by Congress." Katzmann, *Institutional Disability*, 52. This attempt to remedy the lack of intent did not prevent the confusion and controversy that had already begun.

25. Scotch, *From Good Will*, 61.

26. Katzmann, *Institutional Disability*, 79, 191.

27. David Lissey and Sara Massengale, memorandum to Jim Cannon, November 14, 1975. This document can be found in the David Mathews collection, Kettering Foundation archives. For more information, contact archives@kettering.org.

28. Marjorie Lynch, Undersecretary of HEW, memorandum to the Honorable James Cavanaugh, "Section 504 of the Rehabilitation Act," May 28, 1976. This document can be found in the David Mathews collection, Kettering Foundation archives. For more information, contact archives@kettering.org.

29. Scotch, *From Good Will*, 81.

30. Scotch, *From Good Will*, 89.

31. Katzmann, *Institutional Disability*, 99.

32. Katzmann, *Institutional Disability*, 100.

33. Katzmann, *Institutional Disability*, 100.

34. Katzmann, *Institutional Disability*, 100.

35. Scotch, *From Good Will*, 64.

36. Scotch, *From Good Will*, 76. Later, on the question of bilingual education and the rights of public school students who did not speak English, the *Lau* decision

established legal precedent for disregarding cost. Martin Gerry wrote OCR's position paper for that case. Scotch, *From Good Will*, 64.

37. Peter Schrag, *Mind Control* (New York: Pantheon Books, 1978), 214-215.

38. Katzmann, *Institutional Disability*, 85-86.

39. "Nondiscrimination on the Basis of Handicap; Programs and Activities Receiving or Benefiting from Federal Financial Assistance," 41 Fed. Reg. 20296 (May 17, 1976), p. 20296.

40. Rabkin, "Office for Civil Rights," 316.

41. "Paragraph (k) of § 84.3 defines the term 'qualified handicapped person.' Throughout the proposed regulation, this term is used instead of the statutory term 'otherwise qualified handicapped person.' The Department believes that the omission of the word 'otherwise' is necessary in order to comport with the intent of the statute because, read literally, 'otherwise' qualified handicapped persons include persons who are qualified except for their handicap, rather than in spite of their handicap. Thus, a blind person might possess all of the qualifications for driving a bus except sight and could therefore be said to be an otherwise qualified handicapped person for the job of bus driving. In all other respects, the terms 'qualified' and 'otherwise qualified' are intended to be interchangeable." "Nondiscrimination on the Basis of Handicap," p. 20299.

42. Scotch, *From Good Will*, 78-79.

43. Scotch, *From Good Will*, 90.

44. Dave M. O'Neill, "Discrimination Against Disabled Persons: The Costs, Benefits and Inflationary Impact of Implementing Section 504 of the Rehabilitation Act of 1973 Covering Recipients of HEW Financial Assistance," 41 Fed. Reg. 20312 (May 17, 1976).

45. "According to Martin Gerry [director of HEW's OCR], . . . '[Mathews] really had more concern about things that might happen, or the whole legitimacy of the regulation-writing process.'" Scotch, *From Good Will*, 88-89.

46. "Since it appears to be the case that the implications of this legislation have not been elaborated before the general public in sufficient detail, it seems appropriate, before issuing a Notice of Proposed Rulemaking, to solicit public comment on certain key issues which any proposed regulation would, in all likelihood, address." "Nondiscrimination on the Basis of Handicap," p. 20296.

47. I don't recall Richard Scotch interviewing me on this subject. Those whom he did interview in OCR apparently did not comment on the impact of regulation reform on rulemaking for Section 504. Scotch wrote that there was no "official rationale" for not publishing OCR's March version of the regulations. He quotes OCR's characterizations of me as having a "more-or-less" charity mentality toward people with disabilities, failing to understand the concept of rights, and trying to delay the

regulations in hopes they would go away. Scotch does report, however, that others in the Department, specifically the head of Rehabilitative Services, also had reservations about the March draft. Scotch, *From Good Will*, 88-90.

48. Martin H. Gerry, Director, Office for Civil Rights, memorandum to Marjorie Lynch, Undersecretary of HEW, "Re: Summary of Section 504 and Executive Order 11914," July 27, 1976. This document can be found in the David Mathews collection, Kettering Foundation archives. For more information, contact archives@kettering. org.

49. Martin H. Gerry, Director, Office for Civil Rights, memorandum to Secretary David Mathews, "Re: OCR Public Affairs Plan for Section 504 Update," July 2, 1976. This document can be found in the David Mathews collection, Kettering Foundation archives. For more information, contact archives@kettering.org.

50. Scotch (quoting John Wodatch), *From Good Will*, 98.

51. Scotch, *From Good Will*, 102.

52. Scotch, *From Good Will*, 101.

53. Scotch (quoting testimony), *From Good Will*, 98-101.

54. Senate Subcommittee on the Handicapped, letter to HEW Secretary Caspar Weinberger, November 13, 1973. Quoted in Scotch, *From Good Will*, 127.

55. HEW Secretary David Mathews, letter to Honorable Harrison A. Williams Jr., Chairman, Committee on Labor and Public Welfare, United States Senate, January 18, 1977. This document can be found in the David Mathews collection, Kettering Foundation archives. For more information, contact archives@kettering.org.

56. In subsequent maneuvering in the courts, HEW's lawyers were able to make the point that a cabinet secretary has a right to consult with Congress. Katzmann, *Institutional Disability*, 163-164.

57. HEW Secretary David Mathews, letter to Honorable Harrison A. Williams Jr., Chairman, Committee on Labor and Public Welfare, United States Senate, January 18, 1977. This document can be found in the David Mathews collection, Kettering Foundation archives. For more information, contact archives@kettering.org.

58. Katzmann, *Institutional Disability*, 166-171.

59. Katzmann, *Institutional Disability*, 170.

60. Katzmann, *Institutional Disability*, 168.

61. Jürgen Habermas, Chapter 10, "On the Internal Relation between the Rule of Law and Democracy," in *The Inclusion of the Other: Studies in Political Theory*, eds. Ciaran Cronin and Pablo De Greif (Cambridge, MA: MIT Press, 1998), 257.

62. Rabkin, "Office for Civil Rights," 306.

63. Rabkin, "Office for Civil Rights," 338.

CHAPTER XI

SCHOOL DESEGREGATION

As you read, remember that the book's subject is a *with* strategy, even as the focus shifts here to how the government works in educational matters. If there is an area where institutions, governmental and nongovernmental, especially need to work *with* citizens and communities, it is in public schooling.

This chapter and the next delve into the inner workings of government when faced with two highly contentious issues: school desegregation and integration. I should tell you how I define these two terms. Desegregation, prohibiting the exclusion of some people from using public facilities, such as city buses and schools, is a legal matter. Integration is a societal challenge and has to do with getting people who aren't alike to work together for the good of all. The government must do a great deal, though not all, of the work of desegregation. Citizens must do much of the work of integration. Both benefit when there is collaboration.

I can't say whether desegregation or integration was more difficult in the 1970s. Both were. In some places, such as large urban centers, desegregation was still being adjudicated in the courts and significant integration was yet to be attempted. But how desegregation came about had a great influence on the prospects for constructive integration.

COMPETING NATIONAL INTERESTS

In the 1970s, there were various national interests driving the push for school desegregation and integration. These interests were in tension with one another. For instance, ending segregation in schools was intended to prohibit the discrimination that had unjustly denied some children the good education they deserved. There was also a national interest in keeping communities responsible for education because of the critical role that families and their communities play. And the quality of education certainly matters, just as justice and local control do. But these interests were often seen as competing. Should justice be the priority and not local control? Should the quality of education trump all else?

The clash of these interests was so extreme that some people questioned whether Americans could, in fact, rule themselves responsibly, unless that rule was exercised through the courts and government agencies. Some argued that the racial attitudes that led to segregation were so deeply ingrained in society that they could never be eradicated voluntarily. The strongest sanctions had to be applied at the federal level to make people do what was morally right.

Others were of the opinion that democracy is rule by the people, and that local citizens should retain control of local schools.[1] From this point of view, democracy has its roots in school boards and other institutions of self-rule such as juries, municipal elections, and town councils. These give people a direct experience in democracy. The question in the desegregation controversy was whether local control had to be sacrificed because segregated schools were so patently unjust that social justice overrode all other considerations.

The Importance of Framing

In the 1970s, these interests were treated as mutually exclusive in highly adversarial debates. The decision-making was framed in a way that made reaching a sound conclusion impossible. There was little agreement on the name of the issue to be decided. All of the options for action on the problems weren't on the table. Few were willing to give an option that they didn't favor a fair trial. The decision-making seldom involved public deliberation.

The conflict over desegregation that racked the country grew out of an adversarial framing of the issues. Many people, for many reasons, felt outrage or believed things very important to them were being threatened. They blamed those they felt were responsible. It wasn't that the blame wasn't justified. Often it was. The problem was that blaming promoted mutual antagonism. Emotion flamed like a dry forest ablaze.

I'll try to describe the conflict in a way that captures some of this intensity. (If I could use emojis, I would use the ones with angry faces shouting, but old-fashioned exclamation marks "!" will have to do here.) For some, the desegregation issue was an obvious matter of rank, egregious, long-standing injustice! Many African American children had been relegated to inferior schools. How could anyone say that was not obvious discrimination? For others, the issue was educational. Some children were not getting the education they needed! Terrible! And there were unacceptable differences in the academic achievement levels of children. Surely, every child deserved a good education! For still others, especially parents, their greatest responsibility was for the well-being of their children. They believed that they had an unquestionable right to influence, if not control, what happens to their children when they were in school! The best way to do that was by having schools close to them—in their communities. Taking control of local schools away from people's communities was un-American!

Framing the desegregation issue so that people with such strong convictions could move from first reactions and biases to more reflective and shared judgment was extremely difficult because of the intensity of the emotions.

A LOST PERSPECTIVE: SCHOOLS FOR A NEW NATION

Other concerned Americans had their eyes not just on schools and the quality of education but on the kind of country the United States should be. They wanted a country where all citizens would be free from the discrimination that marginalizes people who needed to live and work together. These citizens feared a divided society and divided communities.

People who saw a connection between the public schools and national well-being had a history to draw on. At the nation's founding, schools were seen as the ideal institution for nation building. This essential role was recognized as early as the Land Ordinance of May 20, 1785. The country needed public schools, and the federal ordinance made land available for communities to use for that purpose.[2] The new country had a compelling interest in the "general diffusion of knowledge."[3] It was once a common cause.

George Washington laid out this argument for education when talking about the future of the former colonies. He championed educating young Americans together, though he wasn't likely to have had African Americans in mind. Washington reasoned that young people were at a period in their lives when "friendships are formed & habits established" and that this was a perfect time to overcome stereotypes and forge the cooperative relationships needed for the Union to prosper.[4] The first president saw schools as well suited to cultivating the kind of cohesive society a republic needed. (Today, we add that, obviously, citizens are unlikely to learn to work together if they are segregated.)

Sadly, by the 1970s, Americans weren't united behind the cause of public education. Instead, they became locked into bitter disputes over desegregating schools. Each of the conflicting parties tended to believe there was only one issue—their issue—and only one solution—theirs. Even the claim that there were other issues involved was unacceptable. A country that was so divided was unlikely to make use of its creative problem-solving abilities when they were most needed.

THE STRUGGLE TO MOVE AHEAD

Perhaps influenced by Americans of all races having shared foxholes in the Korean War, in 1954 the Supreme Court had ruled in *Brown v. Board of Education* that legally segregated schools were unconstitutional because the separation of the races could never provide an equal education for everyone.

Incensed by the ruling, massive resistance erupted in the South.[5] President
Eisenhower had to send troops into Little Rock, Arkansas, in 1957 to enforce
the *Brown* decision. Southern governors like George Wallace of Alabama
urged defiance. More riots erupted.

By 1965, despite the political opposition, most school boards in the South
had agreed to prepare desegregation plans that met federal guidelines. And by
1970, much of the overt political opposition to eliminating legally mandated
segregation had collapsed in that region. Still, integration met strong resistance. Violent opposition to eradicating de facto segregation (by custom, not
law) was breaking out in urban centers. The federal courts became the major
actors.

Implementing Court Orders

The eroding opposition to desegregation in some areas didn't end the conflict. To the contrary. In the 1960s and 1970s, racial tensions went from bad to
worse. In 1963, the deaths of four black girls in a Birmingham church bombing
carried out by the Ku Klux Klan stung the conscience of Americans. This
opposition to civil rights was marked by pure evil. Congress, at the insistence
of President Lyndon Johnson, passed the Civil Rights Act in 1964. However,
historians note that riots in major urban areas (Detroit, Newark, and the
Watts neighborhood of Los Angeles) between 1965 and 1967 further polarized
racial attitudes. Understanding what happened in the 1960s requires some
background.

Voluntary Compliance

Before *Brown*, federal judges followed the ruling in the *Briggs* case of 1952,
which had held that the Constitution required the elimination of only legally
imposed segregation.[6] Pledges by school boards to comply with the law were
accepted by the government. Local superintendents and officials in HEW's
Office of Education tended to be from the same professional circles and

treated one another with respect as colleagues. Federal school officials also usually recognized and supported the view that public education was a state, not a federal, responsibility, so they tried to build trust with local officials. Any differences between the federal government and school boards were to be negotiated in hopes that communities would believe that they had more ownership of the changes.

Recognizing that enormous social change was needed, the executive branch had initially favored a strategy of gradual, incremental school deseg-regation. The Kennedy administration encouraged voluntary compliance with civil rights laws affecting employment. This strategy worked to a degree, according to John McKnight, who was carrying out the policy at the Equal Employment Opportunity Commission.[7] That strategy changed over time, however, for reasons that are important to recognize.

In 1965, the Commissioner of Education issued the first guidelines for implementing Title VI of the Civil Rights Act, which prohibited discrimi-nation on the basis of race, color, and national origin in programs receiving federal financial assistance.[8] The guidelines were moderate and generally acceptable to the South. Even opponents of desegregation, like Governor Faubus of Arkansas, who had resisted desegregation in Little Rock in 1957, came to recognize that schools couldn't remain segregated.[9]

Policies Change

In the 1960s, the Johnson administration had dual policy objectives: to not only support school desegregation, but, having declared a war on poverty, to provide more money for poor families and children. Schools were sup-ported by the 1965 Elementary and Secondary Education Act (ESEA). This legislation gave the federal government considerable leverage because it stipulated that federal funds could not be used by segregated schools. Some schools would come to depend on these funds for a quarter to a third of their budgets.[10]

By the latter part of the 1960s, relations between federal and local officials began to deteriorate. And the forces bringing about the change in relationship didn't always have to do with desegregation. Some had to do with the nature of bureaucracies and how they operate; they need structure and certainty. The bureaucracies in this case weren't just at the federal level. Local offices wanted to know exactly what they were required to do under the new civil rights and antipoverty laws. Administrators in the educational bureaucracies favored detailed instructions that would remain stable over the long term. Federal officials also came to operate more bureaucratically in order to meet demands for specific guidelines for interpreting civil rights laws. And officials in Washington wanted relief from the heavy workload imposed by case-by-case negotiations with state and local school systems.

Funding Threats

In 1966, new regulations were written that threatened to cut off funds (and freeze allocations already promised) in order to bring about desegregation in recalcitrant school districts. The 1965 guidelines had relied on freedom of choice, which allowed students to select any school they wanted to attend. But that policy had left most African American students in the same schools. Under the new guidelines, funds were eventually denied to 38 districts for not desegregating. Freedom of choice was no longer a viable policy.[11] Furthermore, the negotiations that were favored in 1965 as a strategy for desegregation had also fallen out of favor, particularly with African American leaders, who considered local school officials (primarily white) to be unsympathetic.

   Recognizing these policy failures, officials in the Johnson administration were troubled. Cutting off funds conflicted with the goal of getting more money to the poor. And the White House counsel considered withholding funds a potent, even dangerous, remedy and recommended great care. An official in the civil rights division of the Justice Department acknowledged that the threat of cutoffs was a "sledge-hammer not a scalpel."[12] President Johnson himself was keenly aware of the practical, political consequences that had to be taken into account when desegregating schools. He got angry when the federal bureaucracy, without his knowledge, threatened Chicago with a termination of funds. The city's mayor, Richard J. Daley, was a powerful figure in the Democratic Party. So senior officials in HEW were sent to Chicago to meet with Daley after he had called the President to protest. HEW eventually accepted Chicago's earlier pledges to investigate and correct problems, and subsequently released the funds—a settlement that critics said was no more than a slap on the wrist.[13]

Changing Attitudes

The reversal in Chicago disappointed advocates of a vigorous prosecution of segregation, but within a few years after the Civil Rights Act of 1964, officials in HEW began calling for more realistic enforcement, a view attributed to Secretary Wilbur Cohen.[14] Cohen had reservations about what the government had been doing and believed that the public did, too. He wanted more federal funds to improve substandard schools serving African American students.[15] Even the staunchest champions of desegregation, like Johnson's Commissioner of Education, "Doc" Howe, came to say that 100 years of segregation couldn't be eradicated in a short time.[16] And journalist Douglass Cater, Johnson's assistant in the White House, pointed out that the procedures being used under HEW's guidelines made the Commissioner of Education police, judge, and jury. Cater favored more government incentives to desegregate rather than threats of punitive actions that would harm schoolchildren.[17]

A NEW ERA: "QUOTAS" AND COURT-ORDERED BUSING

Despite these moderating influences in the Johnson administration, relationships between federal and local authorities continued to deteriorate when the means agreed on for student desegregation (voluntary compliance) failed to deliver large-scale change. As noted, the courts and the federal government were initially satisfied when school districts dropped racial criteria for assigning students and allowed students free choice in selecting a school. However, local pressure was often applied to intimidate African American students so they would not exercise this right. Freedom of choice went out as an option the way voluntary compliance had.

The desegregation debate then changed significantly. Organizations representing parents and other interested parties protested the lack of progress toward integration and insisted that 20 percent of the African American student population be enrolled in integrated schools.[18] I don't think they intended to change the debate by introducing precise, quantified criteria. However, they were frustrated because the *Brown* criteria—"with all deliberate speed"—seemed to take forever. This introduction of quantitative standards for compliance, also called "quotas," would come to dominate the controversy. And conflicts between civil rights advocates and local officials were escalating, which sharpened the political debate.

Likely angered by the outright defiance of politicians like George Wallace, the Supreme Court put its foot down on May 27, 1968, and in the *Green* case insisted on immediate school desegregation. School boards had to come forward with plans that would work and work soon.[19] With freedom of choice discredited, numerical goals or quotas were on their way to becoming the new remedy for segregation in any form.

Another issue also surfaced. How were quantitative standards to be met when the population of children living near the schools didn't match the standards? In the *Swann* decision in 1971, the Supreme Court upheld a district judge's decision that assigning children to the school nearest their home (a neighborhood school) would not end segregation and said that busing was "a starting point in shaping a remedy" (not a quota) to achieve a racial balance in the schools.[20] The court set a flexible ratio of white and black students as the standard for balance: every school's student body should comprise 9 to 38 percent African Americans. This ratio could be reached by busing students, restructuring school zones, or other means. While acknowledging that the Constitution does not require any particular degree of racial integration in public education, the Court did say that numerical ratios would now be used for demonstrating desegregation.

This introduction of a standard for racial balance and the use of busing to achieve it added still other dimensions to an already highly contested issue. Court-ordered busing would eventually become synonymous with desegregation.[21] In 1973, the controversy over mandatory busing became even more widespread after the Supreme Court ruled in the *Keyes* case that de facto segregation in the North was unconstitutional, a decision that extended and reinforced the *Swann* ruling.[22]

Busing was fiercely defended by advocates of desegregation who saw it as the only way to achieve what had now become the objective: no racially identifiable schools. However, court-imposed busing was generating increasing opposition in Congress, as well as on Main Street.[23] A 1972 survey by pollster Robert Teeter showed that while substantial majorities in every region of the country favored school desegregation, most people were opposed to mandatory busing. Black voters, however, favored busing if they saw it as the only means to a good education.[24]

COURT BATTLES

The federal court system was becoming caught in protracted and ultimately unsuccessful efforts to achieve the degree of desegregation mandated by its rulings. Disputes over school desegregation that began in 1955 stayed in the court system for almost a half-century.[25]

Kansas City: Who Pays?

The case of Kansas City, Missouri, stands out because the district court went so far as to impose taxes, contradicting the fundamental American principle that taxation required the consent of the citizenry.

Turning to the federal courts was inevitable, and desegregation could be expensive. Could the courts levy taxes? The circumstances made what some considered a compelling case. Prior to 1955, many of the suburbs around Kansas City would not allow African American students to attend their public schools, so parents of these children moved into the metropolitan area where the school district would accept them. After the *Brown* decision, the Kansas City school district had established neighborhood zones and allowed any student near them, regardless of race, to attend. Its plan also allowed students to transfer out of their zone. However, to prevent the city school district policies from affecting the suburbs, where residents were primarily white, the Missouri legislature had prohibited any enlargement of the school district's boundaries.[26]

Then, when there wasn't significant desegregation in the early 1970s, the federal government entered the picture and charged the city school district with maintaining a segregated system.[27] Later, in *Jenkins v. Missouri*, Judge Russell Clark decided to require improvements in the city schools, which he believed would attract white students from the suburbs.[28] He ordered nearly $2 billion to be spent over 12 years to build or renovate schools and bring test scores up to the national average. The money was used for higher teacher salaries, an Olympic-sized swimming pool with an observation room, field trips to other countries, a model United Nations, a robotics lab, and a zoo. In addition, $900,000 was allocated for advertising to attract white students, and $6.4 million was spent on transportation. (If bus routes didn't run near a white student's home, the school district paid for a taxi to transport the student to and from school.)[29] Still, these students did not enroll in the numbers expected, and a requirement of a 60-40 racial balance meant that many seats remained empty.

Per-student expenditures in Kansas City rose and far exceeded the national average. Tax revenue to cover these expenditures became a problem. So, the court required the state to help fund the integration plan, which upset parents in other Missouri communities because tax revenue was being withheld from their districts and sent to Kansas City. Judge Clark acknowledged that the tax burden could not be placed entirely on the state, but voters in the Kansas City school district had repeatedly rejected tax increases. So, Clark ordered that property taxes in Kansas City be more than doubled. He also ordered a 1.5 percent surcharge on income earned by people who worked in Kansas City but lived elsewhere. Clark admitted that he had to balance taxation without representation against schoolchildren's right to equal opportunity. His justification was that he was siding with the children. Many citizens had a different reaction; they dubbed Clark "King George" and called him "the poster boy for an imperial judiciary."[30]

By the 1990s, the Kansas City case reached the Supreme Court, which ruled that Judge Clark did not have the authority to impose taxes but could order the district to pay its debts. He was also told he could not use state funds to lure students from the suburbs. Instead, he was directed to eliminate any remaining vestiges of discrimination and return control to local authorities as soon as possible. Clark realized that he had created a school system that could not be supported by the tax base, but his court did not have the authority to require funding.

In 2003, a new district judge, Dean Whipple, ruled that the district had complied with the court's orders in a reasonable time. But reports showed that by 2000 the "schools were no more racially integrated than in 1985, and despite a student-teacher ratio of 13 to 1 (among the lowest in the nation), test scores were dismal."[31]

Boston: Trapped in a Box?

The Kansas City case showed there were limits to what even the federal courts, with all their power, could do to bring about desegregation. A similar case in Boston demonstrated how courts can be limited or "boxed in" in other ways. These two cases set the stage for what I want to talk about later, which is the constructive role the community itself must play as a coproducer of justice and social cohesion. (That's the subject of the next chapter.)

The school situation in Boston was already bad when I came to Washington in 1975. The battle lines were so fixed that there was little room to maneuver. Following the *Keyes* ruling, Judge Arthur Garrity from the federal district court in Boston required children in a low-income, white neighborhood in South Boston to be bused to a low-income African American neighborhood, Roxbury.[32] That had occurred in 1974. The two groups involved (Irish Americans and African Americans) had a history of conflict in Boston, having clashed in 1968 in disturbances following the assassination of Martin Luther King Jr.[33] Court-ordered school busing was met with more violence (*Figure 13*).

Because of the violence, Boston Mayor Kevin White and Massachusetts

FIGURE 13. *Mounted police officers tried to control the crowd after a riot broke out outside South Boston High School on Dec. 11, 1974. (Photo by Ted Dully/The Boston Globe via Getty Images.)*

Governor Frank Sargent requested federal marshals to enforce the court's ruling. White asked Judge Garrity; the governor asked President Ford. Both the judge and President Ford turned the requests down on the grounds that the responsibility belonged to state and local enforcement officers.[34] While Ford had opposed segregation, he did not believe in "forced busing" to achieve a racial balance.[35] So, when confronted with what was happening in Boston, he said that he, "respectfully disagree[d] with the judge's order," adding that Bostonians must respect the law. Ford condemned the violence.[36]

For the 1975 school year, in support of local authorities, 100 federal marshals were sent in, along with 50 FBI agents, 6 special prosecutors, and 8 additional field representatives.[37] HEW made $2.6 million in ESEA funds available. And the Department dispatched Herman Goldberg, Associate Commissioner of Education, to monitor the situation in Boston. In addition, I asked Joffre Whisenton, Special Assistant to the Secretary, to see whether he could find citizens groups that the Department could work with. The Community Relations Service of the Justice Department also sent conciliators to bridge what had become a gulf separating the schools from many in their communities. The Service worked to diffuse racial tensions and helped in the formation of the Greater Boston Civil Rights Commission.[38]

In 1975, Judge Garrity asked Edward J. McCormack to head a team charged with drawing up a plan for Boston that was to be more "politically acceptable."[39] McCormack was an influential Bostonian and the nephew of a former Speaker of the House, John William McCormack. The judge, however, kept Roxbury and South Boston in the same district, which was the source of most of the violence. Garrity also increased the number of children being bused from 14,900 to 25,000. And, in reaction to a defiant school board (the Boston School Committee), the judge delved into the small details of running the schools, at one point ordering South Boston to purchase 12 McGregor basketballs and 6 Acme tornado whistles. In schools being changed from elementary grades to higher levels, he directed that the height of urinals be raised.[40]

In addition to efforts at reconciliation by federal officials in 1975-1976, local civic groups also attempted to improve the situation in Boston. They weren't able, however, to offset the already organized and emotionally charged antibusing movement, which had the support of the city's school board. Nonetheless, in some cases, citizens acted constructively on their own. For instance, African American parents raised private funds to transport their children to better, all-white schools.[41]

Boston also had distinctive political dynamics that affected the desegregation crisis. Irish immigrants had worked hard to gain control of local government and were afraid of losing it to the federal government.[42][43] Urban renewal had already disrupted Irish neighborhoods by scattering former residents across the city and replacing them with middle- and upper-class Bostonians.[44] Yet the suburbs, where the affluent lived, didn't bear the brunt of desegregation.[45]

For working-class people, busing their children outside their neighborhood to someone else's schools was the last straw.[46] It deepened the resentment of African American citizens. Reflecting on what happened in

Boston, Garrity described his situation as being "boxed in." The judge said he did not favor busing yet saw no other way to meet the standards for desegregation. He was, it was reported, "pained by the hard choices he had to make."[47]

Beyond Boston

In a sense, the whole country was a courtroom in the mid-1970s. The desegregation cases weren't being tried only in the judiciary, but also in Congress, state legislatures, school boards, the media, and the court of public opinion. Sadly, few, if any, of the conditions needed for sound decisions to emerge from these "trials" were present at the height of the conflict. The issue had become narrowly framed around mandatory busing and racial balance. That framing made it extremely difficult to avoid polarization. Consequently, the political debate remained focused on one institution, the schools; on one factor, race; and on one option, a specific quantitative balance in student bodies to be achieved through court-ordered busing. This implied that there was a single solution to be agreed upon when actually a number of partial solutions or innovations on a variety of fronts might have been more realistic. The political advantage to the narrow framing was that it kept the pressure on abolishing the racial identity of the schools. But this framework also gave those who opposed desegregation a clear target to attack.

Going back over the desegregation cases, reviewers have been struck by the amount of human distress and turmoil that resulted when court rulings, which were often narrowly constructed to respond to a specific situation, were amplified by bureaucratic regulations and then brought to bear on school boards, administrators, teachers, unions, parents, and communities, each with its own concerns and constraints. The outcome of this interaction, with each party doing what it thought best, has been described as tragically absurd. Writing about desegregation in the Cleveland schools in a 1975 article in the *New York Times*, James Reston observed: "Go where you will in the big towns of the United States today and you will find disintegration, racial segregation, economic disruption and political and moral confusion."[48]

FROM DESEGREGATION TO INTEGRATION

My reaction to the desegregation crises was naturally influenced by my experiences before coming to HEW. The University of Alabama was moving from legal desegregation to combining different groups into a coherent whole, which is called "integrating" or coalescing and incorporating. I don't mean homogenizing or eliminating differences. That incorporating had to be done both within the whole of the state as well as on campus.

I'll digress a little bit into details and personalities because they are essential to the story I want to tell. I owe a great deal to what I learned from the people I will cite, and their influence carried over to HEW.

The University, as I said, had been desegregated by a court order in 1963 by Judge Frank M. Johnson. But it hadn't become significantly integrated until the 1970s. During that decade, the number of African American students grew from a small group to more than 1,600, an increase from 2 percent to more than 10 percent.[49] This increase was the result of actively recruiting good students who had been going outside the South for their education. These students began to work their way into campus life, often with the support of their white classmates. Changes in the athletic programs got the most media attention. In 1969, Wendell Hudson broke the color barrier in basketball.[50] Even earlier, walk-ons in football in 1967 paved the way for scholarship players like Wilbur Jackson and John Mitchell a few years later. This experience told me to look on both sides of the divide in cities like Boston for people who would be willing to work for peaceful desegregation and integration.

Breaking the hold of segregation as a legal matter was difficult, and I credit my predecessor, president of the University of Alabama, Frank Rose; his assistant, Jeff Bennet; and deans John Blackburn and Sarah Healy with taking the institution through desegregation without the violence that had stopped Autherine Lucy's enrollment in the 1950s. (There is now a statue of her on campus.) However, when I became president in 1969, I quickly learned that creating a campus where all students could learn to live and work together was a different challenge from legal desegregation—one that could not be met by the courts alone.

Much credit for constructive change goes to the Student Government

FIGURE 14. *Cleophus Thomas, Jr. (left) was elected in 1976 as the first African American President of the University of Alabama Student Government Association. He is seen here with acting UA President Dr. Richard Thigpen (center) and outgoing SGA President Dale Wallace (right). (Photo courtesy of the University of Alabama Libraries Special Collection.)*

Association in the 1970s when students elected the first African American officers, Sylvester Jones as vice president and, later, Cleo Thomas as president (*Figure 14*). Integration also had a cultural dimension. Students like Everett McCorvey in the music department brought their talents to campus. Music programs added spirituals, and the Afro American Gospel Choir was born. The classroom wasn't the only place in colleges and schools for students to learn about one another. Black professors did join the faculty, and they formed the Black Faculty and Staff Association in the 1970s. Among the pioneers was Joffre Whisenton, whom I mentioned earlier. He was the first African American to earn a PhD, and I was one of his graduate advisors.[51]

I also learned that people can change. Ten years after he stood in the schoolhouse door to block desegregation, George Wallace, paralyzed from the waist down after a failed 1972 assassination attempt, crowned Terry Points as the first African American homecoming queen at the University of Alabama (*Figure 15*).

FIGURE 15. *Terry Points, the first African American student at the University of Alabama to be crowned homecoming queen, is congratulated by Governor George Wallace in 1973. (Photo courtesy of the University of Alabama Libraries Special Collection.)*

Did racial harmony result? No. Were there protests and sit-ins? Yes. White students took a little time, but most adjusted to the change. However, expectations were quite different. What seemed too slow a pace of change to some appeared to others as an unseemly rush to accommodate. Building new relationships moved step by step. Change occurs, it has been said, at the speed of trust. And that isn't instantaneous.

I tell this story to make the point that the ultimate goal isn't just desegregation; it's new, constructive ways of working together. And that objective is not something that an external authority can decree. It is a kind of relationship. The parties involved in building that relationship must constantly adjust what they are doing as circumstances will inevitably change. A working relationship isn't homogenization and doesn't eliminate differences; it uses them.

SECOND THOUGHTS

By the mid-1970s, Judge Garrity's disquiet about busing was being shared by more and more people for a variety of reasons. Despite the Supreme Court's rulings in 1971, polls taken the following year showed that most Americans opposed compulsory busing by a three-fourths majority.[52] This opposition was significant when measured against the nearly two-thirds majority that had supported the *Brown* decision in 1954.[53] Although opposition was attributed to deep-seated racism by some, only a small percentage of Americans were opposed to school integration.[54]

Some advocates of desegregation also began expressing reservations about busing. They feared the court's remedy, busing children to achieve a racial balance in schools, was leading to resegregation. Norman Cousins, then editor of one of the country's leading magazines, *Saturday Review*, wrote in 1976, "Busing hasn't desegregated the schools. It has resegregated them." In Washington, he noted, 96 percent of the students were African Americans; in Newark, 72 percent; and in Detroit, 70 percent.[55] Cousins called for addressing fundamental problems in the inner cities: the scarcity of good housing, high levels of poverty, lack of access to justice. And he urged depolarizing the busing issue that had been taken over by liberal and conservative ideologies.[56]

While a majority of Americans favored school desegregation, people began looking for ways to achieve that other than by busing, especially if the buses crossed school district lines. They came up with proposals to extend district boundaries to include a more diverse population and build housing for low-income families in middle-class neighborhoods.

By 1973, even some of the leading advocates of desegregation in the African American community had second thoughts. Atlanta's branch of the NAACP decided that insisting on racial balance was a flawed strategy. Fearing that white flight would resegregate schools, the organization moved away from racial balance as an objective and concentrated on winning control of the schools by electing African American board members.[57] The people in that community didn't want to lose their hard-won influence on the education of their own children. The value of local control had a broader appeal than might be imagined when just listening to states' rights advocates.[58]

The US Supreme Court: Behind the Curtain

Inside the federal court system, there were concerns about what was happening in desegregation, as was evident in Judge Garrity's distress. There were also reservations in the Supreme Court. I'll use Justice Hugo Black to make this point. Black, who supported the *Brown* ruling, had concerns, expressed privately, even though he was instrumental in overturning segregation laws. He became so identified with liberal decisions that I seem to recall that the Alabama legislature resolved not to allow him to be buried in his own state. Black's reservations reflected the tensions among the different American interests that were called into play in the desegregation issue.

Justice Black, like many Americans from rural areas, had no problem with using buses to transport children to a centrally located school serving a dispersed community. But this opponent of segregation also believed that retaining community control of schools was essential. He worried that mandatory busing could cause many people to abandon the public schools. As a strict constitutionalist (who carried a copy in his pocket), Black wanted limits placed on the power of federal judges to order busing because he could not find justification for it in the Constitution. He also didn't believe that the court could force communities to spend money to the extent that citywide busing would require.[59]

Critics have charged just the opposite, that placing such limits on the courts would take the pressure off the federal government and that would result in the resegregation of the schools. Even if it required being coercive, segregation could be stamped out only by confronting those resisting court orders and federal requirements with penalties they couldn't bear.[60]

Black's reservations eventually gave way to other considerations. Chief Justice Warren Burger had insisted that the court present a solid front in the 1954 *Brown* decision. He was fearful of encouraging segregationists. On those grounds, Burger had persuaded Black and the other justices to make the court decision unanimous.[61]

Despite the Supreme Court's position, Congress' opposition to busing grew. In 1974 and 1975, in response to resistance to mandatory busing in the urban centers of the North, two amendments were passed that prohibited transporting children past the nearest or next nearest school and required that other measures to end racial isolation be exhausted prior to busing students, making it a remedy of last resort. These other measures included constructing new facilities, creating magnet schools, and changing attendance zones.[62] These, however, didn't stop the resegregation of urban schools.

THE FORD RESPONSE

As all of these conflicts were swirling around, how did President Ford weigh in? I'm not going to argue that no mistakes were made or that a perfect solution was offered but rejected. Still, what happened then is an important part of this history that needs to be noted.

While Congress was already considering desegregation measures, Ford wanted to offer his own plan. Proposing an "alternative," however, was a lightning rod because it was taken to mean an alternative to busing. I advised him not to get into a situation in which he might be expected to have a solution that would make any busing unnecessary. In some cases, busing might not have dire consequences. The difficulty was, as officials in the Office of Education (OE) pointed out, the issue of desegregation was being framed in a way that made extensive busing inevitable. Children in urban areas lived in their own socioeconomic neighborhoods, and their schools were in these neighborhoods. Consequently, as long as the government required specific racial ratios of students, there was no way to achieve a balance without compelling some students to be transported out of their neighborhoods to another area. Judge Garrity was right about being boxed in; framing the issue this way put the country in a box that inhibited looking for other means to further both desegregation and integration.

Just looking for other remedies, however, was suspect. It was demonized as segregation in disguise. But my experience with integration taught me that progress could and had to be made on multiple fronts. No one remedy, including busing, would address all the questions about public education. Citizens in some communities had been able to bring about peaceful desegregation. I wanted the President to look at what they were doing. (More about that in a minute.)

It is important to keep in mind that the busing crisis of the 1970s came at a time when people's confidence in government was plummeting. I thought the administration's response had to take that into account. The public's perception was that the federal government, in all of its branches, was making school matters worse rather than better. Although Washington needed to come up with an acceptable national strategy, I believed that the implementation had to be local. Yet, given the resistance to desegregation, I recognized that communities, their citizens, and parents shouldn't have unchecked power to make all the decisions about desegregation. Still, I was convinced that the pendulum had swung too far away from the citizenry and their communities. Although quite aware of the resistance that politicians like George Wallace could rally, I knew there were many people of good intent in the country and a host of pragmatists, who, whatever their personal views on race, would support the public schools and work for their communities. Those Americans needed to be enlisted. These were among the considerations I had in mind when participating in developing the Ford administration's plan.

In addition to falling confidence in government, other factors had a bearing on planning for the Ford response. Some were inside HEW. Even within a single department, there could be fundamental differences on the proper role of the federal government. HEW worked through both the Office of Education and the Office for Civil Rights to desegregate schools. These two agencies had different histories and points of view. The officials in OE were largely educators and inclined to lend a helping hand to their fellow professionals in the school systems. From their perspective, the role of government was to support and assist local schools. The OE had at its disposal a modest incentive: funds authorized under two emergency legislative acts.[63]

The Office for Civil Rights was from a different era, and its orientation was naturally legalistic. From its perspective, the role of government was to regulate and enforce. OCR was also close to interest groups rightfully opposing discrimination. The tools at OCR's disposal were largely coercive, principally the threat of cutting off funds. As in other cases, the burden placed on schools and educators to carry out HEW regulations was not a primary concern in OCR; justice for minorities was.[64] I believed the Ford plan had to empower the Office of Education as well as recognize OCR's point of view. The issue, in my mind, was not so much whether the federal government should have punitive powers, but how and when they should be used and what effect they would have. Understanding that effect required a greater role for the Office of Education.

As federal dollars became a larger share of schools' budgets, withholding funding was a potent weapon. However, cutting off funds that came from taxpayers was a convenient target for politicians like George Wallace, who learned how to turn a federal threat to their advantage, without actually sacrificing federal dollars. Railing against the threat brought out more supporters and hardened battle lines. Another limitation to financial threats was that the processes for terminating funding resulted in drawn-out legal battles so that justice delayed was justice denied.[65]

I believed that a less combative, multifaceted strategy would be more effective. And I thought that different cases in different circumstances merited different approaches to the problems. School boards that had dug in their heels in defiance required a firmer response than those open to negotiations.

Reconciling Differences

Although I knew that the Department had to withhold funds when the law required it, I still saw a role for HEW in reconciling differences, arbitrating disputes, and helping solve problems. Threatening local officials early on in negotiations over compliance could be counterproductive because it encouraged defensive resistance. The goal, it seemed to me, was to avoid getting to the point where force was the only alternative. So, I brought in experts to the Department to explain what could be achieved using the mediating strategies being developed in the legal profession. I was astounded by the mountain of suits falling on the Department. While the government can't make itself immune, I believe it should be possible to divert conflicts to other processes like mediation through which better decisions might be made and still follow the relevant laws. In this and other cases, I drew on the experience of friends in labor negotiations and members of the American Bar Association who also saw the necessity for alternative means in settling disputes.[66] Of course, mediation couldn't be effective in all situations because some people benefited from conflict.

Federal pressure did accelerate desegregation, though not without unintended side effects. In Alabama, despite pressure from Governor Wallace, most local school systems had consented to comply with the law prohibiting segregation by the spring of 1965. To stem this defection, Wallace pressured the legislature (along with the congressional delegation) to support him in legal maneuvers to block compliance without losing federal funds. HEW's threat to cut off educational funds gave Wallace the springboard he needed to rally support for the local control of schools. (However, he meant state control, which was different from community control.) A federal court ruling in New Orleans that upheld HEW's right to terminate funding did nothing to deflate the political groundswell the governor was orchestrating. In fact, the governor used the ruling to broaden his appeal in order to combat increasing opposition to him within his own state.[67] George Wallace was also well on his way to making a serious bid to become President of the United States.[68] He came to symbolize the political era in the US that historian Dan Carter has characterized as the "politics of rage," a description that might also fit the environment in 2020. This phrase certainly fits the politics that came to characterize the effort to desegregate schools; arguments were cast in moral terms by the combatants on both sides.[69]

WHAT'S NEXT?

I've said from the beginning of this account of the desegregation crisis that a *with* strategy had something positive to offer. I want to focus on that in the next chapter. Despite the toxic political climate in the 1970s, some communities were able to use local, citizen-led groups to pave a way forward in education. What they did and the role the federal government might have played by working *with* these groups has implications for today's resegregated schools.

NOTES

1. Histories of education in the United States sometimes describe local schools as "district schools," meaning a school "organized and controlled by a small locality financed by some combination of property taxes, fuel contributions, tuition payments, and state aid." Carl F. Kaestle, *Pillars of the Republic: Common Schools and American Society 1780-1860* (New York: Hill and Wang, 1983), 13. See Lawrence Cremin quoting Horace Mann in 1837. Mann described the public schools as "each being governed by its own habits, traditions, and local customs." There was, Mann reported, "no common superintending power over them." As state superintendent in Massachusetts, Mann was determined to exercise more power through the state government, but he and superintendents elsewhere always had to contend with an entrenched tradition of local control. Lawrence A. Cremin, *American Education: The National Experience, 1783-1876* (New York: Harper and Row, 1980), 155.

    Also see the discussion of the centralizing thrust of integration strategies and the corresponding rejection of localism as backward and biased in Kimberlé Crenshaw, Neil Gotanda, Gary Peller, and Kendall Thomas, *Critical Race Theory: The Key Writings That Formed the Movement* (New York: The New Press, 1996), 133-135.

2. "There shall be reserved for the United States out of every township, the four lots, being numbered 8, 11, 26, 29, and out of every fractional part of a township, so many lots of the same numbers as shall be found thereon, for future sale. There shall be reserved the lot No. 16, of every township, for the maintenance of public schools within the said township; also one third part of all gold, silver, lead and copper mints, to be sold, or otherwise disposed of, as Congress shall hereafter direct." Library of Congress, Documents from the Continental Congress and the Constitutional

Convention, 1774-1789, Land Ordinance of 1785, http://memory.loc.gov/cgi-bin/query/r?ammem/bdsdcc:@field(DOCID+@lit(bdsdcc13401)).

3. Thomas Jefferson, "A Bill for the More General Diffusion of Knowledge," in *The Papers of Thomas Jefferson*, vol. 2, ed. Julian P. Boyd (Princeton: Princeton University Press, 1950), 526.

4. Joseph J. Ellis, *Founding Brothers: The Revolutionary Generation* (New York: Vintage Books, 2002), 154.

5. *Brown v. Board of Education of Topeka*, 347 U.S. 483 (1954).

6. Gareth Davies, *See Government Grow: Education Politics from Johnson to Reagan* (Lawrence, KS: University Press of Kansas, 2007), 121; and Briggs v. Elliott, 342 U.S. 350 (1952).

7. Rachel E. Dixon, *Voluntary Compliance and the Work of John McKnight* (Dayton, OH: Report to the Kettering Foundation, January 2018); David Cayley, "Community and Its Counterfeits: Part Two of an Interview with John McKnight," *Mouth Magazine* 107, no. 9 (2008): 38-53.

8. The accounts of desegregation strategy in this section were drawn from Gary Orfield, *The Reconstruction of Southern Education: The Schools and the 1964 Civil Rights Act* (New York: Wiley-Interscience, 1969).

9. Orfield, *The Reconstruction of Southern Education*, 119.

10. Orfield, *The Reconstruction of Southern Education*, 108.

11. Orfield, *The Reconstruction of Southern Education*, 115.

12. Orfield, *The Reconstruction of Southern Education*, 117. HEW also raised the sensitive issue of faculty desegregation. Chicago officials said that having black teachers instructing white students was far more sensitive a matter than student integration. Yet black students, their parents, and civil rights activists insisted on faculty integration. This issue would still be unresolved by the mid-1970s.

13. Orfield, *The Reconstruction of Southern Education*, 195.

14. Orfield, *The Reconstruction of Southern Education*, 195-196.

15. Gary Orfield, *Must We Bus? Segregated Schools and National Policy* (Washington, DC: Brookings Institution, 1978), 285.

16. Orfield, *The Reconstruction of Southern Education*, 204.

17. Dean J. Kotlowski, *Nixon's Civil Rights: Politics, Principle, and Policy* (Cambridge, MA: Harvard University Press, 2001), 26-27.

18. Orfield, *The Reconstruction of Southern Education*, 144.

19. *Green v. County School Board of New Kent County*, 391 U.S. 430 (1968).

20. *Swann v. Charlotte-Mecklenburg Board of Education*, 402 U.S. 1 (1971).

21. In 2019, the *New York Times* published an extensively documented article arguing that school busing wasn't the real issue. The real problem was the white racism that kept busing from integrating schools. The author, Nikole Hannah-Jones, writes about

the Charlotte-Mecklenbury schools in North Carolina, where busing was made to work and there were achievement gains for both black and white students until litigation reversed the desegregation order. She also contends that busing had to be used because black and white families seldom lived in the same neighborhoods. Nikole Hannah-Jones, "It Was Never about Busing," *New York Times*, July 12, 2019.

22. *Keyes v. School District No.1*, Denver Colorado, 413 U.S. 189 (1973).

23. "A majority of Americans continue to favor public school integration, but few people—black or white—think that busing is the best way to achieve that goal, the Gallup Poll reported yesterday. . . . Another part of the survey indicated that much of the opposition to busing was not based on racial animosity. Other reasons for the opposition, according to survey findings, are the belief that busing is an infringement of personal liberties, worry about busing children to schools in different neighborhoods and concern that busing will increase local school taxes." "Gallup Finds Few Favor Busing for Integration," *New York Times*, September 9, 1973, 55.

24. Memorandum for the Attorney General, folder "February 27, 1972–Attorney General–Surveys on Race and Busing," Box 64, Robert Teeter Papers, Gerald R. Ford Library, https://www.fordlibrarymuseum.gov/library/document/0027/1691443.pdf.

25. This section on Kansas City was based on an analysis of court rulings, legislative records, and newspaper files done by Kristin Cruset, a researcher at the Kettering Foundation. Kristin Cruset, memorandum to David Mathews, March 27, 2009. This document can be found in the David Mathews collection, Kettering Foundation archives. For more information, contact archives@kettering.org.

26. Gotham, K.F. "Missed Opportunities, Enduring Legacies: School Segregation and Desegregation in Kansas City, Missouri," *American Studies*, 43(2) (2002): 5-41.

27. Investigations, charges, and countercharges went on for four years and ended in January 1976 when an HEW administrative law judge ruled that the city had not dismantled its dual system. The school district took the position that it could not comply without expanding its jurisdiction into the annexed suburbs and took the case to the federal district court in 1977. Following the Supreme Court ruling in the *Milliken* case, which prohibited imposing a burden on suburbs that could not be shown to have taken actions resulting in segregation, the district judge dismissed the suburbs as defendants in the case.

28. *Jenkins v. Missouri*, 593 F. Supp. 1485 (WD Mo. 1984).

29. Paul Ciotti, "Money and School Performance: Lessons from the Kansas City Desegregation Experiment," Policy Analysis No. 298 (March 16, 1998), 2-15, https://www.cato.org/policy-analysis/money-school-performance-lessons-kansas-city-desegregation-experiment.

30. Ciotti, "Money and School Performance,"12. Court cases did not end by any means with Kansas City. In 2006, the tensions led to a legal battle involving officials of the Louisville and Seattle schools, on the one hand, and plaintiffs representing parents on the other. That year, four other former Secretaries of HEW and Secretaries of the Department of Education and I filed a brief with the Supreme Court as *amici curiae* supporting decisions of the local school boards in Louisville and Seattle to prevent racial isolation by regulating pupil assignments. David Mathews, Joseph A. Califano Jr., Shirley M. Hufstedler, Lauro Fred Cavazos, and Richard W. Riley filed a Brief of Former United States Secretaries of Education and Secretaries of Health, Education, and Welfare Who Served Five Former Presidents as *Amici Curiae* in Support of Respondents in *Community Schools v. Seattle School District No. 1, et al.* and *Crystal D. Meredith, Custodial Parent and Next Friend of Joshua Ryan McDonald v. Jefferson County Board of Education, et al.*, Nos. 05-908, 05-915. The brief was filed on October 10, 2006. These boards were being sued by plaintiffs acting on behalf of white students who were not permitted to transfer out of schools on the grounds that the transfers "would have an adverse effect on desegregation compliance" and would be working against the goal of maintaining racially diverse schools. Also see *Parents Involved in Community Schools v. Seattle School District No. 1*, et al., and *Meredith, Custodial Parent and Next Friend of McDonald v. Jefferson County Bd. of Ed.*, et al., 2007. The former Secretaries pointed out that the country had a compelling interest not only in preventing the racial isolation, but also in preserving local control. And the decisions on preventing racial isolation in Seattle and Louisville had, indeed, been made by local boards, whose authority had been affirmed in the 1970s by the Supreme Court. See *Milliken v. Bradley*, 418 U.S. 717 (1974) and *Dayton Board of Education v. Brickman* (Dayton I), 433 U.S. 406 (1977). The ruling in the *Milliken* decision in 1974 is quite explicit that while local control is not sacrosanct, "no single tradition in public education is more deeply rooted than local control over the operation of schools; local autonomy has long been thought essential both to the maintenance of community concern and support for public schools and to the quality of the educational process." *Milliken*, 418 U.S. at 741-742. The school boards in these cases, however, had used race as a consideration in making school assignments in keeping with the national interest in cohesion within diversity. Objecting, plaintiffs sued on the grounds that even a limited use of race is unconstitutional. In a 5-4 ruling on June 28, 2007, the Supreme Court agreed with the plaintiffs and ruled in their favor.

31. Abigail Thernstrom and Stephan Thernstrom, *No Excuses: Closing the Racial Gap in Learning* (New York: Simon and Schuster, 2003), 164.

32. *Morgan v. Hennigan*, 379 F. Supp. 410 (D. Mass. 1974).

33. Not to overstate, Kettering researcher and editor Kristin Cruset noted in her analysis

that the rioting in Boston was limited—21 injured, 30 arrested, $50,000 in damage—compared to other cities like Washington, DC, and Chicago, where people died and damage was in the millions.

34. Jack Tager, *Boston Riots: Three Centuries of Social Violence* (Boston: Northeastern University Press, 2000), 205-206.

35. An examination and critique of Ford's stand on desegregation in Congress and as President is Lawrence J. McAndrews, "Missing the Bus: Gerald Ford and School Desegregation," *Presidential Studies Quarterly* 27, no. 4 (Fall 1997): 791-804.

36. Ronald P. Formisano, *Boston Against Busing: Race, Class, and Ethnicity in the 1960s and 1970s* (Chapel Hill, NC: University of North Carolina Press, 2004), 80.

37. Paul M. Goldstein, "School Integration and Busing Policy during the Ford Administration" (undergraduate honors thesis, University of Michigan, 1998), 33.

38. Community Relations Service, US Department of Justice Community Relations Service (CRS), "New England Regional Director Martin A. Walsh to Retire after 35 Years' Service," http://www.usdoj.gov/crs/pr06302003.htm.

39. J. Anthony Lukas, *Common Ground: A Turbulent Decade in the Lives of Three American Families* (New York: Vintage Books, 1985), 248, 260. Other Massachusetts officials were also drawn into the busing controversy, including the state's two US senators, Ed Brooke and Ted Kennedy. Lukas reported on their response:

> Neither man actually advocated busing. In April 1965, Ed Brooke—then the first black to serve as Massachusetts Attorney General—said, "I don't believe any parent, black or white, wants to have his children bused from a superior school to an inferior school. It's just not natural. The sane and sensible approach is the destruction of the ghetto." Ted Kennedy was equally skeptical. On *Meet the Press* in March 1964, he told a reporter, "If your question is asking me whether I oppose 'busing' students, I do." But as support for busing became a touchstone of commitment to racial equality, both senators gradually altered their positions, and when Arthur Garrity handed down his decision, Kennedy and Brooke rallied around the embattled judge.

40. Lukas, *Common Ground*, 250-251. Garrity was dealing with Louise Day Hicks, who chaired the school board and was one of the leaders of the antibusing movement. The board defied not only the federal judge but also the state legislature, which had prohibited racial imbalance.

41. Formisano, *Boston Against Busing*, 37-38.

42. The violence in Boston showed how much social class friction contributed to the problems of desegregation. In that city and across the country, blue-collar citizens had become increasingly estranged from a government that their families had traditionally served as its most stalwart patriots. Working-class young men, white and black, were also doing a disproportionate share of the fighting in Vietnam. And economic problems in the country made matters worse. A long period of steady growth

in jobs and wages had ended, and inflation had set in; prices increased, along with taxes. Women joined the workforce to maintain standards of living. While incomes for working-class whites had gone up between 1961 and 1968, those for minorities had grown even faster. Part of the increase for Americans living below the poverty line came from government transfer payments of $121 billion. When the economic boom ended, low-income people were hit hard, but whites resented what they considered the unearned assistance that black citizens received from transfer payments. Adding to the class tensions, technology reduced the number of entry-level jobs that whites and minorities competed for. Dan T. Carter, *The Politics of Rage: George Wallace, the Origins of the New Conservatism, and the Transformation of American Politics* (New York: Simon and Schuster, 1995), 348-349.

43. Formisano, *Boston Against Busing*, 11, 15, 226-227.

44. Tager, *Boston Riots*, 189.

45. Tager, *Boston Riots*, 193, 227.

46. Tager, *Boston Riots*, 201-202.

47. Lukas, *Common Ground*, 251. I also used the review of this literature on Boston done by Kettering Foundation researcher Kristin Cruset. Community Relations Service, US Department of Justice Community Relations Service (CRS), "New England Regional Director Martin A. Walsh to Retire After 35 Years' Service," https://www.justice.gov/archive/crs/news-2003.htm, cited in Kristin Cruset, memorandum to David Mathews, "Answers for Race and Public Schooling, #13 (n.d.).

48. James Reston, "The Cities of America," *New York Times*, November 23, 1975.

49. "The University of Alabama 1969-1979," University of Alabama Archives, p. 9. In their book *After the Dream: Black and White Southerners Since 1965*, Timothy J. Minchin and John A. Salmond say, "By the fall of 1974, HEW's own data highlighted that just 4 percent of the students at 10 major southern state universities were black. Ironically, the best-performing institution was the University of Alabama where Governor Wallace had staged his 'stand in the schoolhouse door' in 1963. At the main Tuscaloosa campus, 6.4 percent of students were now black, a gain that was largely credited to the actions of top university administrators." Timothy J. Minchin and John A. Salmond, *After the Dream: Black and White Southerners Since 1965* (Lexington, KY: University Press of Kentucky, 2011), 154.

50. Andrew Gribble, "Wendell Hudson, Alabama's First Black Scholarship Athlete, Still Contributing to Tide Athletic Department" AL.com, October 16, 2013, https://www.al.com/sports/2013/10/wendell_hudson_alabamas_first.html. A number of other black athletes followed Hudson into the program, and by his senior year, he was one of four black starters on the men's basketball team, along with Leon Douglas, Charles Cleveland, and Ray Odums.

51. Other early faculty members included Archie Wade, Art Dunning, Lena Prewitt,

Dorsey Blake, Harold Bishop, and Leon Chestang. Some stayed at the University, like former BFSA President Samory Pruitt, who is now Vice President for Community Affairs. Space prevents a complete list but for more, see the University of Alabama Black Faculty and Staff Association webpage at http://bfsa.ua.edu/history.html.

52. Opinion Research Corporation, *Nixon Poll*, March 1972, obtained through Roper Center for Public Opinion Research, University of Connecticut.

53. Gallup Organization, *Gallup Poll (AIPO)*, March 1959, obtained through Roper Center for Public Opinion Research, University of Connecticut. Other scholars raised questions about these findings. See Milton Rokeach and Sandra J. Ball-Rokeach, "Stability and Change in American Value Priorities, 1968-1981," *American Psychologist* 44 (May 1989): 775-784.

54. Some scholars believe that federal pressure to desegregate schools would have worked in all branches of the government had the pressure been kept on. Gary Orfield was impressed by signs that predispositions against busing had decreased over time. He cited Harris polls showing that throughout the 1970s, 73-78 percent opposed busing but that the percentage had dropped to 53 percent by 1986. Fully 41 percent said they favored busing. The attitudes of those directly involved, the families and students who experienced busing, were decidedly favorable. Orfield concluded: "The experience with busing is much more positive than is widely believed and . . . white opinion resisting busing is by no means monolithic or unchangeable." Orfield argued implicitly that school boards freed from court orders should retain busing as a tool for desegregating US public schools, but school officials are loath to continue busing for desegregation if the court-ordered policy is widely seen as a failure in the community. Gary Orfield, "Public Opinion and School Desegregation," *Teachers College Record* 96, no. 4 (Summer 1995): 654-669.

   Also see Richard A. Pride, "Public Opinion and the End of Busing: (Mis) Perceptions of Policy Failure," *Sociological Quarterly* 41, no. 2 (Spring 2000): 208: "Strong public support for integrated public schools was problematized by an equally strong opposition to busing, the principal tool used to achieve that goal."

55. Norman Cousins, "Busing Reconsidered," *Saturday Review*, January 24, 1976, 4. I had known Norman since he visited the University of Alabama in the late 1960s and shared his concerns about resegregation.

56. Cousins, "Busing Reconsidered," 4.

57. Formisano, *Boston Against Busing*, 223.

58. Gary Peller, "Race-Consciousness," in *Critical Race Theory: The Key Writings That Formed the Movement*, eds. Kimberlé Crenshaw et al. (New York: The New Press, 1996), 135. I also recall African American educators in Alabama who said that they gave up ownership of their schools, which were often closed after desegregation, in hopes that their children would get a good education in the better-funded white

schools. Yet, as the schools resegregated, they felt they had lost on all fronts. The schools weren't providing a good education, and they had little control over them. For more details, see *Connections: Communities, Schools, and the People Who Made Them* (Auburn, AL: Truman Pierce Institute and Caroline Marshall Draughon Center for the Arts & Humanities, Auburn University, 2009).

59. Bob Woodward and Scott Armstrong, *The Brethren: Inside the Supreme Court* (New York: Simon and Schuster, 1979), 110.

60. According to Gary Orfield, resegregation can be avoided with appropriate programs to stabilize integrated neighborhoods. He also states that enforcement and severe discipline are necessary when violations are found. Orfield, *Must We Bus?*, 437-438. See also, "Even a brief exercise of national authority can relieve local leaders of the political burdens of implementing a deeply resented change and can create a new status quo which some local leaders will defend. . . . I am convinced that the use of governmental power to break up the remnants of the American caste system is the most pressing public issue of this generation." Orfield, *The Reconstruction of Southern Education*, viii-xi. And, according to a paper by Erika Frankenberg and Kendra Taylor, "Segregation fell more sharply in districts under court order." Erika Frankenberg and Kendra Taylor, "ESEA and the Civil Rights Act: An Interbranch Approach to Furthering Desegregation," *RSF: The Russell Sage Foundation Journal of the Social Sciences* 1, no. 3 (2015): 38.

61. Roger K. Newman, *Hugo Black: A Biography* (New York: Pantheon Books, 1994), 601-602; and Woodward and Armstrong, *The Brethren*, 184.

62. Marvin Esch, Republican House member from Michigan, authored the first amendment in 1974, and Senator Robert Byrd, Democratic Whip from West Virginia, the second in 1976.

63. Joseph N. Morgan and Edith K. Mosher, "The Story of Emergency School Aid, a Legislative Step-Child: Policy-Making in a Transitional Period" (paper presented at the annual meeting of the American Educational Research Association, Chicago, IL, April 1974).

64. Adding to the difficulty, legislators, justices, and other public administrators, not just those in OCR, were beginning to rely more and more on hard data, which was leading to more oversimplifications of complex problems. See Dwight Waldo, "Public Administration in a Time of Revolutions," *Public Administration Review* 28, no. 4 (July-August 1968): 362-368. Reprinted in Jay M. Shafritz and Albert C. Hyde, *Classics of Public Administration*, 2nd ed. (Chicago: The Dorsey Press, 1987). Trying to measure progress on morally charged issues with quantitative indicators wasn't the only contradiction I found troubling. While the government should not fund a school that insists on breaking the law, the stated objective was to promote voluntary compliance. As Doug Cater in the Johnson administration had pointed out, if funds were actually withheld, it would hurt the children that the law intended to aid.

65. See the Center for National Policy Review's report *Justice Delayed and Denied: HEW and Northern School Desegregation* (Washington, DC: Center for National Policy Review, 1974).

66. Stan Murphy organized this search for alternative means. Stan Murphy, telephone conversation with Paloma Dallas, August 10, 2009.

67. Warren Trest, *Nobody But the People: The Life and Times of Alabama's Youngest Governor* (Montgomery, AL: NewSouth Books, 2008), 398.

68. Jeff Frederick, *Stand Up for Alabama: Governor George Wallace* (Tuscaloosa, AL: The University of Alabama Press, 2007), 152-160.

69. Carter, *The Politics of Rage*.

CHAPTER XII

A *WITH* STRATEGY FOR
EDUCATING ALL CHILDREN

The last chapter described the struggle to desegregate the public schools and implement the Supreme Court's 1954 *Brown* ruling outlawing segregation. That struggle is ongoing. The overarching objective is a good education as a right for every child in schools that can also draw on the education provided by families and available throughout communities. I think of education as a collective, democratic right, which is not quite the same as the personal rights we are born with as individuals. The beneficiary of this right is democracy itself. Democracies can't function without an educated citizenry. The schools are one of the institutions that provide this education.

WITH IN A POLARIZED ENVIRONMENT

Despite the importance of a good education for all, the country has been deeply divided over how to achieve it. And, because many schools have become resegregated today, the question remains of how to reach that objective. After the 1954 ruling, through which progress was made in some communities, it was the result of citizens working with one another in multiracial coalitions and with governing institutions. What happened wasn't a model of unblemished success, but what the coalitions did is still relevant. They are examples of what a *with* strategy can do. Local, often informal, multiracial coalitions were helpful in moving beyond a moralized impasse to a more pragmatic approach to problem solving.

Citizens With Citizens

I am most familiar with what happened in the 1960s and 1970s, when some people felt compelled to seek out those on the other side of the desegregation issue in order to prevent violence and educate all children well and safely. These citizens, who came from different parts of their communities, weren't sure what to do, but their instincts told them that the results they hoped for were possible only if people worked together.

That is still happening today. A few years ago, a study cited New York as the most segregated city in the country.[1] There, some citizens—mostly parents and teachers—started a bottom-up initiative to address the problem.[2] (I mention this because it counters a widespread assumption that change can come only from the top down.)

The groups I am talking about often began as informal gatherings of concerned citizens. They might have no more structure than an agreement to meet regularly at a local restaurant or some other neutral site. When conflicts were especially threatening, the groups were invisible; they gathered late at night because they were bringing people together who would be attacked for meeting with "the enemy." Some of these groups later created formal multiracial associations or coalitions. Examples in Alabama were Selma One and Mobile United (which still exists). These local groups formed by citizens' initiatives were effective because they had authenticity and credibility.

Reframing Issues

One role the coalitions played was reframing the school desegregation issue by broadening the focus to include more than schools alone. They added the community itself and its well-being as a consideration. The objective included keeping the community from being torn apart. This reframing was difficult to do nationally in the 1960s and 1970s because the issue of desegregation was typically presented as a struggle between something good (either states' rights or social justice) and something evil (a federal takeover of schools or "segregation forever"). In this kind of moralized combat, any compromise was unthinkable; it would only encourage the opposition. Nothing could be done that might give comfort to the enemy.[3]

To be sure, not all citizens' groups were effective. Some were window dressing or purely advisory. My impression was that the committees in which citizens themselves decided that they had important work to do were the most influential, although they were not always successful as they began their work. Initially, they had to build support and cross imposing dividing lines. The multiracial groups were an essential counterforce to organizations like the Ku Klux Klan (KKK), which were effective in that they could turn a frustrated, angry segment of the population into a formidable force.

Other causes that local citizens' coalitions coalesced around, in addition to education and public schools, were respect for the law and economic progress (which required outside investments). These considerations admittedly seem bland when compared with the super-heated rhetoric of the times.[4] Just obeying the law may have been an unlikely rallying cry, but it appealed to moderates on opposing sides of the racial divide. The compelling rationales also drew on Americans' pragmatic bent. Practical problem solving eventually (and I emphasize *eventually*) proved appealing in times of raw emotions and frustrating moral dilemmas.

Perhaps you can see why I think the story of these multiracial groups— who formed them and why—is worth remembering today. A number of our public schools have become resegregated, plagued by gaps in academic performance, and suffering from alarming dropout rates. Broad-based coalitions, including businesses, religious congregations, educational institutions, and civic organizations, down to the neighborhood level, could be very helpful in dealing with these problems now.

Paying the Price of Progress

Speaking frankly, cooperation in multiracial groups, which is essentially a *with* strategy, had costs for the people who were involved. Supporting one another as members of the coalitions helped deal with these costs. African Americans who participated in coalitions with other races faced attacks from within their own ranks as being subservient to whites. Even though they faced criticisms, one of the most effective things civil rights leaders did was to speak to everyone, not just their followers, as Americans bound together by democratic values like human rights.

White participants in the coalitions also faced severe criticisms. Some were shunned by people who had been friends for years. Some even had to leave their homes and the towns where they lived. And that wasn't the worst that happened. Leaders and moderates on both sides were high-priority targets for militants prone to violence. Collaboration was treason.

Citizens With *Governments*

The value of citizens' groups in reducing racial tensions had been mentioned as early as 1955 in the Justice Department's brief to the Supreme Court.[5] And President Nixon recognized that peaceful desegregation needed agreement between opposing factions.[6] His strategy was top down. In 1970, Nixon cabinet members set up state committees made up of business and other leaders in six southern states to negotiate desegregation plans. The meetings were held at the White House, and the President himself participated.[7] However, most of these state committees were the result of government, not community, initiatives. These were useful, though different politically from locally initiated groups.

At the state level, many of the government officials working toward peaceful desegregation included "New South" governors like William Winter of Mississippi and Jimmy Carter of Georgia. I got to know them at meetings of the Southern Growth Policies Board. They were quite unlike Alabama's George Wallace.

Although their states had large blocks of Wallace sympathizers, these New South governors were politically astute enough to encourage community coalitions of citizens to build support for peaceful desegregation. These were like the multiracial groups that Martin Luther King Jr. had turned to in the early days of the Civil/Human Rights Movement. For instance, Governor Reubin Askew of Florida formed a citizens' committee on education in 1971. In writing the history of this effort, Gordon Harvey reported that Askew "wanted communities to become more involved in the everyday life of schools and even to formulate policy."[8] According to Harvey, "The governor favored a committee of, by, and for citizens" to look beyond "predetermined answers."[9] Other organizations, like the Florida League of Women Voters, joined the cause in 1973, as did key legislators Jack Gordon and Bob Graham, later a US Senator. In 1973, the Florida assembly, perhaps sensing that a good education for all had widespread appeal, passed a bill that both reformed and increased state school funding.[10] The same thing happened in other southern states and perhaps elsewhere.

The case for citizens' coalitions like those in Florida was made quite persuasively in an essay written in 1972 by Curtis Graves, an African American legislator from Texas.[11] His support for these coalitions grew out of his experience with organizing Southerners in the 1960s to oppose segregation. Graves thought the lessons learned could be used in forming multiracial coalitions. In fact, he had been elected to the Texas legislature because of the work of a multiracial coalition in Houston. This state government collaboration with local citizen efforts is an excellent example of a *with* strategy at work.

Across State Lines

To generate political support for what local groups and reform-minded governors were doing, citizens formed their own multiracial committees on a regional basis.[12] I was involved in one of these, the L.Q.C. Lamar Society, whose "members" included my predecessor at the University of Alabama, Frank Rose; a classmate of mine, Brandt Ayers, editor and publisher of the *Anniston Star*; and historian and civil rights leader John Hope Franklin. These Southerners used the Lamar Society to promote a public dialogue they hoped would lead to "practical solutions to regional problems too long overlooked."[13] (Note the appeal to pragmatism.) In a book of essays published by the Society in 1972, author Wille Morris wrote that the organization urged ending racism, a "primeval obsession," that had shaped the region's consciousness in the past.[14] The Lamar Society argued that clinging to the resentment that had built up in reaction to the punitive measures taken against the South after the Civil War, and not taking responsibility for its own problems, the region had done more damage to itself than the North had ever done.

Some Progress

Not because of multiracial coalitions alone but through many other efforts, the increase in school desegregation in the South by 1970 was dramatic. When the school year began that fall, the number of African American children in racially isolated schools had dropped from 68 percent in 1968 to 18.4 percent.[15] The nation's most segregated region had become its most desegregated. Who was responsible? The courts? Federal agencies? Political leaders like the New South governors? Civil rights advocates? Citizens' coalitions? Probably all in combination and none in isolation from the others. This confluence of forces was not always intentional, yet, nonetheless, the forces were often complementary, with different groups playing different roles.

Did racial prejudices vanish in the South? Of course not. Still, by the 1970s, there was a growing sense in the region that old ways of relating were ending and new ones had to be established. Unfortunately, once desegregation was no longer a central issue, many of the citizen coalitions atrophied and were not available when the schools began to resegregate. The decline of these multiracial groups may also have been a factor in the return of racial problems in the country.

THE FORD PLAN AND A COMMUNITY
ENGAGEMENT STRATEGY

In a policy statement on June 24, 1976, President Ford reaffirmed that he opposed segregation and would not tolerate defiance of Supreme Court rulings. He was emphatic in saying that he and all who served with him would enforce the law.[16] Ford also acknowledged that busing had been useful in achieving desegregation in some cases but argued that its overuse by lower courts had turned a simple judicial tool into a measure that was creating widespread resentment and interfering with a good education for all. This was consistent with the position he had taken in his vice presidential confirmation hearing in 1973, when he told the Senate that he believed in integration but not forced busing to achieve racial balance. In 1976, he added that he considered de facto segregation as unlawful as de jure segregation.[17]

I found President Ford eager to find politically viable ways to eradicate segregation. He opposed a constitutional amendment to prohibit busing.[18] And he seemed secure in his conviction that he had something constructive to say on the school issue, although he rejected the argument that he was obligated to rally support for busing because it was the law of the land.[19] By 1976, he had moved away from calling only for better education.

While open to new ideas and the advice he was getting from staff and cabinet members, there was a clear trajectory on civil rights in Ford's career dating back to the 1950s. He supported the 1954 *Brown* decision, voted to cut off funds for school construction if schools didn't comply, and favored the Emergency School Aid Act (ESAA) in 1972, which assisted schools with desegregation costs, except for transportation.[20] However, Ford did not support all desegregation efforts. He was critical of the 1971 *Swann* decision, which sanctioned busing, and a 1972 district court ruling to allow busing across district lines in Detroit. He also disagreed with Garrity's ruling in Boston in 1974, while publicly condemning violence in the city. (In a change from the year earlier, the Ford administration did send federal assistance to Boston, which I mentioned in chapter XI.)

A National Commission to Encourage Multiracial Coalitions

Before announcing his plan, President Ford listened to proposals from the cabinet secretaries. Proposals included for the government to do more research, query school administrators, hold seminars, and create a clearinghouse. The proposal I sent was different. The federal government had, in the past, created nongovernmental agencies that worked collaboratively with local groups of citizens. I thought one should be formed to mobilize the latent pragmatism and good intent on issues of desegregation. My model was the National Academy of Science. And my examples of agencies that worked to stimulate local efforts were the National Endowment for the Humanities (NEH) and the National Endowment for the Arts (NEA). These were precedents for adding a section in the Ford bill to create what I called a National Community and Education Commission (NCEC) (*Figure 16*).[21] The Commission was to work with local multiracial coalitions that were already established and encourage others to form. The primary mission was to ensure that children of all races and ethnicities would learn together in the best of schools. The assumption was that the whole of a community, not just its schools and their administrators, had to be engaged. Communities have a host of educational institutions in addition to schools—libraries, museums, youth clubs, music programs. And communities could benefit from citizens forming multiracial groups to work *with* all these educating institutions, including the schools.

To give President Ford and the White House staff a better idea of what a national commission could do, citizens' coalitions were invited to meet in the cabinet room on Saturday, June 12, 1976 (*Figure 17*).[22] It went well, and I followed up with a recommendation to enlarge the commission to 100 members and reduce its staff to a minimum so that professionals would not take over the work citizens should do. The commission was to assist multiracial groups early on in preparing for desegregation. ("Preparing" involved more than planning; it included building community support.)

Did Ford consider the benefits of busing as he was making his decisions?[23] He did approve a recommendation to review the research on busing. And the White House was advised of the numerous studies underway in HEW concerning desegregation—research done by the Office of Education, the

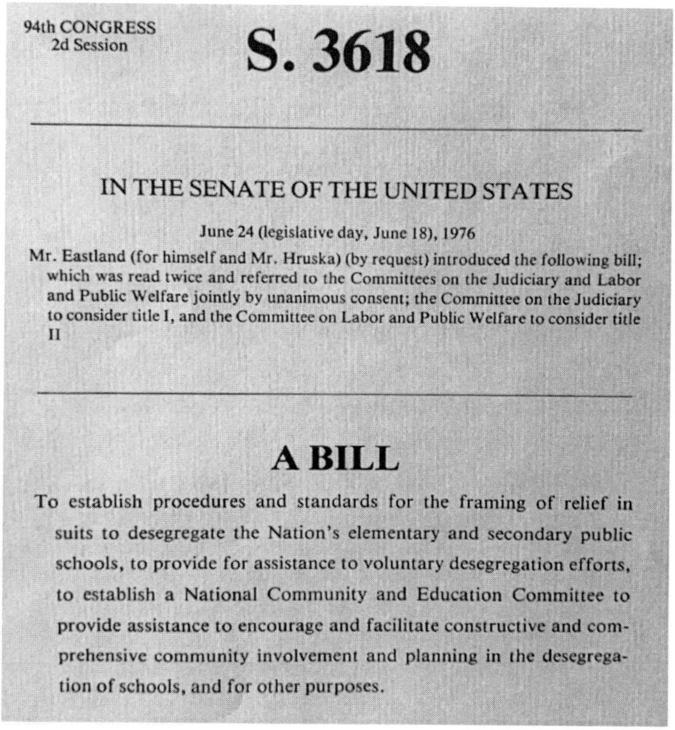

94th CONGRESS
2d Session

S. 3618

IN THE SENATE OF THE UNITED STATES

June 24 (legislative day, June 18), 1976

Mr. Eastland (for himself and Mr. Hruska) (by request) introduced the following bill; which was read twice and referred to the Committees on the Judiciary and Labor and Public Welfare jointly by unanimous consent; the Committee on the Judiciary to consider title I, and the Committee on Labor and Public Welfare to consider title II

A BILL

To establish procedures and standards for the framing of relief in suits to desegregate the Nation's elementary and secondary public schools, to provide for assistance to voluntary desegregation efforts, to establish a National Community and Education Committee to provide assistance to encourage and facilitate constructive and comprehensive community involvement and planning in the desegregation of schools, and for other purposes.

FIGURE 16. *In 1976, the establishment of the National Community and Education Commission was proposed as a section to the Ford Administration's desegregation plan. (From David Mathews' collection at the Kettering Foundation.)*

National Institute of Education, and the Assistant Secretary for Planning and Evaluation.[24] In a memorandum to the President in March, I pointed out that this research showed busing was working in certain cases, particularly when the community believed that the extra burden of travel was equally shared.[25] (The review also found that the busing studies were inconsistent.[26])

In 1976, President Ford sent his omnibus School Desegregation Standards and Assistance Act to Congress. It did not call for the elimination of any busing but rather for limiting its use to unlawful acts of discrimination. The act would also have restricted court-ordered busing (an "interim and transitory remedy") to five years. Achieving a specific racial balance was not required,

FIGURE 17. *Members of multiracial citizens' coalitions from around the country met with President Ford at the White House on June 12, 1976. Attendees included citizens from Pontiac, MI; Kansas City, MO; Louisville, KY; Dallas, TX; and Omaha, NE. (From David Mathews' photo collection at the Kettering Foundation.)*

but ending racial isolation was.[27] In addition, the act included provisions for a National Community and Education Committee, a version of HEW's National Commission plan to encourage communities to form multiracial coalitions (committees) that would work on desegregation and integration. The first section of the bill came from the Justice Department, and the second was based on HEW's recommendations.

Although Congress was too divided along party lines to pass the Ford bill, it served to define Ford's position.[28] And I thought bringing the constructive influence of citizens into the debate, while not the perfect solution, was a significant step in the right direction.[29]

Putting the commission into operation would have had to be done in the President's second term, which wasn't to be. But I had worked closely with then-Governor Jimmy Carter on the Southern Growth Policies Board when public education was an issue. So, I was pleased to see that when he became

President, a community strategy got consideration, although a national committee was never created.

MORE POSSIBILITIES

After making my proposal for a commission, I continued to look for any and
all measures that communities could take to end racial isolation. I began to
get the results from research that I had pledged to consider within a month or
so after I arrived at HEW. According to the studies, magnet schools to attract
students from throughout a city could promote integration if they were in
accessible locations and assertive in recruiting minority students (which
most weren't at the time). Magnets weren't likely to have a significant impact
on the number of minority students participating, yet they provided a rationale other than race for bringing young people together. And even though
written off by some as "not working," magnets in states like New York, the
Department staff reported, had been successful when tried on a small scale,
as in Rochester.[30]

Other promising measures to both end racial isolation and improve education included parental involvement in desegregation planning, creation
of a multiethnic curriculum, more use of sports and other extracurricular
programs to demonstrate positive integration, and incentives to build multi-
racial/multiethnic neighborhoods.[31]

LOOKING BACK

People of different races voluntarily joining forces isn't unheard of, but neither is it common, when people are in the middle of conflicts. Multiracial
coalitions were experiments in likely adversaries working together. Were
the coalitions recognized for what they did? A great deal depended on
whether these groups were voluntary associations initiated by communities
or imposed by a court or other external authority. The voluntary ones I was
familiar with did much better.

A 1984 study was less positive, but the reasons given were revealing because they reflected a misunderstanding of what citizen coalitions were to do.[32] The study reflected the way "Squares" see "Blobs." The coalitions were judged not effective in planning and didn't produce "detailed reports and recommendations." These criticisms appear to assume citizens' coalitions were administrative agencies. The locally initiated groups I knew about didn't so much make plans as provide a venue for competing parties to construct a scenario for peaceful desegregation. That often involved dealing with issues of funding, local control, and all the other sensitive subjects in school desegregation.

The more serious criticism was that they didn't deal with blatant cases of segregation. And yet the groups I was familiar with did operate where racial divisions were very sharp, as in Selma, Alabama, when it was racked by deadly racial conflict.

Beyond Segregated Schools

The tragedy of focusing on just schools and battling over desegregating them, largely by legal means, was that it was easy to lose sight of a larger objective. That was building a nation where people of all kinds knew how to work together as Americans for the benefit of all.[33]

I lived through the efforts to desegregate the University of Alabama from the time I was an undergraduate to the time I was president. The challenge wasn't just to end illegal segregation in educational institutions; the larger goal was to create a new state where all its people would join forces for the common good. That goal was called "integration," as distinct from the legal problem of desegregation. However, I'm not sure "integration" is the right word. I like simply "working together" better.

My experience in Alabama came with me to Washington and HEW. It taught me not to expect a single solution or even a detailed plan decided on beforehand. What actually happened in the 1970s was constant trial and error on a number of fronts. The only constant was continuous engagement of varied and opposing groups in the pursuit of a better future that could be seen only dimly in a turbulent present.

The point I want to make is that the country still needs more experimentation in nation building that returns education to the key role it once played. There have to be multiple initiatives in education because there is no one way to do everything that needs to be done.

A willingness to experiment is essential because it is democracy's way of learning what is best. Furthermore, a democracy must allow for what experimentation allows for, which is the possibility that decisions could be wrong. In fact, they often are. Consequently, conclusions have to be considered provisional and open to revision. Such democratic doubt, however, doesn't fit well with the need for absolute certainty. But that is what highly partisan politics demands.

WHY NOT EXPERIMENT?

The US has such a rich legacy of inventors and inventive people, why wasn't that available to draw on in the school desegregation/integration crisis? I have been puzzled by that for some time. Perhaps it has to do with what I wrote about earlier—the extreme divisions brought about by pitting national imperatives against one another and not recognizing their interdependence. Maybe it had to do with focusing on a means to an end (busing) and not the objective itself, a good education for all children in which they could learn to work together. Or could it be that people were so intent on the righteousness of their goals that they paid too little attention to the effects that the way they went about achieving them were going to have on the results we wanted?

The case I was trying to make for encouraging experimentation has some grounding in our nation's history. Daniel Boorstin observed in *The Genius of American Politics* that Americans have usually been less fixed on a certain notion of what *must* happen (the "isms" that attracted Europeans) and have been more open to the idea that "*anything* might happen."[34] Consequently, we have been sympathetic to experimentation, and the country has often moved forward by trial and error. Another historian, Henry Steele Commager, found something similar in analyzing our national character:

Being "practical, democratic, individualistic, opportunistic, spontaneous, hopeful, pragmatism was wonderfully adapted to the temperament of the average American."[35]

Conflicting Imperatives

Little is more American than the right of people to protest peacefully when they are aggrieved. But eventually, people have to come together to make needed changes. That is especially difficult when people are pulled in different directions.

Pitting Democratic Values against One Another

Earlier I said the school desegregation issue suffered from being framed as a contest between good and evil. There was evil, and there was good. Yet the tendency to separate and prioritize democratic values rather than to recognize their interdependence was not helpful. This was particularly true of the relationship between our country's interests in rights—such as everyone's right to be treated fairly—and the value placed on another right—people's right to rule themselves.[36] The argument was made that the injustice of segregation was so egregious that it had to be eliminated at the expense of self-rule or local control if necessary. That argument loses sight of the interdependence of social justice and democratic self-rule. It is only in democracies that justice and human rights are valued. But, in the polarized environment of the 1960s and 1970s, even the effort to show this interrelation was attacked as being either a denial of the value of social justice or the value of self-rule.

Placing one democratic value above the other can be particularly damaging to public schools because one of their principal missions is to teach young people the importance of both self-rule and justice. That lesson is lost when local schools discriminate, and it is lost when schools are placed under external rule.[37] What students see in the way their schools are governed is a more profound civic lesson than any in a classroom.

Conflating Means and Ends

Australian philosopher John Dryzek insists that policymaking must be open to considering both the values to be served (ends) *and* the actual effects of the processes used to implement a policy (means).[38] To restrict the discussion to only one dimension can be perilous, if not disastrous. Dryzek uses the case of mandatory busing in the United States to achieve social justice as an instance when a policy debate was closed to considerations of actual effects. He noted, "busing provoked opposition even from those who shared the goal of desegregation."[39]

Another mistake is just the opposite: treating the way to do something, the means, as undebatable objectives or ends. Mandatory busing was one means or way to reach a goal, which was ending segregation and paving the way to working together more effectively by drawing on our differences. However, in the school desegregation debate, the means—busing—was given the same standing as the end itself—justice. When a critical examination of busing was placed off-limits, it was impossible to experiment with additional means for ending segregation. The goal, ending unequal treatment, was in danger of being equated with one particular means, mandatory busing. Allowing ends to justify means, as John Dewey observed, is as fundamental a mistake in politics as it is in philosophy: "The idea that 'the end justifies the means' is in as bad repute in moral theory as its adoption is a commonplace of political practice."[40]

Dewey's Commonplace in the Senate

I ran into the problem of treating means as ends during my confirmation hearing in 1975. In explaining my reservations about relying on compulsory busing alone, I didn't tell the senators what seemed obvious, which was that the Department was legally obligated to support busing when it was ordered by the courts.[41] That oversight was my mistake. Attitudes toward busing were often used as a litmus test for racism.[42] For some, questioning busing was the same as opposing desegregation. As scholars like Dan Carter pointed out, this stereotype didn't begin to lose some of its hold until President Jimmy Carter's administration.

Fortunately, Nat Colley, a friend and fellow Alabamian, who served with me on the Kettering Foundation board and was an attorney for the NAACP, came to my aid at the hearing. He enlisted the support of Clarence Mitchell, chief Washington lobbyist for the NAACP. I was grateful for his counsel. On the second day of the Senate hearings, I emphasized that I certainly recognized the authority of court rulings.[43] I also said I would study other ways of integrating the schools and was careful not to rule out any busing.[44] I didn't have my own remedies already crafted at that time; my point was that the country needed to be more open to considering other means.[45] Rather than expecting any one policy to do everything, I thought we had to consider multiple interventions, backed up with incentives.[46]

LOOKING AHEAD: COMMUNITIES AS EDUCATORS

To broaden the debate over schools, it would have helped to look at how the community itself can educate, even in the parts of a community that don't appear to have any educational resources. I say that because communities are not usually recognized for this ability; still, citizens anywhere can be complementary producers of learning. That is what the citizenry uniquely has to offer in a *with* strategy for education. For instance, a community is a civic education laboratory. Young people learn a great deal from what they see happening, good or bad.

An example of a community educating comes from the work of Jack Shelton and PACERS. Chapter XV will describe how PACERS used community history, as told by a town's senior citizens, to teach and how the schools used this resource.

Recently, I saw still another example of a community educating. In this case the "teacher" was a historical society. Youngsters from different schools came together at a historic park to participate in a living exhibition of Native American culture.[47] With guidance from the ancestors of the Creeks who had once lived in the area, the students played the same stickball game that once was played by competing tribes, listened to Indian folklore, discovered how to prepare native food, and learned craft skills prized in another culture. This happened in a community that had experienced considerable racial segregation. But all these children were playing together when the community educated through a reenactment of past events. This is but one example; surely there are many more possibilities to use a community to educate in ways that give young people opportunities to get to know those who are different.

When former US Senator Lamar Alexander was governor of Tennessee, he launched an initiative based on the proposition that "communities fix schools."[48] And Pat Harbour, a senior associate at Kettering, has collected enough stories of citizens who aren't professional educators but who nonetheless teach to fill a book.[49] In addition, there is a case to be made that the role of the community isn't just to support the schools; communities can educate and the role of the schools is to support them in doing that![50]

WHAT'S NEXT?

Up to this point, I have used cases to show when it was and wasn't possible for governing institutions to work more *with* citizens and for citizens to collaborate more *with* institutions. In the school desegregation crises, citizens working with citizens played a decisive role. The next chapter will take up a case in which Washington, a state capitol, and citizens were all open to a *with* strategy, but other forces intervened.

NOTES

1.   Eliza Shapiro, "Then as Now, a Fight over School Segregation," *New York Times*, April 15, 2019, 20A; John Kucsera and Gary Orfield, *New York State's Extreme School Segregation: Inequality, Inaction and a Damaged Future* (Los Angeles: Civil Rights Project/Proyecto Derechos Civiles, March 2014).

2.   Winnie Hu, "From Grass Roots, a Plan to Open Doors to Every Student," *New York Times*, May 18, 2018, A25. This story is not a fairy tale about citizens solving problems that officials can't. Disagreements over possible solutions were strong. Yet the point of the story for me is that citizens came together to create the conditions under

which more children would have an opportunity to get a good education. Citizens brought about change that went beyond what schools and city officials can do alone.

3. Dan T. Carter, *The Politics of Rage: George Wallace, the Origins of the New Conservatism, and the Transformation of American Politics* (Baton Rouge: Louisiana State University Press, 2000), 473.

4. For a thorough and insightful account of the role of citizens' coalitions, see John Egerton's story of what happened in Memphis, Tennessee. John Egerton, *Promise of Progress: Memphis School Desegregation, 1972-1973* (Atlanta, GA: Southern Regional Council, 1973).

5. In November 1954, Herbert Brownell Jr., Attorney General, and other members of the Justice Department submitted "Brief for the United States on the Further Argument of the Questions of Relief" for the October Term, 1954, in the case of *Brown v. Board of Education*, p. 21.

6. Tom Wicker, *One of Us: Richard Nixon and the American Dream* (New York: Random House, 1991), 485.

7. Secretary of Labor George Schultz led a presidentially initiated project in 1970 to bring together white civic leaders (largely businessmen) and black leaders (like officers of the NAACP) to negotiate agreements to promote peaceful school desegregation. I don't want to make light of a laudable federal initiative but rather to compare it with the multiracial, community-generated initiatives that I was familiar with. George Schultz, "How a Republican Desegregated the South's Schools," *New York Times*, January 8, 2003, A23.

8. Gordon E. Harvey, *A Question of Justice: New South Governors and Education, 1968-1976* (Tuscaloosa, AL: The University of Alabama Press, 2002), 93.

9. Harvey, *A Question of Justice*, 94.

10. Harvey, *A Question of Justice*, 108-109.

11. Curtis M. Graves, "Beyond the Briar Patch," in *You Can't Eat Magnolias*, eds. H. Brandt Ayers and Thomas H. Naylor (New York: McGraw-Hill, 1972), 41.

12. The Nixon administration also encouraged the formation of statewide coalitions in the South (largely of business elites). Wicker, *One of Us*, 486-487, 504.

13. H. Brandt Ayers, "You Can't Eat Magnolias," in *You Can't Eat Magnolias*, eds. H. Brandt Ayers and Thomas H. Naylor (New York: McGraw-Hill, 1972), 17.

14. Willie Morris, "Introduction," in *You Can't Eat Magnolias*, eds. H. Brandt Ayers and Thomas H. Naylor (New York: McGraw-Hill, 1972), xi.

15. Wicker, *One of Us*, 487.

16. Gerald Ford's opposition to segregation went back to his support for his teammate, Willis Ward, the first black athlete playing University of Michigan football. Brian Kruger, *Black and Blue: The Story of Gerald Ford, Willis Ward and the 1934 Michigan-Georgia Tech Football Game* (Detroit: Stunt3 Multimedia, 2011)

17. James Cannon, *Time and Chance: Gerald Ford's Appointment with History* (New York:

HarperCollins, 1994), 233, 246. A more critical take on Ford's record on busing can be found in McAndrews, *Missing the Bus*, 791-804.

18. As House Minority Leader, however, Ford had favored a constitutional amendment. See Gary Orfield, *Must We Bus?* (Washington, DC: Brookings Institution, 1978), 249.

19. On education in general, Ford's position was dictated by his determination to hold down federal spending during a time when the nation's economy was faltering. But a struggle was going on between the executive and legislative branches, as well as between the courts and the other two branches. This contest over power often overshadowed all other issues. The 1976 and 1977 appropriations from Congress added billions to the administration's request; Ford vetoed both but was overridden. His fiscal conservatism opened him to the charge that he said he favored better education but did not support it in his budget, a charge that doesn't take into account his overriding concern about the economy. Also see Davies, *See Government Grow*, 103.

20. Up until unveiling his own bill, he cited proposals made by Representative Marvin Esch as the alternatives to busing he supported. In fact, his first signature as President in 1974 had been on a bill that contained a compromised version of the Esch amendment. McAndrews, *Missing the Bus*, 793-794. Esch wanted to prohibit courts or federal agencies from ordering busing for integration purposes to any but the school closest or next closest to the student's home. (The House passed the Esch amendment, but the Senate changed it and Esch ended up opposing what he proposed. Paul M. Goldstein, "School Integration and Busing Policy during the Ford Administration" (History Honors thesis, University of Michigan, Ann Arbor, April 20, 1998), 23-24.

21. I had originally suggested that the commission be created by Executive Order, but the President preferred using legislation.

22. Meeting with Community Leaders Agenda, 06/12/1976, folder "Busing General 6/76 (5)," Box 13, Bobbie Greene Kilberg Files, Gerald R. Ford Presidential Library.

23. In developing his policy to deal with the crises surrounding desegregation, President Ford naturally turned to the Attorney General, Ed Levi, for advice. Ed had been Dean of the law school and the President of the University of Chicago. He was the one who favored putting limits on mandatory busing: confining its use to eliminating intentional segregation, constraining the extent of the busing to correcting just for the segregation caused by unlawful actions, and restricting the time allowed for a school system to be under court order. (The authority to so limit the lower federal courts was in Congress' power because federal law determined the jurisdiction of these courts.) Also see David Kirp, "School Desegregation and the Limits of Legalism," *The Public Interest* 48 (Summer 1977): 117.

24. Memo, 05/20/1976, folder "Busing-General 3/76-5/76(4)," Box 13, Bobbie Greene Kilberg Files, Gerald R. Ford Presidential Library. This memo from the Gerald R. Ford Library includes a previous memorandum from me to James M. Cannon dated,

March 29, 1976, with an attachment entitled "On-Going Department Studies and Activities Related to Desegregation."

25. Three letters from Secretary Mathews, 03/02/1976, folder "Busing–General 3/76–5/76(4)," Box 13, Bobbie Greene Kilberg Files, Gerald R. Ford Presidential Library. The reference here is to the document entitled, "Memorandum for the President" dated, March 29, 1976.

26. Private conversations with the former Director of the National Institute of Education, Dr. Harold Hodgkinson, September 2008.

27. The precise language in the bill said: "The purpose of relief directed to the effects of unlawful discrimination in the operation of the schools is not to compel a uniform balance by race, color, or national origin that would not have existed in normal course from individual voluntary acts, but is, rather, to restore the victims of discriminatory conduct to the position they would have occupied in the absence of such conduct, and so to free society and our citizens from the conditions created by unlawful acts." "School Desegregation Standards and Assistance Act of 1976," S.3618, 94th Congress, 2nd Session, June 24, 1976.

28. While President Ford didn't mention the need for experimentation, he had advocated in his many speeches on school desegregation improving student-teacher ratios, upgrading schools in deprived areas, and relying more on neighborhood centered schools. Paul M. Goldstein, "School Integration and Busing Policy during the Ford Administration" (History Honors thesis, University of Michigan, Ann Arbor, April 20, 1998), 33.

29. My proposal said: "The Commission's role would not be to serve as a court-appointed intermediary between parties in a legal suit related to desegregation. Mediation would be a proper role for the Commission only in instances where it was conducted informally and with the voluntary participation of the major elements of the community. Similarly, the Commission would not be empowered to act for any state of federal agency in an enforcement or compliance capacity." From the "Establishment of the National Community and Education Commission: A Major Initiative in School Desegregation," p. 2. This document is attached to a May 20, 1976, memorandum from Mathews to President Ford.

30. Memorandum by Virginia Y. Trotter, Assistant Secretary for Education, for Secretary Mathews, September 23, 1975, with attached paper, "Methods of Achieving Desegregation," National Archives.

31. Today, the US Department of Education is offering a program entitled Magnet Schools Assistance to improve diversity. It provides grants to assist in the desegregation of public schools by supporting the elimination, reduction, and prevention of minority group isolation in elementary and secondary schools with substantial numbers of minority group students. See US Department of Education, Magnet Schools

Assistance, Office of Innovation and Improvement, 84.165A, https://www2.ed.gov/programs/magnet/index.html.

32. Jennifer Hochschild, *The New American Dilemma: Liberal Democracy and School Desegregation* (New Haven, CT: Yale University Press, 1984).

33. The need for people who have many identities to also have a shared identity as Americans is the subject of historian Johann N. Neem's books. In *Democracy's Schools*, he writes, "Americans at the time considered public schools vital for preparing new citizens for participation in a democracy. Moreover, at a time of rising immigration, they were seen as necessary to bring together an increasingly diverse society. 'Our public schools are the most democratic institutions that this peculiarly democratic country affords,' proclaimed E. Hodges, superintendent of schools in Fond du Lac, Wisconsin, in 1854. Schools should treat all children equally, educating them not just in the 'rudiments,' but instilling them with the knowledge necessary for citizenship. In a society divided by religion, ethnicity, party, and wealth, public schools would 'harmonize the various discordant elements that are found in society' because students would 'sympathize with and for the other.' In public schools, diverse people would come to think of each other as fellow Americans." Neem, Johann N. *Democracy's Schools: The Rise of Public Education in America*. (Baltimore: Johns Hopkins University Press, 2017), 139.

34. Daniel Boorstin, *The Genius of American Politics* (Chicago: University of Chicago Press, 1953), 6.

35. Henry Steele Commager, *The American Mind: An Interpretation of American Thought and Character Since the 1880s* (New Haven, CT: Yale University Press, 1950), 97.

36. The right of self-rule has sometimes been called "popular sovereignty," but this is often equated with direct democracy and slights the concept of *public* sovereignty. Popular sovereignty is also confused with states' rights, which are another matter and may not result in self-rule at all.

37. The decline in local control, in both state and community, has been attributed to a number of changes in American democracy, not just to the desegregation crisis. In his studies of federal policy in the latter part of the 20th century, Hugh Graham found that the political system changed as less visible political actors, often "second-tiered civil servants," shaped policy without public debate or regard for public opinion. They and the federal courts brought about far-reaching changes in authority and power. Partly as a result of these shifts, Gareth Davies concludes in *See Government Grow* that there was a significant weakening of the American principle of dividing authority between levels of government between 1960 and the early 1970s. See Hugh Graham's *The Civil Rights Era: Origins and Development of National Policy* (New York: Oxford University Press, 1990) as well as Gareth Davies, *See Government Grow: Education Policies from Johnson to Reagan* (Lawrence, KS: University Press of Kansas, 2007).

38. John S. Dryzek, *Discursive Democracy: Politics, Policy, and Political Science* (New York: Cambridge University Press, 1990), 146-147.

39. Dryzek, *Discursive Democracy*, 146-147.

40. John Dewey, "Logic: The Theory of Inquiry," in *The Later Works, 1925-1953* 12, ed. Jo Ann Boydston (Carbondale, IL: Southern Illinois University Press, 1986), 490.

41. I had tried to convey my views on desegregation, integration, busing, respect for the law, and the role of the Department to the Senate at my confirmation hearing in July of 1975. By this time, Congress was already on record restricting the use of busing and leading democratic senators from northern states were saying that mandatory busing wasn't working. They were not just responding to popular pressure. James Coleman, the sociologist whose studies had shown the positive effects of integrating poorer black students into schools attended by middle-class whites, had just released another study warning against the unintended consequences of extensive busing. He believed it contributed to middle-class flight out of the cities to the suburbs. James S. Coleman, Sara D. Kelly, and John A. Moore, "Trends in School Segregation, 1968-1973" (Washington, DC: Urban Institute, 1975). Also see "Residential Segregation: What Are the Causes? (Testimony of Gary Orfield, March 22, 1996)," *Journal of Negro Education* 66, no. 3 (Summer 1997): 204-213; and "The Role of Social Science in School Desegregation Efforts," *Journal of Negro Education* 66, no. 3 (Summer 1997): 196-202.

42. Carter, *The Politics of Rage*, 447-448.

43. Tom Raum, "Mathews Calls Remark Hasty," *Washington Post*, July 19, 1975. Also see "Mathews Has No Alternative Plan: HEW Nominee Says Bus Stand Perhaps Hasty," *Houston Chronicle*, July 18, 1975.

44. Some of the documents from studies of new ways that might bring about the integration of the public schools are in a collection of memoranda and concept papers on desegregation that is in the Ford Presidential Library at the University of Michigan.

45. David Mathews, interview by George Herman, Nancy Hicks, and Fred Graham, *Face the Nation*, CBS News, September 14, 1975.

46. Transcript, Hearing Before the Committee on Finance, United States Senate, Ninety-Fourth Congress, First Session on Nomination of Forrest David Mathews, Nominee to be Secretary of Health, Education, and Welfare, July 15, 1975 (Washington, DC: US Government Printing Office, 1975). Transcript, Hearing before the Committee on Labor and Public Welfare, United States Senate, Ninety-Fourth Congress First Session on Additional Consideration of F. David Mathews to be Secretary of Health, Education, and Welfare, Thursday, July 17, 1975 (Washington, DC: US Government Printing Office, 1976).

47. In the interest of full disclosure: this program was organized by the Clarke County Historical Society in Alabama. My wife and I, along with others in our family, are members. The park was created by my grandfather.

48. Governor Alexander's slogan "Communities Fix Schools" has been the theme of
     other successful efforts to use community-based strategies to improve student
     achievement. See Jennie Carter Thomas, "How Three Governors Involved the Public
     in Passing Their Education Reform Legislation," Report to the Kettering Foundation,
     Janaury 19, 1993. This document can be found in the Kettering Report File
     Collection, Kettering Foundation archives. For more information, contact archives@
     kettering.org.

     The work of 19 community-organizing groups is described in a study by Eva Gold,
     Elaine Simon, and Chris Brown, *Successful Community Organizing for School Reform*
     (Chicago: Cross City Campaign for Urban School Reform, March 2002).

49. See a study of the citizens who aren't professional educators but who nonetheless
     teach, in Patricia Moore Harbour's *Community Educators: A Resource for Educating
     and Developing Our Youth* (Dayton, OH: Kettering Foundation Press, 2012).

50. Edmund Gordon revived the idea that education begins in the homes and turned
     the current assumption that communities should supplement the work of schools
     on its head. He believes that schools should supplement the education provided
     by the community. Edmund W. Gordon, Beatrice L. Bridglall, and Aundra Saa
     Meroe, eds., *Supplementary Education: The Hidden Curriculum of High Academic
     Achievement* (Lanham, MD: Rowmand and Littlefield, 2004).

     In *Reclaiming Public Education: Common Sense Approaches*, Bob Cornett, a
     former state budget director for Kentucky, describes how the small commu-
     nities in Eastern Kentucky learn and educate. Bob Cornett, *Reclaiming Public
     Education: Common Sense Approaches* (Dayton, OH: Kettering Foundation,
     2015), https://www.kettering.org/catalog/product/reclaiming-public-education-
     common-sense-approaches.

CHAPTER XIII

THE GOVERNMENT ISN'T ALWAYS THE OBSTACLE

Even with state and federal encouragement, a *with* strategy can be blocked by other forces. The case here has to do with health care and medicine, which are related although not the same. While our health is certainly influenced by what medical professionals do, other forces—economic, social, legal, and so on—also have an impact.

I've tried to simplify the narrative as much as possible, but details are essential because they explain the nature of these forces. The setting is the state of Alabama in the 1970s. The major characters are four institutions of higher education. One is a new state university in Mobile, the University of South Alabama (USA). Another is the state's oldest university, the University of Alabama (U of A), which was placed in Tuscaloosa by the legislature. The other two universities were once branch campuses of the University of Alabama. Later, by board action, both became full-fledged universities, one in Huntsville (UAH) and the other in Birmingham (UAB). While USA has its own separate board of trustees, U of A, UAB, and UAH all report to the same board, which was made up of very distinguished Alabamians. These aren't the only institutions of higher education in the state; in fact, there are a good many, including another senior institution, Auburn University.

If all of these institutions and the interplay among them aren't enough of a challenge to keep track of, there are also four medical programs involved. The state's School of Medicine was part of UAB, Mobile had a new medical school at USA, and in 1972, the University of Alabama asked the legislature for and was given authorization for a College of Community Health Sciences (CCHS). (Notice that the word in the name is *health*, not *medicine*.) That same year, UAH also received a legislative appropriation for a medical program.

You see what I mean about details. This story has more characters and more internal dynamics than a daytime television soap opera. And that's not all. The American Medical Association (AMA) is a central, if not the most significant, character, acting through its accrediting agency, the Liaison Committee for Medical Education (LCME).

I am part of the story, too, because I was president of the University of Alabama at the time, and I persuaded the legislature to appropriate funds for CCHS. I make this self-disclosure because I recognize that there are other interpretations of what happened that are different from mine. I cared deeply about CCHS and can't pass myself off as an objective narrator. I am also an Alabamian. Being from a small town in a rural area, I have been particularly sensitive to their problems, which included inadequate medical and health care.

HEALTH CARE IN THE UNITED STATES

The US has some of the most advanced medical care in the world. That distinction is a great achievement, and it benefits people all over the world who require specialized treatment. However, this country also has rural areas and urban cores with health problems associated with developing countries. That was the case in Alabama in the 1970s. People died unnecessarily because their illnesses weren't identified and treated early on. They needed more than just good *medical* care. They needed good *health* care, which is more comprehensive because the illnesses people suffered from were not just medical. They were related to economic distress (poverty), lack of social services, inferior education, poor nutrition—the list goes on. Because problems in health care come from many different sources and many different people and institutions are involved, good care is more likely when all the affected parties collaborate in a *with* strategy.

In the 1970s, federal health agencies in Washington had several policy goals. One was to make affordable care available to all Americans. Another was to support research on life-threatening diseases like cancer. And a third was to prevent illness whenever possible. These are compatible objectives; they reinforce one another. Nonetheless, in practice, these federal goals could be drawn into unintended conflict by forces outside the government.

Calls for Reform

In the 1960s, the federal government developed new policies supporting communities in their struggle against the problems that imperil the health of citizens. Changes were made in laws, in budgets, and within medical education. These built on, and contributed to, a movement to reform the health-care system.

Setting the stage in 1959, the Surgeon General's Consultant Group on Medical Education had issued the Bane Report, which pointed out that medical schools were becoming centers for research and the training of specialists, while the number of physicians going into primary medical care was decreasing.[1] Other reports followed, warning that doctors were being trained to treat patients who were seriously ill in hospitals but that community-based care for ambulatory patients was not getting the attention it deserved. The vast majority of people who sought care were in this latter category. These people had chronic health problems that required ongoing attention.[2]

In 1967, the National Advisory Commission on Health Manpower insisted that the health-care system needed an overhaul.[3] The critical problems, the commission argued, weren't because of specialization but because of inattention to the behavioral sciences and other disciplines that might be used to address the economic, social, and psychological phenomena affecting people's health.

By the 1970s, the decline in the number of primary care doctors was reaching crisis levels in rural areas and inner cities. The specialized practices in hospitals weren't going to work in those locations; medical practice had to be redesigned and aligned with other professional practices, even nonmedical ones.

As these attempts at reform were getting underway, medical specialization, along with breakthroughs from new drugs and technologies, were enabling the medical system to work what seemed miracles—open heart surgery, for example. These miracles gave even more prestige and power to specialists.[4]

New Fields Emerge: Family Practice

Despite the growth of specialties, the crisis in primary care was so alarming that new fields like family medicine emerged. In 1964, Dr. William R. Willard (*Figure 18*), who would later become the first dean of the U of A's College of Community Health Sciences, wrote a report for the American Medical Association (AMA) arguing that health care had to be provided within the context of a patient's environment, including their family and community.[5] He wanted a new generation of doctors who would have both undergraduate clinical experiences in treating patients after their basic courses and a three-year graduate residency program designed especially for family physicians. Many of these proposals were also in the recommendations of the 1966 Citizens Commission on Graduate Medical Education.[6] An agenda for change was developing.

Some doctors trained in centers for biomedical research and specialized practice, however, were quite critical of family physicians. They argued that anyone with a serious problem needed to see a physician trained in dealing with that illness. No generalist could hope to keep up with the rapidly developing medical sciences. Consequently, family physicians were dismissed as no more than ill-prepared internists. Yet family practitioners were not arguing that they could be all-sufficient generalists. They knew that they had to refer their patients to specialists when more complex illnesses presented. They also realized that doctors were needed in the many towns that were

FIGURE 18. *Dr. William R. Willard, known as the father of family medicine for his role in establishing it as a specialty, was the first dean of the College of Community Health Sciences. (Photo courtesy of the University of Alabama Libraries Special Collection.)*

too small to support highly specialized physicians and full-service hospitals (*Figure 19*).

Reaching beyond the Medical Sciences: Community Health

Family practice was controversial, but another new field, community health, was even more contested. Community health drew on evidence that the local environment had a bearing on the physical well-being of its residents. It adhered to the philosophy that "individuals (and their ill-health) cannot be understood solely by looking inside their bodies and brains; one must also look inside their communities, their networks, their workplaces, their families, and even the trajectories of their life."[7] Community health care was based on the premise that a community's physical structure and social

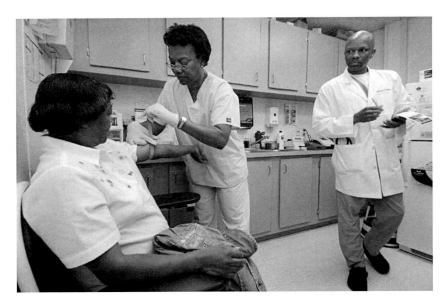

FIGURE 19. *A family practitioner sees a patient in his office in a rural clinic. (Photo by Rick Falco/Vision Project.)*

cohesion directly relate to the health and well-being of its people. This premise recognized that citizens and communities have contributions to make, which would require collaboration with others outside the field of medicine.[8]

Supportive Federal Policies

In the 1960s, several federal policies aimed at fighting poverty also had an impact on health care. Better health was one of the objectives of these policies, as it had been in the Depression recovery programs of the New Deal.[9] In 1964, the Economic Opportunity Act created the Office of Economic Opportunity (OEO) and paved the way for numerous community initiatives. The OEO gave grants to establish community health centers that would provide comprehensive care to underserved rural communities and urban neighborhoods.[10]

The OEO also funded medical schools, hospitals, health departments, and community groups to plan and administer these health centers. With community participation, policymakers intended for neighborhood health centers to serve as models for the reorganization of health-care services. Federal policy promoted comprehensive care and preventative medicine.[11]

Dr. Jack Geiger, director of the first local health centers program in the United States, made the case for community health in terms that reflected the mind-set for a *with* strategy, "Communities of the poor, all too often described only in terms of pathology, are in fact rich in potential and amply supplied with bright and creative people. . . . They . . . have the capacity to attack the root causes of ill health through community development and the social change it engenders."[12] Geiger's argument that even the poor have abilities is significant because it is one of the key assumptions in a *with* strategy, which is that citizens and communities with needs are not without resources and abilities. Otherwise, collaboration would be impossible.

THE SITUATION IN ALABAMA

While national reforms embraced proposals to create new fields of practice and new designs for health-care delivery, most of Alabama's political leaders in the 1960s were focused more narrowly on just increasing the number of doctors. They believed that more physicians would increase competition for patients, which would drive medical professionals into the smaller towns and rural areas. In 1966, the state legislature took steps to address what its members saw as an undersupply of physicians. Legislators asked the Birmingham-based School of Medicine's accrediting agency, the LCME, for advice. This was the first but not the last role the LCME would play in Alabama politics. In 1967, consultants from the LCME recommended creating several new programs, including a two-year program in basic sciences for premed students at the U of A, which was in Tuscaloosa. The consultants also advised that all these new programs be coordinated.[13] I don't recall much, if any, recognition of the importance of better health care.

Two Crises

The state certainly needed more physicians, in fact, 1,100 more. In Cleburne County, for instance, there were only two doctors for the entire population. And because 74 percent of the members of the state medical association received their training outside Alabama, the state was in the unenviable position of trying to entice doctors to come from other states. Equally disturbing, the average local physician was working 20 hours in excess of the standard 40-hour workweek.[14]

I knew firsthand what it was like to live where there was only one doctor. In Grove Hill, it was Ralph Neal Sr. He was an excellent physician, but his practice was becoming increasingly taxing. The era of the family physician who made house calls was clearly over. That was especially true in rural areas where not only were physicians retiring, but small community hospitals were closing—a trend that would continue.

As I said, the other crisis in the state was in health, not just medicine. And physicians alone couldn't solve it. Persistent poverty and an unequal distribution of medical personnel across the state resulted in many counties having developing-world health statistics, such as high rates of infant mortality. These problems were noted in a report by Clifton Meador, who was dean of the School of Medicine in Birmingham from 1968 to 1973. While advocating for more internships and residencies, Meador argued that the state's problem was both "too little medical care for the sick and too little preventative care for the well."[15] That was a significant statement because it went beyond the policy of just adding more physicians.

THE UNIVERSITY OF ALABAMA MARCHES TO A DIFFERENT DRUMMER

The case I am about to present deals with a health-care initiative launched in Tuscaloosa by the U of A. This effort recognized the role of communities in health and led to the creation of a new institution, appropriately named the College of Community Health Sciences.[16] CCHS was designed to be a part of a university-wide "armada" of supporting schools in fields ranging from law and business to social work, education, and psychology—with nursing added later. The reason for having such a far-reaching armada was that the problems adversely affecting people's health were coming from many sources. So, any remedies had to come from many locations.

As I've said, what happened to CCHS is a case study in the power of intervening forces. There were no villains. All the actors in the story acted in what they saw as their best interest. Yet the possibility of carrying out anything close to a *with* strategy was not to be fully realized at the time.

The approach to health promoted by the College of Community Health Sciences was very collaborative, especially in its relationship to communities.[17] However, as this case makes clear, neither supportive federal policies nor a college equipped to address Alabama's health crisis would have the power to carry the U of A's armada to its destination.

The Vision

The history of CCHS goes back to discussions within the U of A that were leading to an alternative to the consultants' plan for a two-year basic science program for premed students. Clinical education, the last rather than the first part of a medical student's training, seemed a better fit with the resources of the institution and the needs of the state. First discussed in 1969, Meador's analysis of the state's needs was shared by Dr. John Burnum, a Harvard-trained physician in Tuscaloosa, who was a member of the U of A planning committee.[18] Their agreement was significant because John represented the local physicians, who would need to support an initiative like CCHS.

The Armada

Gradually, the recommendation to expand premed studies in Tuscaloosa gave way to a plan for a two-year program in clinical medicine. And clinical medicine became part of a broader plan for a university-wide, multifaceted initiative to improve health care for all Alabamians, with an emphasis on those in rural areas.[19] I had participated in this planning before I became U of A president and was enthusiastic about the new direction.

Having rejected the LCME's recommendations for expanding premed education, we received badly needed support in 1970 from Dr. John Phin of James Hamilton Associates. He agreed with the plan to go into clinical medicine. Phin pointed out that the state's mental health initiatives were in Tuscaloosa and could provide clinical opportunities. Phin also recommended that the U of A develop programs in health education, nonsurgical medical management, and the delivery of health care. Furthermore, he suggested a family practice program. This program would be unique to Tuscaloosa and would not conflict with the mission of the School of Medicine in Birmingham but rather would complement it. Cooperation and coordination with UAB, UAH, and CCHS could be handled through written agreements.[20]

The logic behind the shift in the University's planning was what I mentioned earlier: the problems of health care came from everywhere and so must the solutions. As a comprehensive university, the U of A was the obvious institution to respond to this challenge. The institution had faculty in all the relevant fields. If collaboration among all the professionals in the armada began on the campus, it could carry over to the state. In this way, the U of A hoped to counter the state's fragmented system of health care.

This institution-wide strategy did not mean the University thought it could do everything by itself. To the contrary, the institution counted on the support of the School of Medicine at UAB and wanted to develop ties with both the new medical program in Huntsville at UAH as well as the new medical college in Mobile at USA. Auburn University, the state's land-grant institution, had faculties in pharmacy and Extension that could contribute significantly to a statewide coalition. Cooperation with local hospitals and agencies was equally important.

So, rather than following the LCME's recommendations, the U of A developed a different response to the state's health and medical crises, one that hoped to draw from reforms in the medical profession as well as new federal programs that linked health care with communities. The concept that guided the creation of CCHS reflected the community health model proposed by pioneers such Jack Geiger. Dr. Douglas Scutchfield, who would join the

CCHS faculty, was clear about the logic behind the model: "Just as you can't teach clinical medicine without a patient, you can't teach community medicine without working on the community."[21]

THE POLITICS OF MEDICAL EDUCATION

As the planning for CCHS evolved, a struggle developed in Alabama between forces that, on one side, were dedicated to expanding health care and, on the other, were protective of the excellent medical research and specialization in the School of Medicine at UAB. The dynamics of this political conflict would have a significant impact on the prospects for collaboration. I thought that what CCHS was attempting to do and what the School of Medicine had done were complementary, not competitive.

Why was there conflict? Why didn't the School of Medicine follow Dean Meador's logic and take up the problem of too little preventative care, which might have taken the school on the path that the U of A followed? (Meador was no longer dean after 1973.) According to Dr. Richard Rutland, who interned in Birmingham at the School of Medicine, the institution was never receptive to the argument for new fields like family practice championed by physicians like Dr. Willard. On the other hand, there was some support at the School of Medicine. Dr. Rutland recalled a few faculty, like Ben Branscomb and the Finleys, Sarah and Wayne, who encouraged the new programs that would develop at CCHS.[22] (The Finleys also cofounded the first medical genetics program in the southeastern United States.)

Agreement, Then Surprise

Despite differences in medical philosophy, the U of A and UAB were to sign an agreement to cooperate in March of 1971. However, on the eve of the announcement, UAB officials abruptly and surprisingly withdrew from the agreement. The reasons for the sudden change seemingly had to do with one of the intervening forces: institutional competition. We were told that the withdrawal of support resulted from UAB's realization that a new, four-year, medical school in Mobile would take funds away from the School of Medicine. (Neither CCHS nor the medical program at UAH, however, were to be four-year schools.) State funding for USA's new medical school would create a problem for Birmingham because UAB was competing for a large federal grant that required millions in a state match.[23] Notice the irony: Government policy was both compatible with what CCHS was planning and supportive of the School of Medicine's research that served specialization. At the federal level, it made sense to aid both. But locally, there was conflict over state funding as well as over reforms in medicine.

UAB's withdrawal of its support didn't sit well with the people around the state who saw the benefit in the CCHS plan. They created a citizens' organization, Alabama Community Medicine, that urged legislative funding for the College.[24]

The State Legislature Acts

The political climate in the state favored doing more to deal with the crises in both medical and health care, even if the distinction wasn't clear. The gubernatorial election in 1970 showed strong public support for addressing the lack of access to care. Governor George Wallace campaigned on the issue and was determined to act on his campaign promise. His opponent, Albert Brewer, was also firm in his support for expansion.

In April 1971, notwithstanding UAB's objections in March, the Alabama House of Representatives swiftly authorized a $50 million bond for expanded care. Most of the money went to UAB and to the new four-year medical school at USA. The U of A received $4 million for CCHS as a two-year school in health care. UAH also received funding for a two-year school.[25]

WILLARD AT THE HELM

Finding leadership for CCHS was the next step, and that was taken when Dr. Willard accepted the position of dean in 1972. Having the winner of the

AMA's Abraham Flexner Award for Distinguished Service as its leader was as auspicious a beginning as any college could hope for. Willard had come to be known as a founding father of family medicine.[26]

Community Medicine

Dean Willard not only championed family medicine, he was a pioneer in the new field that was even more controversial, community medicine. One of Willard's most important insights was that communities had to be involved in a new way of professional practice. He believed that "medical education should encompass all aspects of treating disease, not merely in patients but in communities as a whole." That required the "integration of health services into the . . . community."[27]

This philosophy implied that CCHS also had to be integrated into its own academic community, which was the U of A. Bill Willard understood the implications of his ideas for the entire institution, and I found him comfortable with the idea of an armada.

Pioneers like Willard had solid examples of what linking community with health care could accomplish. He had become familiar with the community medicine program at the University of Kentucky (UK), where he had been dean before coming to Alabama. At UK in 1960, Dr. Kurt Deuschle created one of the first programs in this field. Kentucky's medical students learned to shift their focus "beyond the health of the individual to that of the community as a whole."[28] They had to take into consideration a range of social and economic realities that were implicated in health problems. In confronting these factors, students were to develop skills that would take them outside the doctor's office and into a relationship with other community actors. They were encouraged to treat citizens as agents with work to do, not simply as passive patients, which is one of the defining characteristics of a *with* strategy. Dean Willard carried this philosophy to CCHS by bringing one of his students from Kentucky, Dr. Douglas Scutchfield, to introduce community medicine into the CCHS curriculum.[29]

Despite the opposition of the School of Medicine at UAB, but fortified by a legislative appropriation, Willard began recruiting faculty to carry out the vision of CCHS—among them, some of the best family physicians practicing in the state. Willard identified the other faculty he wanted to recruit: internists, pediatricians, obstetricians, and gynecologists, along with specialists in psychiatry. He anticipated having a model family practice program linked to primary care centers throughout the state.[30]

Willard recognized that the U of A had no intention of expanding into a four-year medical school. Believing that expansion would detract from the primary mission of CCHS, he agreed with that decision. The new dean intended to draw residents looking for opportunities in family practice and community medicine from UAB, USA, and other medical schools across the country. He pledged to "cooperate closely" with the School of Medicine at UAB as well as the two-year school at UAH. Willard also agreed to accept UAB students interested in a clinical experience in family practice. The CCHS dean wanted every member of the faculty to be "qualified for a faculty appointment by the appropriate department chairman at UAB." To cement the relationship, Dr. John Packard, a graduate of Yale and Harvard, transferred from UAB in 1973 to become an associate dean at CCHS.[31]

THE QUESTION OF CONTROL

The forces that would cause serious problems for CCHS were set in motion soon after it opened in 1972. The Academy of Family Physicians, perhaps unintentionally, put a new issue on the legislative agenda: coordination of the medical programs in Birmingham, Huntsville, and Tuscaloosa. Why not in Mobile at USA as well? It seems that the proposal came from the dean of the new school in Mobile, which had a separate board from UAB, UAH, and the U of A.[32] UAH was alarmed by the possibility that the legislature might encroach on its control. Legislators seemed on the verge of mandating a system with a chancellor for all three institutions but not a statewide system for higher education, which other states had.

The three-institution board lost no time in responding to the academy and the legislature. In 1972, a committee of trustees asked the vice president of UAB to prepare a plan for medical education and the next day created a special committee to receive the recommendation. The report of the special committee made it clear that UAB was to be in control of all medical programs. It also referred to the three institutions reporting to the board as campuses in a "system."[33]

Though it didn't speak to the unique mission of CCHS, the board's responses resolved the questions raised by the academy and the legislators. Dean Willard believed that a "lack of coordination" was a political issue used for a variety of purposes rather than a real problem. But he pledged to cooperate. After all, the medical deans at the three universities had already begun to meet regularly and work together. The deans respected one another as professionals, resolved issues deliberatively, and saw no need for centralized, bureaucratic coordination for programs that had different objectives from those of the medical school in Birmingham.

Some citizens saw the board's report as the first step toward removing the independence of the medical programs in Tuscaloosa and Huntsville. They argued that the 1969 legislative action was to establish three medical programs at three universities, not three branches of a system, which the legislature had not authorized.

Reframing the Issue

The board's report showed that a significant change was occurring in the debate in Alabama. What began as a debate over one problem—the health of the people—had shifted to another, the control and coordination of an academic division—medicine. Obtaining recognition for the unique role of CCHS required broadening the issue being discussed by the board to deal with the state's health crises. As long as the issue revolved largely around control and coordination, the value of what CCHS could do for the state would remain a peripheral consideration.

THE POWER OF ACCREDITING AGENCIES

I wrote my master's thesis on academic accreditation, which plays a useful role by protecting the quality of education. That protection is certainly in the public's interest. What I didn't realize or recognize in my 1959 thesis was that an accrediting body can become the equivalent of a special interest group with its own agenda. (I don't know of any comprehensive accrediting association that regulates the various accrediting associations to prevent this from happening. However, now that I think of it, that may not be a bad idea.)

While the Academy of Family Physicians was making its way to the Alabama legislature to voice its concerns about coordination, the LCME, as an agency of the American Medical Association, returned to the scene. It would become one of the most powerful of those external forces. (Recall that the LCME had been instrumental in developing the plan that the U of A had rejected.)

The LCME exercised its power in Alabama by launching the academic equivalent of a nuclear threat—the loss of the School of Medicine's accreditation. The committee refused to accredit three separate medical programs, insisting that the three had to be treated as branches of the school in Birmingham. The LCME had a track record of opposing new medical education programs in other states, which resulted in disputes as disruptive as the one in Alabama. Why wouldn't examining each program individually be as or more likely to protect academic quality? Even UAB posed the question of separate accreditations to the LCME.

Early in 1974, the approaching accreditation of the School of Medicine in Birmingham resulted in adding new levels of bureaucracy to exercise the control by UAB, which the LCME insisted upon. The medical school added an executive dean as its way of meeting this requirement. Bureaucratic regulation would eventually replace what had been professional agreements to cooperate.

Later that year, the council of presidents for the U of A, UAB, and UAH developed a memorandum of understanding that was given to the board of trustees as a recommendation for coordination.[34] The presidents believed that this was the way the governance should work—cooperatively, not bureaucratically—and they were in reasonable accord. The memorandum pointed out that the U of A and UAH both had legislative mandates for medical education, which the board had accepted, and that each institution's program was directly funded by the lawmakers.

The seven unique missions of CCHS were attached to the president's memorandum with a note showing that some of these missions were part of long-established and accredited nonmedical programs at the U of A. The memo acknowledged, still again, UAB's right to consent to faculty who would be teaching its undergraduate medical students and to approve the curriculum for them in Tuscaloosa and Huntsville. Budget requests were to be developed through joint consultation, and the UAB vice president was to have full knowledge of the resources available for medical education at the other two institutions. In sum, everything that needed to be done to protect the accreditation of the School of Medicine at UAB would be done.

Just prior to the restatement of missions, the board had received a report from consultants saying that the coordination of medical education was a matter for the state as a whole and beyond the scope of the trustees' authority. The new medical school in Mobile under the administration of USA needed to be included. These consultants advised the board that, while UAB should control any programs that led to the MD degree, there was "not a necessity for extending that coordination to other health programs." And the consultants pointed out that the MD program was consuming a disproportionate amount of board attention. They recommended that the board give more consideration to "other pressing matters."[35] Their report appeared to have little or no impact.

THE WILL OF THE PEOPLE?

The work that CCHS was committed to do was consistent with what the elected leaders of Alabama wanted to do and had been approved by allocating taxpayers' dollars. The mission of CCHS was also consistent with what the people of the state wanted for their well-being. However, the academic accrediting agency was able to override both what the legislature intended and what most Alabamians favored. LCME's threat to withdraw accreditation was an all-powerful outside force.

In April 1976, as Willard predicted, the LCME issued a report that was quite critical of CCHS. The disdain for the efforts of Dean Willard and his faculty could not have been more explicit. The board of trustees quickly agreed with the LCME ruling that UAB's School of Medicine should be fully responsible for the quality of all the medical educational programs. The deans of what were now "branch campuses" would be administratively responsible to executive control in Birmingham. Shortly after this decision, Dean Willard resigned.

FOR THE RECORD

The contributions that CCHS had made to Alabama in a relatively short time (1973-1979) could be seen by the time of Dr. Willard's departure. The most significant one, given the mandate from the legislature, was that 40 family practice residents had or would complete their three-year residency program before 1980, and 27 of these physicians established practices in Alabama. The record of service was also extensive. Yet the community medicine program that was key to Bill Willard's plan was not able to reach its full potential.

In 1990, Willard's legacy was still evident when Dr. John Wheat initiated a program at CCHS to recruit students from rural backgrounds in hopes that they would return to rural areas to practice. They did. The Rural Health Leaders Pipeline Program has been quite a success. By 2015, more than 60 percent of the Rural Pipeline doctors were in primary care in rural communities.[36] More recently, the local health clinics promoted by the College played a critical role in combating the COVID-19 pandemic.

I didn't use the phrase "*with* strategy" in the 1970s. Nonetheless, looking back, I remain convinced that good health care is impossible without collaboration involving federal agencies, state medical schools, the citizens in their communities, professionals in medicine, and the other professionals needed to combat the many problems that threaten people's health. I wish I had been better at countering the competing forces and making the argument for better health care. But the CCHS case speaks directly to the question of why a *with* strategy is needed and some of the obstacles to anticipate.

WHAT'S NEXT?

In making the distinction between health care and medical care, I don't want to avoid the question of the public's role when there are medical issues that call for the best science has to offer and the soundest advice that professionals can give about dangers to people's safety. Having just been faced with a deadly attack from the COVID-19 virus, we have seen what citizens will and won't do. People have reacted in different ways, raising questions about personal rights and responsibility for others and their communities.

This book doesn't have clear answers about what should be done in the future or what all the implications are for the role of citizens and their relationship with the relevant governing institutions. It does present a range of cases when the public's safety was in question in hopes that a broader perspective will be more helpful in the long run than looking at just one traumatic event.

NOTES

1. Frank Bane (Chairman), *Physicians for a Growing America: Report of the Surgeon General's Consultant Group on Medical Education* (Washington, DC: US Government Printing Office, 1959).
2. Ted Davis, "The Genesis of the University of Alabama in Huntsville's School of Primary Medical Care," (master's thesis, the University of Alabama in Huntsville, 1980), 10-17.
3. J. Irwin Miller (Chairman), *Report of the National Advisory Commission on Health Manpower* (Washington, DC: US Printing Office, 1967).
4. Neal Holtan, "Recommended Reading on the History of Medical Specializations," *Minnesota Medicine* 87(8) (August 2004): 28-30.
5. Dr. Willard chaired the American Medical Association's Ad Hoc Committee on Education for Family Practice. In 1964, the committee issued a report called *Meeting the Challenge of Family Practice.* See Edward Black, *A History of the College of Community Health Sciences, 1966-1973* (Tuscaloosa, AL: Report to the College of Community Health Sciences at the University of Alabama, 2001), 1-2, 25.
6. Davis, "The Genesis," 14-16.
7. Jonathan Lomas, "Social Capital and Health: Implications for Public Health and Epidemiology," *Social Science and Medicine* 47, no. 9 (1998): 1182.

8. Kurt Deuschle and Frederick Eberson, "Community Medicine Comes of Age," *Journal of American Medical Education* 43(12) (December 1968): 1229-1237.

9. Michael R. Grey, *New Deal Medicine: The Rural Health Programs of the Farm Security Administration* (Baltimore: John Hopkins University Press, 2002).

10. Fitzhugh Mullan and Leon Epstein, "Community-Oriented Primary Care: New Relevance in a Changing World," *American Journal of Public Health* 92 (11) (November 2002): 1749.

11. The first of the community health centers, located in Boston and in Mound Bayou, Mississippi, explored ways to address the underlying factors that led to many diseases. These factors included poverty, malnutrition, and lack of transportation. In H. Jack Geiger, "Community-Oriented Primary Care: A Path to Community Development," *American Journal of Public Health* 92 (11) (November 2002): 1713-1716. In 1990, Dr. Regina Benjamin opened a center in Alabama, the Bayou La Batre Rural Health Clinic. Partly because of the work done there, Dr. Benjamin was installed as United States Surgeon General in 2009.

12. Geiger, "Community-Oriented Primary Care," 1716.

13. This report emphasized the low physician-to-population ratio in Alabama and lagging medical school enrollments since 1952. The report recommended increasing the number of admissions to 125 in the School of Medicine at UAB, adding a new four-year medical school in Mobile at USA, and establishing a two-year clinical school at UAH. Davis, "The Genesis," 27-30.

14. David Mathews, "Statement to the Conference on Community Medicine" (speech to the Symposium on Clinical Training for Community Medicine, Tuscaloosa, AL, March 11, 1971). The statistics for the speech were taken from the report, "Expansion of Medical Education Programs in the State of Alabama," prepared by the Booz, Allen, and Hamilton Commission (November 20, 1967), 12, 16. These documents can be found in the David Mathews collection, Kettering Foundation archives. For more information, contact archives@kettering. org.

15. Clifton K. Meador, "Medical Education and Health Care Delivery in Alabama," University of Alabama School of Medicine, c. March 1971, p. 1. Files in the Office of the President of the University of Alabama in Birmingham.

16. For a detailed history of CCHS, see a monograph on the College that I wrote jointly with Laura Hall Downey, "National Health Policy and Community Needs" (2006). This document can be found in the David Mathews collection, Kettering Foundation archives. For more information, contact archives@kettering.org.

17. In this chapter, I drew on documents written by Laura Hall Downey, such as the monograph we wrote jointly, "National Health Policy and Community Needs."

18. John F. Burnum, letter to David Mathews, June 26, 2000. This document can be found in the David Mathews collection, Kettering Foundation archives. For more information, contact archives@kettering.org.

19. Arthur T. Potter, letter to Legislative Delegation, West Alabama Area Comprehensive Health Planning Council, and the Press of West Alabama, May 7, 1969. See also John F. Burnum, letter to David Mathews, October 20, 1969. This document can be found in the David Mathews collection, Kettering Foundation archives. For more information, contact archives@kettering.org.

20. Charles Moore, summary of James Hamilton Associates report by Dr. John Phin, November 24, 1970. This document can be found in the David Mathews collection, Kettering Foundation archives. For more information, contact archives@kettering. org.

21. Douglas Scutchfield, memorandum to CCHS faculty, February 19, 1975. This document can be found in the David Mathews collection, Kettering Foundation archives. For more information, contact archives@kettering.org.

22. Dr. Richard O. Rutland Jr., "The Beginnings of the College of Community Health Sciences" (speech, Department of Behavioral and Community Medicine and RAHA, Tuscaloosa, AL, April 6, 1995).

23. Author unknown, memorandum, "Proposed Expansion of Medical Education in Alabama," no date, 3, 7, 10. Included in David Mathews, letter to Dr. C. T. Moore, April 20, 1971. This document can be found in the David Mathews collection, Kettering Foundation archives. For more information, contact archives@kettering. org.

24. Victor Poole, a banker from Moundville, led this effort.

25. Black, *A History,* 18.

26. Black, *A History,* 26.

27. Black, *A History,* 23-24.

28. Black, *A History,* 2.

29. See Edward Black's description of the Deuschle project; Black, *A History,* 2-3.

30. Willard also continued to point out that the challenges facing the state clearly transcended the field of medicine per se, so he wanted to use existing faculty from the social, behavioral, and biological sciences. Eventually, the new dean hoped to include programs for nurse practitioners and physician assistants who would be trained to work alongside family doctors. William Willard, memorandum "UAT Community Medicine Program—Objectives, Character and Preliminary Planning Considerations," July 6, 1972, 2, 3, 5, 6-7, 8. This document can be found in the David Mathews collection, Kettering Foundation archives. For more information, contact archives@kettering.org.

31. In addition to Dr. John Burnum (Harvard) and Dr. Dick Rutland (Tulane), who was president of the Alabama Chapter of the American Academy of Family Physicians (AAFP), the faculty drew from excellent academic institutions such as Johns Hopkins and Vanderbilt, along with the Universities of Michigan, Virginia, and North Carolina. Some of these physicians had published scholarly studies. For example,

Dr. Bob Pieroni had written a textbook and 20 journal articles. See Black, *A History*, 36-38; Rutland, "Beginnings," 14; and Biographical Synopsis of Physician Faculty of the College of Community Health Sciences, October 18, 1974. This document can be found in the David Mathews collection, Kettering Foundation archives. For more information, contact archives@kettering.org.

32. At some point, Academy leaders met with Dr. Bucher, the dean of the new medical college in Mobile. The Academy's understanding came from Bucher's statement that "three medical schools, each reporting to a different president, when coordination is imperative . . . is obviously a disaster." Bucher made no mention of the fourth school in this mix to be coordinated and that was his own. The Academy went to members of the legislature "to stimulate legislation to correct this deplorable arrangement." Legislators met with the Academy members, and one, Senator Roland Cooper, a very powerful politician, wanted to create a chancellor for all of the three institutions with medical programs (other than Mobile) and pledged to create a study committee with that end in mind. Ibid. These events were preceded by a meeting in 1972 between the Academy and UAB brought on by the rejection of a family practice program at the School of Medicine the year before. The UAB leadership had told the Academy that such a program was "impossible at the present" but that this type of practice was ideally suited for the new schools in Tuscaloosa and Huntsville. LeRoy Holt, letter to Ehney A. Camp, August 9, 1972. This document can be found in the David Mathews collection, Kettering Foundation archives. For more information, contact archives@ kettering.org.

33. Report of the Special Committee of the Board for System Medical Programs (known as the "McCall Report") to the Board of Trustees of the University of Alabama, adopted by the Board on November 18, 1972, 43. Recommendation (C) is shown as amended by Board action January 18, 1975. Nothing in the McCall Report recognized the distinction between the UAB program of undergraduate medical education and the University of Alabama program for rural health care or the residencies for graduates of any four-year medical school. It dealt exclusively with the clinical programs for a small group of UAB undergraduates in medicine. Protecting the accreditation of UAB was the top priority. Tuscaloosa trustee Ernest G. Williams expressed no reservations on behalf of CCHS and later in 1975 supported the creation of a system with full authority vested in a chancellor, who would be Joe Volker, UAB president. Ernest G. Williams, letter to John Burnum et al., September 26, 1979. In time, the system would move from medical education to all other education in the institutions in Tuscaloosa, Huntsville, and Birmingham. These documents can be found in the David Mathews collection, Kettering Foundation archives. For more information, contact archives@kettering.org.

34. McCall Report, 41; Ernest G. Williams, letter to John Burnum et al., September 26, 1979.

35. Excerpt from Unnamed Consultant Report (April 13, 1974), 55. This document can be found in the David Mathews collection, Kettering Foundation archives. For more information, contact archives@kettering.org.

36. "RMS XX, the University of Alabama Rural Medical Scholars, 2015-2016," *The Scope of Family Medicine* (Fourth Quarter 2015): 10. Also see Harold Reed, *Fayette County Medicine: A History of Quality Health Care in Rural Alabama* (Lulu Publishing Services, 2014).

CHAPTER XIV

WITH THE PEOPLE WHEN THEIR SAFETY IS THREATENED

The first chapters described the troubled relationship between the citizenry (the public) and the governing institutions. This chapter will concentrate on those institutions that are responsible for our health and welfare. In the past, what has happened to our confidence in them and our respect for their authority? And what is the role of citizens? Do they produce anything that is valuable to professionals and medical institutions? What can people contribute by working together that will benefit them and the institutions?

Rather than focusing on one dramatic and terrible case, the COVID-19 pandemic, this chapter looks at a range of cases that all have implications for our safety. That may provide some perspective for what has just begun—sorting out what can be learned from COVID.

One of those cases, the threat of a pandemic in 1976, is very relevant; fortunately, it did not occur. The virus involved didn't mutate into a deadly form, but it wasn't possible to know for sure what would happen in advance. This case also shows how much time it takes for our decentralized system of health care to respond. And it tells how people have reacted in the past to the advice to be vaccinated.

Working *with* the people is valuable under these conditions, but I want to begin by acknowledging what institutional professionals already know. A *with* strategy isn't relevant in all cases, and how it is used will vary.

IS A *WITH* STRATEGY ALWAYS NEEDED?

Most of us are rightly concerned about what is added to our food or injected into our bodies. And the federal government is responsible for protecting us. But how far does that responsibility go, and when does the public need to be involved?

Would a rose's scent change if you called a rose a melon? Probably not. Does the same logic apply when talking about "chips" made from potatoes? Does what they are called really matter? And who should decide? This was actually a question brought before the Department in 1975. There was no crisis and why the federal government, in all its majesty, was involved may puzzle you. It did me. Nonetheless, as I learned, HEW had to act.

The question was whether a popular snack, Pringle's, could be called "potato chips" (*Figure 20*). The answer came from HEW's Food and Drug Administration (FDA). The FDA ruled that the label "Pringle's Newfangled Potato Chips," which were made from dehydrated potatoes, must be described on their packaging as "potato chips made from dried potatoes." This description had to appear in type that was "not less than one-half the size of the largest type in which the words 'potato chips' appear."[1] This Solomon-like ruling protected the sanctity of the word "chip," reserving it to mean a slice from a whole, intact potato. (Today, this snack is labeled simply as "Pringles," with no reference to potato chips.)

Did the citizenry need to collaborate with the government in this case? I don't think so. But what about when dealing with a popular food dye?

How Red Must a Cherry Be?

Another case in which the government had to act had to do with food coloring. Americans must like the color red in the food they eat. Preserved

FIGURE 20. *The FDA had to intervene in a dispute between potato chip manufacturers and Procter & Gamble over whether Pringle's Newfangled Potato Chips could be labeled as "potato chips." (1970s Pringles Cans, Kellogg Company Archives.)*

cherries have to be bright red. Some M&Ms, too. We love red velvet cupcakes. Most of these reds once came from the food coloring Red Dye No. 2. Then HEW's Food and Drug Administration found research showing that No. 2 could cause cancer. But this was far from an open-and-shut case. Some scientists argued that No. 2 was safe in the small amounts used. And food companies claimed that the alternative, Red Dye No. 40, would turn cherries, soft drinks, and candy an unappealing brown. What were the implications for the public in this decision? Should the citizenry be involved? And, if so, in what role?

Even though we are very concerned about what we eat and expect the government to protect us on questions like the safety of food dyes, the government relies on scientists to sort through conflicting claims and decide what the preponderance of evidence shows. In this case, the decision was to substitute No. 40 for No. 2. (The cherries, fortunately, did not turn brown.)

Should citizens have made that decision? Doubtful. Scientists are usually the best judges of the evidence that is available in such cases. However, people deserved the clearest explanation possible about why scientists decided that the danger of cancer was enough to favor Red Dye No. 40 as an alternative.

Truly Public Issues

When should the public, unquestionably, be involved? It all depends on what is at issue in the issue. The real issue from a public perspective in the dye case wasn't just about red coloring; it was about food safety. The public's outlook is usually wider and less technical than that of government officials and experts. The broader issue, food safety, touches on many things people care deeply about: the responsibilities of government, their own personal control, and the degree of risk. The dye issue needed a name that captured these concerns. The citizenry did have work to do, and it was to rename the issue so that there could be public deliberations on the standards for food safety. Citizens renaming an issue in terms of what people see as most valuable makes it possible for them to productively engage *with* the government rather than simply complaining *about* the government. That is particularly important when people are fearful. The government and the public need a different relationship *with* one another in such situations.

The public has a good deal of choice work to do on the issue of food safety because of the trade-offs that must be considered. What, if any, risks are acceptable when the scientific evidence is inconclusive?[2] What control should people have over what they eat, and how much control should the government have? A deliberative environment is necessary when controversies threaten to disrupt the public's need to move from first reactions to more considered judgment.

ENCOUNTERING A NEW FORM OF LIFE

Some scientific issues pose low levels of danger. Others just the opposite; the threat to life is enormous. The following case is such an example. It involved using deoxyribonucleic acid, better known as DNA, to recombine the building blocks of life into new organisms, which, if dangerous, could be unstoppable. In 1972, researchers found that they could transfer genes from one plant or animal to another, even those of different species. This was made possible by the discovery of enzymes capable of breaking DNA strands at specific sites and "of coupling the broken fragments in new combinations . . . thus making possible the insertion of foreign genes into certain cell particles (plasmids)."[3] These plasmids could then be used "to introduce the foreign genes into bacteria or into cells of plants or animals in test tubes." Once transplanted, the genes could "impart their hereditary properties to new hosts."[4] This is called "genetic engineering," and it caused quite a commotion.

Despite the potential for these modified genes to work medical miracles, people were afraid they could die if a harmful new gene that couldn't be killed escaped a lab. In the 1970s, some saw using recombinant DNA (rDNA) in generic engineering as scary as the worst horror movie.

Developing Guidelines

The National Institutes of Health (NIH) at HEW was responsible for setting guidelines for this research. The way the NIH responded provides one of the best examples of engaging the public, using the engagement practices that were available at the time. The rDNA issue was complex, and developing guidelines was quite a bumpy ride. The lab experiments used a strain of *E. coli* that had a sterling safety record, and the NIH attempted to reassure people using scientific information.[5] Public concerns, however, were serious enough to require temporarily halting the research, as scientists continued to debate guidelines.[6] Their meetings resulted in proposed guidelines to be presented to NIH for approval in December 1975.

Dr. Don Fredrickson, head of NIH, published these guidelines in the *Federal Register* in 1976 and opened them to public review. He then organized a hearing in Washington in February and included more participants than those who were involved in the earlier meetings of experts.[7] Seventeen interest groups attended. Even though the general public had little voice, I thought the Department was moving in the right direction.[8]

In addition to the February meeting, the NIH asked for and received numerous written comments, which were used to make changes to the guidelines. Another meeting was held in April 1976. And the Department provided more opportunities for general public comment when a new version of the guidelines was printed in the *Federal Register* on July 7, 1976.[9] The notice made it clear that HEW wanted "further . . . public comment and consideration" and that the publication of the guidelines should not be confused with the normal procedures in rulemaking in which further comment would *not* have been invited.[10] The discussion of policy considerations in the *Register* was also very explicit about the "strong disagreement" over the possible hazards of rDNA research.[11]

Fredrickson wanted scientists to be especially open because "the scientific community must have the public's confidence that the goals of this profoundly important research accord respect to important ethical, legal, and social values of our society."[12] The unstated assumption, however, was that this could be done by assurances from government officials.

The federal government was doing what it does best. The 1976 guidelines set up physical and biological barriers to protect lab workers, the surrounding communities, and the environment from possible, though as yet unknown, dangers.[13] Despite these efforts, when people learned about this research, they were still frightened. The issue for citizens went beyond the scientific and technical questions dealt with inside government and by the scientific community. It had implications that required the exercise of public judgment.[14] Among the tensions that needed to be worked through were those between the value placed on saving lives using genetic engineering and protecting the public from possibly dangerous new life forms. The things people valued, along with the tensions among them, were quite evident.

Who Is in Control?

Responses to the proposed guidelines surfaced a particularly sensitive concern that could have been weighed in public deliberations. It had to do with control over experimentation. The question was not only whether the controls were technically sufficient, but who should have them? Was the public to have a role in making this decision, and what should that role be?

The importance of the question of control was highlighted by Dan Yankelovich in his research on trends in public opinion. He found that "all of our surveys over the last decade show that every year, more and more people are coming to believe that the part of their lives that they are able to control is diminishing."[15] He went on to add that the individual's autonomy was being reduced, not only by governments, but also by other institutions. So, people were becoming "more determined to control the remainder." It is significant that this quotation appeared in a 1977 article arguing that the public's reluctance to accept the government's health advice was linked to a "growing distrust of authority." That reluctance would still be evident a half-century later.

How was the trade-off to be made between public control and the necessary latitude for laboratories to move ahead in potentially lifesaving research? Although this issue was ripe for public deliberation, more conventional hearings were all that was available at the time. The city council of Cambridge, Massachusetts, held open meetings about the issue because Harvard was building a lab for genetic research. An article about the hearings noted that citizens took "unprecedented steps to involve themselves in decision-making regarding biological research."[16]

What does this case have to say about *with* and what the public could add by collaborating with the health agencies? My answer is that the citizenry—using civic organizations, libraries, and schools—could have provided a more deliberative environment. (I say "more" because I'm sure there was naturally occurring deliberation among the public.) The conditions were favorable. Government officials wanted to hear from both special interest groups and the general public. What was missing were opportunities for public deliberation rather than just informed discussions in expert terms. It would be years before there were enough forum sponsors who understood the need for public meetings with a deliberative structure.

The Outcome

What happened in 1976? I didn't take every issue to President Ford and was inclined to go it on my own unless I saw that he would be affected or needed to take a position. I thought the recombinant DNA issue was one of those instances. On June 18th, I notified him that the Department was about to issue guidelines with the intent to "afford protection with a wide margin of safety to workers and the environment."[17] Although aware of the controversial nature of this issue, the President approved the HEW plan to proceed with this recombinant DNA research in the laboratories of the NIH and those of their grantees and contractors. He did so because of the potential benefits, such as treating disease, producing better crops, and creating bacteria that could ingest oil spills in the sea.[18]

DEALING WITH A POTENTIAL PANDEMIC: THE CONSTRAINTS OF TIME

Some of the crises in Washington could have benefited from public deliberations and using a *with* strategy, but there were time constraints. In the spring of 1976, the Ford administration faced the possibility of a catastrophic flu pandemic. A decision had to be made as soon as possible because of the time it would take to be prepared. There was no vaccine that would protect people from this virus.

At Fort Dix, New Jersey, following an overnight military exercise, a soldier fell ill and died. And within a short period of time, 230 more young, healthy recruits became ill. Thirteen of them developed a severe respiratory illness and had to be hospitalized.[19] Tests found that the young men were sick with an influenza virus that appeared to have similarities to the flu virus that caused the devastating pandemic that swept the world in 1918–1919. This virus was labeled "swine flu" because it was thought to have come from pigs. It was markedly different from the flu viruses that were circulating in the population in the 1970s. More worrisome, most Americans had no immunity to this new virus. Furthermore, the virus seemed capable of spreading from person to person because the soldiers had had no contact with pigs. These factors, as well as the duration of the Fort Dix outbreak, raised warning flags for the upcoming flu season.[20] Although public health experts could not be certain there would be a pandemic, they strongly warned the government of the possibility.

Deciding What to Do

Should the government prepare for a worst-case scenario, develop a vaccine as quickly as possible, and encourage everyone to be inoculated? Or should officials adopt a wait-and-see strategy, perhaps produce a vaccine but not use it until there were confirmed cases of swine flu? The constraints were the time needed to develop a vaccine—at least six months if all went well—the time required to immunize a large number of people before they were exposed to the virus, and the ability of a decentralized public health system to respond quickly.

Flu is dangerous even when it isn't caused by an especially virulent virus. Many people want to be protected from such an illness. But personal control is another concern for people. Some were as hesitant to be vaccinated then as some were in 2021. The only way to protect the country as a whole is by large-scale inoculation so that a virus won't spread readily from person to person. However, protecting the country as a whole is in tension with respecting an individual's right to choose.

This issue also presented both the public and government officials with another tension-filled choice: Who should get vaccinated first? It takes time to develop the serum that goes into an inoculation. And health professionals can't treat everyone at once. So, should children get first priority or the elderly? Unlike the situation in 2020–2021, older Americans who had come into contact with this strain of flu as children would have had some immunity, but younger Americans would not. What about the health professionals themselves? If the virus decimated their ranks, who would care for those who were ill? This issue was full of tough choices. Yet, in the spring of 1976, a decision had to be made immediately in order to have vaccines ready for the coming flu season in the fall.

The Government Responds

What actually happened? In light of the infections at Fort Dix, the federal health agencies, with the Center for Disease Control and Prevention (CDC) in the lead, began to prepare for a return of the new virus in the fall. Fortunately, there was a history to draw on. Protective antigens against the 1918–1919 flu had been put into vaccines from 1955 to 1969 (largely for the military), and there were no reports of negative side effects over this extended period of time. This was one indication that a new vaccine against swine flu would be safe.

A committee of experts from outside the Department (the Advisory Committee on Immunization Practices) determined that there was indeed the possibility of a serious outbreak in the fall. Even though some committee members thought the outbreak might not be catastrophic, they didn't think the government should take the chance. Respected specialists like Edwin Kilbourne, the virologist who created the first influenza vaccine in 1960, favored immediate vaccinations and not stockpiling for use if an outbreak became evident. Waiting, Kilbourne believed, would be too late if the flu were already spreading. Furthermore, there was evidence of a new strain, and new strains touch off pandemics. The experts recommended producing enough vaccine for all.

When I brought the situation to President Ford's attention on March 22, 1976, the White House staff had already done its job by laying out the uncertainties and the downsides of accepting HEW's recommendation to begin preparing for immediate vaccinations. I told the President that accepting the recommendation would be criticized no matter what happened. If there was no outbreak, we would be painted as alarmists who exaggerated the threat. If a pandemic occurred, there could be some glitches in the way the healthcare system responded and we would be charged with mismanagement. I volunteered to make the call myself, but Ford, probably recalling his military experience, believed that it was his duty to take the lead as President. There were media inferences that he saw the situation (or was advised to see it) as an opportunity to appear heroic in an election year, but I never heard any such advice.

How did the government deal with the public? In this situation, given the time it took to develop a vaccine, a decision had to be made as soon as the evidence allowed. Given the findings from the advisory committee, the government opted for a campaign to inform and vaccinate citizens. The willingness of people to be vaccinated was key. And the government believed that on this subject Americans would want to hear from the medical experts just as they listened to their personal physicians.

Before announcing the decision and to be doubly diligent, the White House and HEW staff brought in a wide range of experts to a sizable meeting on March 24 to review the situation. Eminent physicians, Jonas Salk and Albert Sabin, were included, not only because they had developed polio vaccines, but also because they were rivals who often disagreed publicly. In this case, both Salk and Sabin urged mass immunization. I recall the President going around the room questioning the scientists and then calling for a show of hands, which was unanimous. At the end of the meeting, Ford took the unprecedented step of encouraging anyone who had reservations to meet him privately afterwards. He waited in his office; no one came. At that point, the President announced his decision to the press.

To his credit, Dr. Theodore (Ted) Cooper, Assistant Secretary for Health, made a valiant effort to reach the citizens who were the most suspicious of the government. For example, there was a rumor circulating that the flu vaccinations were going to be used to harm African Americans.[21] I recall Ted going outside the usual PR channels to reach not just local health agencies but also nongovernmental organizations like churches because they were trusted by many people. These outreach efforts helped make vaccination history (Figure 21). In the 10 weeks between October 1 and December 16, 1976, "almost fifty million Americans were vaccinated—an unprecedented accomplishment."[22]

Fortunately, the flu virus that season was not deadly. However, an expanded surveillance system did find a spike in Guillain-Barré Syndrome (GBS) and, in December 1976, HEW suspended the vaccination program for further scrutiny. (Unable to find any link, vaccinations were resumed in February 1977.) GBS can occur without any association with vaccines, although there have been cases after some shots. As far as I know today, research has still not been able to show conclusively a link between the 1976 vaccine and this syndrome.[23]

The Need for Public Deliberation

What role might the citizenry have played to create a deliberative environment for dealing with the issue of vaccinations? Because of the fear surrounding vaccines, the issue certainly needed public deliberation. The

FIGURE 21. *President Ford receives his swine flu inoculation on October 14, 1976, from White House physician Dr. William Lukash. (Photographer: David Hume Kennerly. Courtesy Gerald R. Ford Library.)*

things people valued were clearly in tension: the personal right to choose conflicted with the need to protect society as a whole. The obstacle to deliberation was a lack of time. The government had to respond in a matter of weeks. And there were few civic organizations prepared to frame this issue for deliberation.

Although deliberation was not possible in this case, it was possible later on. In dealing with another flu outbreak in 2005, government officials did turn to public deliberation for guidance. The Centers for Disease Control and Prevention used deliberation to help decide whether vaccines should be targeted to the most vulnerable (health workers, for example) or to society as a whole. Rather than just relying on polls and interviews, CDC officials teamed up with civic organizations to find out how people made decisions when they were confronted with questions about priorities in vaccine distribution.[24] This was helpful because the results of deliberation aren't like those from polling. Forums help people see how complex an issue is, why people hold on to their opinions, and what prompts them to take into account opinions that don't agree with theirs. What happened in 2005? Government officials recognized that their policies had to give more attention to those most critical to the functioning of society, not just those at high risk medically.[25]

Issues within Issues

Using public deliberation the way CDC did in 2005 is more difficult when there are issues within issues, which was the case in 1976. One of the other issues in the swine flu case had to do with how far the government should go in protecting the manufacturers of vaccines from litigation, particularly if the complaints turned out to have little legal merit. Ideally, public deliberations would have been helpful because the issue raised the question of what role the government should play. But the vaccine manufacturers would stop working if they could not get coverage to protect themselves against baseless lawsuits for damages. And if that happened, the country wouldn't be protected in time for flu season.

In late spring of 1976, the swine flu program was encountering the first of its major obstacles because of this issue. Ted Cooper and I, now joined by William Howard (Will) Taft IV, our General Counsel, shifted back and forth, talking to vaccine manufacturers, lawyers, and Congress. The manufacturers were in an untenable position and time precluded extended negotiations. Congress would have to provide the protection the manufacturers required. I then turned my attention to getting support on the Hill.

This time, Congress acted quickly. With the help of the President, the House and Senate passed a torts claim bill for swine flu in August.[26] That cleared the way for the first inoculation on October 1.[27]

THE LEGACY OF SWINE FLU

Possible pandemics threaten quite regularly, and I am often asked what we learned from the swine flu case. The most important lesson is to be prepared for the worst case. Our health-care system is very decentralized, and fitting all the parts together is extremely difficult even under conditions that are never ideal. We saw how difficult that coordination was in 2020 and 2021. Another lesson, which I mentioned earlier, was putting the medical experts out front. But politicians also have to be supportive and speak to the nonscientific concerns people have as human beings. For example, people wrestle with the tension between protecting themselves personally and making sacrifices to protect the common good. Also, many people aren't sure they can trust the information they are getting, so it was important to do what Ted Cooper did—enlist trusted authorities. Getting the facts out to the public is necessary, but just relying on facts is a mistake. People's disbelief has to do with not trusting the source. In addition, facts reflect the concerns of authorities and experts, which aren't always the same as the concerns of citizens.

Fortunately, the 1976 virus did not reappear in the fall flu season, and it did not mutate into a deadlier form. However, viruses constantly mutate, and no one now can know what new strains might emerge. That is another reason to be prepared for the worst case.

Because the country was lucky in 1976, the swine flu program was ridiculed as a "fiasco" when the virus did not turn out to be extremely deadly. That label was unfortunate because it may have made future health-care professionals hesitant to take bold steps early on to be prepared and to encourage political leaders to warn the public of the possibilities.[28]

FINANCING SOCIAL SECURITY: A SLOW-MOVING CRISIS

Not all crises threaten our health. Keeping the Social Security Administration (SSA) secure was (and still is) imperative. It would be catastrophic if it failed. The possibility of that happening frightens senior citizens and those nearing retirement age. Yet raising Social Security taxes is unacceptable to a great many younger working people. This issue was so controversial in the 1970s that the conventional political wisdom was for politicians to avoid it like it was the electrified "third rail" of a train track. The delay intensified the concern of the two age groups and created a political crisis.

In 1976, I, along with the two other Social Security trustees, the Secretaries of Labor and the Treasury, received a sobering warning from Bruce Cardwell, Social Security Commissioner. Bruce had a reputation for being an able and reliable civil servant, and he reported that the system was facing a financial crisis. We took his warning seriously. Social Security tax revenue would not cover all retirement payments, leaving a $5.7 billion deficit that would have to be covered from the Social Security Trust Fund. As trustees, we reported the problem to President Ford, and he sent remedial legislation to Congress that would have raised Social Security payroll deductions. The legislation failed to pass, and the issue carried over to a new Congress and a new administration.[29] In this case, there was time for the public to work *with* the government to create a deliberative climate to deal with the conflicting concerns. The obstacle was the lack of civic organizations with experience in framing issues for deliberation.

What might public deliberation on this issue have looked like in the 1970s? We can get answers from the early 1980s because the system's financial problems continued and National Issues Forums (NIF) deliberations on the issue had taken place by that time. In the NIF meetings in 1982, the tensions among the things people valued, such as financial security after retirement and control of personal income (no tax increases), were still evident. There were also tensions over how much responsibility the government should have for retirement income and how much responsibility individuals should take.[30] (Social Security was not designed to replace all retirement expenses; people still have to save.)

The deliberations on Social Security were often emotional; people had strong feelings. But in the forums, younger people were asked if, in keeping their money, they would be willing to accept full responsibility for the expenses of aging parents. They hesitated. And the tone of the meetings changed. Hearing the hesitation, senior citizens softened their opposition to any alterations. The age gap dividing seniors from active workers remained yet became less of a factor. People began to weigh the costs and consequences of proposals such as extending the age of retirement and capping benefits. The government decision was still hard to make, but the public deliberations showed the issue might not be a deadly political third rail. The people in the forums were more inclined to recognize that difficult trade-offs had to be made. They knew there would have to be sacrifices; they just wanted the sacrifices to be borne equitably.[31]

This weighing of options created a different public voice. It wasn't the voice of agreement but rather that of citizens making up their minds about what they could live with. Congress in the next administration did act. Maybe these deliberations helped convince legislators that reforming Social Security wasn't a third rail after all.

LEGISLATIVE AND PUBLIC DELIBERATION

In dealing with the Social Security crisis and many other cases in this book, the role of Congress was crucial. The failure to act could turn a problem into a crisis. Timely action could prevent one. That raises the question of whether a deliberative citizenry can work *with* a legislative body to make it more deliberative.

Worrisome Trends

Hearing a deliberative public voice, while possible, does face some obstacles. And reports show that government decision-making is becoming less open and deliberative. Recently, the Congressional Management Foundation found that "Congress has abandoned the deliberative process."[32] This makes it all the more important that there be deliberations in the public arena.

That is true even when the public may begin grappling with an issue in a way that government officials think is off the mark or irrelevant. People start talking about personal experiences and telling stories they have heard. As insignificant as these seeming diversions may appear, this is the way the citizenry makes decisions. Stories about experiences show what is deeply valuable. Most people don't talk in abstractions. What they hold dear is buried in their stories. They may be about trying to stay healthy, because that is deeply valuable. Or the stories might be about relatives who became poor once they were too old to work. The stories are about basics, like being secure, being treated fairly, being free to act, or being in control. Deliberation also moves people to look at difficult trade-offs. Good medical care, for example, usually requires costly drugs and equipment.[33]

What Can Help Elected Representatives

Citizens doing choice work can give officeholders insights that they can't get from other sources. That can also help counter polarization and may show a way forward or highlight what is politically permissible when there is an impasse. That was the case on the Social Security issue. However, for legislators to get the benefits from public deliberation, they have to be in an environment where they aren't being attacked and can think about what they are hearing rather than constantly preparing to defend themselves. There are now better ways to create such conditions without sanitizing the people's interactions with officeholders. I will say more about that shortly.

Recognizing Differences in Perspectives

When there is public deliberation, legislators can identify the differences between the way an issue is seen from a government perspective and the way the citizenry sees the issue. For example, on health-care costs, there are significant differences between the perspectives of the government and those of citizens. The government sees the increasing costs of health care as a budgetary problem, which it is. For citizens, on the other hand, these costs are personal and include the "expense" of navigating an increasingly complex system of doctors, hospitals, and insurance companies.

Insights into Public Thinking

Officeholders are inundated with information on public opinion, but it is impossible for them to see inside people's heads when they are wrestling with trade-offs. Hearing citizens doing deliberative choice work allows officials to find out how people are thinking when they really have to think, which happens when citizens are confronted with difficult trade-offs. Knowing how the citizenry goes about making decisions can provide valuable information for officeholders and administrators because they, too, have difficult trade-offs to make. In some cases, officeholders may disagree with how citizens see an issue or the options they favor. In these situations, public deliberations can tell officials how the citizenry goes about making up its mind so they can engage this thinking where they believe it errs.

Short of Agreement—The Politically Permissible

When citizens in forums show that there is a general direction to move forward, as they did on the Social Security issue, it doesn't give government officials or legislators a set of orders to carry out. Still, they should have a clearer sense of what is and isn't supportable. That's important. As Abraham Lincoln recognized, "With public sentiment, nothing can fail; without it nothing can succeed."[34]

Social Security was one of those issues in which public deliberations on the difficult trade-offs didn't result in full agreement, but the forums showed where there was a way forward to address the funding crisis. In this case, participants in deliberations were able to distinguish what was totally unacceptable from what they might not prefer yet could live with. That delineates a space in which a range of political actions is permissible.[35]

Long-Term Change

While there are cases of insights from forums that can be quite helpful on issues that are on a legislative or regulatory docket, the major effects of public deliberation are long-term, which coincides with the way policy shifts really occur. Major policy changes evolve over time. This effect has been documented in *The Rational Public* by Benjamin Page and Robert Shapiro.[36] Their analysis of a wide variety of policy issues over a period of 50 years shows that the public's attitudes were, on the whole, consistent, rational, and stable. In this sense, the decisions were sound. As the authors explained, the opinions that matured over decades were consistent in that the policies people favored corresponded to what people considered valuable. They were rational in that there were clear reasons for them; for example, people favored more spending on employment when unemployment was high. And public preferences were stable in that they changed incrementally in understandable responses to changes in circumstances. Why were public policy preferences, over time and on the whole, so consistent, rational, and stable? Page and Shapiro believe that it is because the "cool and deliberate sense of the community" eventually prevailed on most issues.

A caveat: Over time, even a sound decision at one point can prove to be absolutely wrongheaded because the circumstances have changed.

Deliberation With

When citizens share what happened in their deliberations with officeholders who are also deliberating, the government is working *with* the people. A *with* strategy has been used in several ways to bring officeholders and citizens together to compare the outcomes of public deliberation with legislative deliberation. One of these exchanges began in 1983 at the opening of the Ford Presidential Library. Former presidents Ford and Carter presided over a meeting comparing legislative with public deliberations on Social Security financing. Such exchanges have continued during presidential elections in Kettering's annual A Public Voice programs in Washington and in states where citizens have deliberated on the same issues that their legislatures were facing.[37]

An experiment in Hawaii showed the potential for this kind of collaborative exchange on a controversial issue: allowing gambling in a tourist paradise. Added revenue was attractive; the possibility of crime and corruption wasn't. In this case, legislative leaders worked with faculty at the University of Hawaii to organize deliberative forums.[38] The purpose of the forums wasn't to tell the legislature how to vote; it was for legislators to see how people were thinking when they had to think, which was needed for weighing the trade-offs. The information about how Hawaiians went about making up their minds was not available from polls.[39]

Some officials now recognize that finding a different way to listen to the public is crucial. It serves their self-interest to engage people without getting attacked in raucous public meetings. Fortunately, there has been some progress in doing that using online deliberation.[40] Whatever the means, the necessity of communicating with citizens is inescapable. To quote former Secretary of State Dean Rusk, "At the end of the day, the American people are going to have to decide. No president can pursue a policy for very long without the support and the understanding of the Congress and the American people. That's been demonstrated over and over again."[41] Rusk, who served during the unpopular Vietnam War, had reason to say what he did.

More recently, members of Congress have been in an experiment using online deliberation to listen to citizens. The results were reported in a 2018 book titled *Politics with the People.* It shows the potential to help counter the loss of public confidence when government authorities (legislators) join citizens in the work of deliberation.[42] Michael Neblo, one of the authors, noted the positive results of exchanges that allowed elected officials to hear citizens engaged in "thoughtful deliberation" in online forums.[43] This experiment involved 13 sitting members of Congress who were dissatisfied with the often acrimonious and unproductive town meetings but recognized their duty to consult with their constituents. Using a new online deliberative town hall technology developed for NIF, both the citizens and the representatives behaved differently in what proved to be a "more satisfying and constructive" experience.[44] Hopefully, these deliberative exchanges will spread to state legislatures as well. They reflect democratic values like openness and reflective judgment, which are the defining characteristics of a *with* strategy. Legislative bodies, from city councils to state houses, to the federal Congress, must be deliberative bodies if they are to remain legitimate in a democracy.

WHAT'S NEXT?

Chapters VII to XIV looked at what has enabled officials in governing institutions to work *with* the people and what made that impossible or highly unlikely. A *with* strategy also requires the citizenry to do its share of the collaborative work. So, the next chapter shifts the focus to look again, and in more detail, at the question of whether citizens have not only the ability but also the resources to work *with* governing institutions. The chapter will build on what has been said about people's faculty for judgment, which is essential in deliberative decision-making. (What deliberation is, how it works, and where it can occur has already been covered in chapter IV and elsewhere.) Chapter XV is more about the resources citizens can use to make a difference—provided they recognize what these resources are and where they can be found.

NOTES

1. John Egerton, "Pringle's vs. the Real Thing: Is the Lowly Potato Chip a Match for P&G?" *New York Times*, November 30, 1975.

2. I realize that people's concerns on scientific issues may not be eliminated by "definitive" evidence because as research continues, the findings may change and conflict in a short period of time. While a substantial minority (37 percent) lose trust in scientific findings on food safety when evidence conflicts, a majority (61 percent) accept the changes as part of the research process. The counter to this loss of trust may go beyond just adding more research data. Monica Anderson, "Most Americans Take Conflicting Food Studies in Stride," Pew Research Center, December 2, 2016, available at https://www.pewresearch.org/fact-tank/2016/12/02/most-americans-take-conflicting-food-studies-in-stride/.

3. "Recombinant DNA Research, Guidelines," 41 Fed. Reg. 27903 (July 7, 1976), pp. 27903-27904. Found at the Gerald R. Ford Library.

4. "Recombinant DNA Research, Guidelines," p. 27904.

5. "Recombinant DNA Research, Guidelines," p. 27907.

6. One of the earliest of these meetings was held at the Asilomar Conference Center in Pacific Grove, California, in February 1975, and a very select group of scientists attended. Some of these scientists wanted strict guidelines, while others wanted permissive ones. Three more meetings were held in 1975 in order to reconcile these differences and come up with a set of guidelines.

7. Secretary David Mathews, memorandum to President Gerald Ford on the publication of guidelines, June 18, 1976. Found at the Gerald R. Ford Library.

8. Susan Wright, *Molecular Politics: Developing American and British Regulatory Policy for Genetic Engineering, 1972-1982* (Chicago: University of Chicago Press, 1994), 184-185.

9. "Recombinant DNA Research, Guidelines."

10. "Recombinant DNA Research, Guidelines," p. 27902.

11. "Recombinant DNA Research, Guidelines," p. 27904.

12. "Recombinant DNA Research, Guidelines," p. 27903.

13. The guidelines prohibited what were thought to be the most dangerous types of recombinant DNA research: cloning derived from certain pathogenic organisms, the formation of recombinant DNAs "containing genes for the biosynthesis of potent toxins"; "deliberate creation from plant pathogens of recombinant DNAs that are likely to increase virulence and host range"; and the transfer of drug resistance traits to "microorganisms that are not known to acquire" them "naturally" if they "could compromise the use of a drug to control disease agents in human or veterinary medicine or agriculture." They also prohibited deliberate release into the environment of any organism containing a recombinant DNA molecule. Last, they recommended that experiments with more than 10 liters of culture "with recombinant DNAs known to make harmful products . . . not to be carried out." See "Recombinant DNA Research, Guidelines," pp. 27914-27915.

14. See Wright, *Molecular Politics*; and Clifford Grobstein, "Asilomar and Public Policy Formation," in *The Gene-Splicing Wars: Reflections on the Recombinant DNA Controversy*, eds. Raymond A. Zilinskas and Burke K. Zimmerman (New York: MacMillan Publishing Company, 1986).

15. Yankelovich saw Americans as not wanting to give the government a license to "enter every nook and cranny of their personal lives." Richard D. Lyons, "Refusal of Many to Heed Government Health Advice Is Linked to Growing Distrust of Authority," *New York Times*, June 12, 1977.

16. The result was two resolutions. The first asked for a three-month moratorium on laboratory experiments so more hearings and testimony could be considered. The second resolution established the Cambridge Laboratory Experimentation Review Board, which consisted of both scientists and citizens. Barbara Culliton, "Recombinant DNA: Cambridge City Council Votes Moratorium," *Science* 193(4250) (July 23, 1976): 300.

17. David Mathews, memorandum to President Gerald Ford, regarding the publication of guidelines, June 18, 1976. Found at the Gerald R. Ford Library.

18. "Recombinant DNA Research, Guidelines," p. 27904.

19. Joel C. Gaydos et al., "Swine Influenza A Outbreak, Fort Dix, New Jersey, 1976," *Emerging Infectious Diseases* 12(1) (January 2006): 23-28.

20. Many in the administration were old enough to remember that, in 1918, a flu virus that wasn't initially a cause for alarm turned deadly in a matter of months. It is estimated to have killed between 50 and 100 million people worldwide, including 675,000 Americans. Niall P.A.S. Johnson and Juergen Mueller, "Updating the Accounts: Global Mortality of the 1918-1920 'Spanish' Influenza Pandemic,"

Bulletin of the History of Medicine 76 (1) (Spring 2002): 105-115. The consequences of such an outbreak today would be dire. As one report pointed out,
"Were a pandemic as severe as that of 1918-19 to occur, over 142.2 million people
would die, and the world's GDP would suffer a loss of $4.4 trillion." Michael T.
Osterholm, "Unprepared for a Pandemic," *Foreign Affairs* 86, no. 2 (March/April
2007), http://www.foreignaffairs.com/articles/2007-03-01/unprepared-pandemic.

21. Concerns of African Americans were discussed in a *New York Times* interview with
    an HEW official, Dr. Delano Meriwether, himself an African American. Richard D.
    Lyons, "Refusal of Many to Heed Government Health Advice Is Linked to Growing
    Distrust of Authority," *New York Times,* June 12, 1977.

22. Fitzhugh Mullan, *Plagues and Politics: The Story of the United States Public Health
    Service* (New York: Basic Books, 1989), 182-185.

23. Felix Leneman, "The Guillain-Barré Syndrome: Definition, Etiology, and Review
    of 1,100 Cases," *Archives of Internal Medicine* 118(2) (August 1966): 139-144. The
    causes of this rare condition aren't known, but it is usually triggered by an infectious
    illness.

24. The Keystone Center, *Citizen Voices on Pandemic Flu Choices: A Report of the Public
    Engagement Pilot Project on Pandemic Influenza* (Keystone, CO: The Keystone Center,
    2005). The Keystone Center did a subsequent report on this research: *The Public
    Engagement Project on Community Control Measures for Pandemic Influenza* (Keystone,
    CO: The Keystone Center, 2007). The CDC also employed public engagement strat-
    egies as part of the 2009 H1N1 flu vaccination program.

25. The Keystone Center, *Citizen Voices on Pandemic Flu Choices,* 28.

26. After attempts to reconcile liability issues with manufacturers and insurers failed, I
    told Representative Paul Rogers, who chaired the House Health Subcommittee that
    held hearings on the liability problem, that we would need protective legislation.
    A swine flu tort claims bill went to the House and Senate August 1, when we still
    weren't sure what had caused the disease afflicting the Legionnaires, and I met with
    the subcommittees and urged action. Although the House subcommittee initially
    responded in support of the bill, once it became clear that the Legionnaires' disease
    was not swine flu, action was postponed. The President then prodded Congress to
    follow up. Edward Kennedy, chair of the Senate Health Subcommittee, held a short
    hearing and the Senate's version of the bill was approved on August 6. The bill passed
    in the Senate on August 10 and was subsequently passed in the House.

27. Because of the time it took to solve these problems, we were behind on the sched-
    ule we wanted to follow, and there were still disputes with manufacturers over exact
    delivery dates, although millions of doses were in bulk form. In late August, I again
    urged all manufacturers (including the dropout who rejoined) to redouble their
    efforts. In September, states began to receive their first shipments. A more detailed

account of this case can be found in "The Swine Flu Case of 1976," an unpublished monograph by the Kettering Foundation. This document can be found in the David Mathews collection, Kettering Foundation archives. For more information, contact archives@kettering.org.

28. For more details of the events surrounding the 1976 Swine Flu vaccinations, see David Mathews, interview by Latif Nasser for *Radiolab*, June 6, 2020. A transcript of this interview can be found in the David Mathews collection, Kettering Foundation archives. An unpublished report on this case, which describes problems like the Guillain-Barré Syndrome, is available in the Kettering Foundation archives. Contact archives@kettering. org.

29. Edward Cowan, "One Way or the Other, Social Security Will Need Help," *New York Times*, March 7, 1976, https://nyti.ms/1XVU6wR. Also see "Social Security Tax Rise Rejected by House Panel," *New York Times*, March 12, 1976, https://nyti. ms/1XVUaNa. And also see "Congress Clears Social Security Tax Increase," *CQ Almanac 1977*, 33rd ed. (Washington, DC: Congressional Quarterly, 1978), 161-172.

30. Public Agenda Foundation, *Retirement and Social Security* (Dayton, OH: Domestic Policy Association, 1982).

31. Domestic Policy Association, *A Report on Its First Year* (Dayton, OH: Domestic Policy Association, 1983).

32. Kathy Goldschmidt and Lorelei Kelly, "Congress Just Doesn't Know Enough to Do Its Job Well. Here's Why," Washington Post, November 14, 2017, https://www.washingtonpost.com/news/monkey-cage/wp/2017/11/14/congress-just-doesnt-know-enough-to-do-its-job-well-heres-why/. See also Kathy Goldschmidt, *State of the Congress: Staff Perspectives on Institutional Capacity in the House and Senate* (Washington, DC: Congressional Management Foundation, 2017).

33. This framing was the subject of an NIF book entitled, *Health Care: How Can We Reduce Costs and Still Get the Care We Need?* (National Issues Forums Institute, 2015).

34. Paul M. Angle, ed., *The Complete Lincoln-Douglas Debates of 1858* (Chicago: University of Chicago Press, 1991), 128.

35. Public Agenda Foundation, *Retirement and Social Security*.

36. Benjamin I. Page and Robert Y. Shapiro, *The Rational Public: Fifty Years of Trends in Americans' Policy Preferences* (Chicago: University of Chicago Press, 1992). Shapiro revisited this research in 2008 and found that changes in the media landscape and increased partisanship appear "to have affected public opinion in unfortunate ways." Today, partisans disagree over what information is factual, and "the public is only as wise as the available information enables it to be." Robert Y. Shapiro and Yaeli Bloch-Elkon, "Do the Facts Speak for Themselves? Partisan Disagreement as a Challenge to Democratic Competence," *Critical Review* 20, issues 1-2 (2008): 116-117.

37. From Bob Daley, "Listening for, and Finding, a Public Voice," *Connections* (2015):

34-37: "*A Public Voice '91*, a one-hour public affairs television program was taped on April 15, 1991, at the National Press Club. It was the first time *A Public Voice* was used formally to describe forum outcomes. Bob Kingston was the moderator. Four members of Congress, four members of the press, and four members of the public joined him. By September 5, 1991, 123 public television stations and 49 cable systems had broadcast the program and it was being distributed by community colleges to their local public access channels. The program continued to be produced in much the same format as the first one from 1991 through 2007. At its peak, *A Public Voice* was broadcast by nearly 300 public television stations across the country every year."

38. Delores Foley, *Sustaining Space and Developing Leadership for Public Deliberation Workshop: History and Impact of the Deliberative Dialogues Project at the University of Hawaii at Manoa,* Report to the Kettering Foundation, July 11, 2006. Reports on three NIF forums, on the topics of money and politics, gambling, and death with dignity.

39. Les Ihara, Jr., "Opportunity for State Legislators," *Connections* (July 2003): 19.

40. Michael Neblo, "Town Halls, without the Screaming or Scripting," OpEd, *Boston Globe*, August 30, 2009, http://archive.boston.com/bostonglobe/editorial_ opinion/oped/articles/2009/08/30/town_halls_without_the_screaming_or_ scripting/.

41. Philip Geyelin, "Dean Rusk's Pursuit of Peace," *Washington Post*, February 8, 1984.

42. Michael A. Neblo, Kevin M. Esterling, and David M. J. Lazer, *Politics with the People: Building a Directly Representative Democracy* (New York: Cambridge University Press, 2018).

43. Neblo, "Town Halls, without the Screaming or Scripting."

44. Neblo, Esterling, Lazer, *Politics with the People*, 5.

CHAPTER XV

RESOURCES FOR WORKING TOGETHER

This chapter picks up where chapter IV left off—with questions about the ability and willingness of citizens to do their share of the work in a *with* strategy. If you are willing to entertain the idea that citizens have innate powers like deliberative reasoning they can call on, then there is still the question of whether they have the resources needed for the work they must do.

Deliberative decision-making is only part of deliberative democracy. The decisions have to lead to action, and citizen action requires resources. These resources are in people—in their experiences, knowledge, skills, and talents, which become more powerful when they are combined in associations. These associations are themselves resources, even the loosely organized, informal ones without a street address. Where can people find the resources? Start in communities.[1]

There has been a tendency to look nationally for resources. That is understandable, and I'm not saying the opposite. There has also been a tendency to think of what is local as merely parochial and of less value. With all due respect, I beg to differ. Local resources are powerful, and they can become available nationally through interconnected networks.

THE COMMUNITY AS A RESOURCE

There is another trend that might be called rediscovering the importance of communities. In the United States, there has always been an appreciation for the role of communities. In our colonial era, the town meeting was a means of self-rule. Thomas Jefferson spoke favorably of the local units of self-government in his praise of "wards."[2]

Now, in the 21st century, scholarly articles and books, along with news stories, have been filled with favorable references to neighborhoods, "ordinary" people, and local engagement. "Think Locally, Act Locally" is a headline I came across in the *New York Times*.[3] Columnist David Brooks reported on small cities that were being revived because "people in local communities are working together effectively to get things done."[4] Thomas Friedman concluded that American politics can still work from the bottom up.[5]

An article in the *Atlantic* by James Fallows cited a poll indicating that 70 percent of Americans trusted their local governments. Fallows used this data to show that in "underpublicized ways . . . America is moving forward locally and regionally."[6] Communities, even those with diverse populations, were given credit for the "reinvention of America." He and Deborah Fallows toured communities across the US from 2013 to 2016 and reported that, while many news stories gave the impression that the country was "going to hell," the view locally was usually positive.[7] "The closer [people] are to the action at home, the better they like what they see."[8] Perhaps this was a result of frustration with Washington, but, whatever the reasons, constructive change at the community level appeared more likely.

More recently, however, some of the praise communities received earlier has been tempered a bit. We have seen that communities are subject to the same troubles that affect the nation. For instance, even established local churches have been hit by a wave of divisiveness.[9] Yet we have learned a great deal now about the influence communities have, for better or worse, on everything from our health to the education of our children—even to our social and economic well-being.

RECOGNIZING UNTAPPED ASSETS

Citizens have multiple resources in many fields, so why do so many people doubt they can make a difference in what happens in the US? Part of the answer may have to do with the way "resources" are understood. The perception that only resources like money are powerful has stopped more civic initiatives than any tyrant ever could. Sadly, many people don't always recognize the value of their resources.

John McKnight and Jody Kretzmann, who started Asset-Based Community Development (ABCD), tell a story about what happened to a local economy when resources that hadn't previously been noticed were recognized. Like all cities, Chicago has blighted neighborhoods that are beset by poverty, drug use, and violence. Yet, in one of these neighborhoods, Kretzmann and McKnight documented resources or assets and demonstrated ways they could be used to counter problems like poverty. They interviewed residents in a low-income area to identify any experiences that residents had that could lead to marketable skills. Among those interviewed, the most common experience was in health care. After identifying 50 people who believed they had a capacity to work in this field, ABCD placed an advertisement in the local paper "Health Care Workers Available." Within one week, all 50 were employed within eight blocks of where they lived.[10]

McKnight and Kretzmann also found that people's ability or power to form nongovernmental associations (the Blobs described in chapter III) creates a valuable resource—the associations themselves. Although conventional wisdom holds that voluntary organizations can't survive in the inner city because people are consumed with day-to-day survival, the two researchers found more than 300 small associations in just one economically impoverished neighborhood.[11] These groups not only provided mutual support but also played crucial political roles (in the broadest sense of "political"). Not being bureaucratic, they could respond quickly to problems, drawing on a wide range of talents or skills. They created a legion of local problem solvers who knew how to get things done.[12]

PUTTING RESOURCES TO USE

The resources of communities show up in numerous areas, even ones where we depend on professional expertise: in health, education, social welfare, and economic well-being. We respect and depend on these skilled professionals, but they aren't all powerful.

In Health and Safety: The Unique Medicine of a Caring Community

A *with* strategy can be very beneficial in health care for a number of reasons. As discussed in chapter XIII, one reason is that health care is more than medical care, and only people and their communities can provide what is needed—the healing balm of human compassion. John McKnight argues that "our neighborhoods are the primary source of our health. How long we live and how often we are sick is determined by our personal behavior, our social relationships, our physical environment and our income. As neighbors, we can do what medical systems and doctors alone cannot."[13] Supporting evidence also comes from Elinor Ostrom's research: hospitals, clinics, and the medical professionals who work in them can't be as effective as they should be without the assistance of citizens who produce "goods" that complement what institutions and professionals provide.[14] Organized human compassion, like the prayer groups in my hometown's churches, is one of these goods.

Systems of Support and Networks of Nurture

Medical institutions like hospitals care *for* people, but families, friends, neighbors—sometimes even strangers—care *about* them. I am not arguing that caring communities can replace medical professionals and hospitals, but many Americans are healthier because of the role people in their communities play in health.

For instance, just the way individuals are seen in a community—which is as neighbors rather than patients—can make a difference. A friend told me a story about a home he renovated that required workers—carpenters, plumbers, and a painter. The home was in a rural area, so there weren't many social service agencies and hospitals. The painter had a drinking problem and might have been known from a professional perspective as an alcoholic, but in the town, he was Joe, the painter. Another of the workers (I think it was the carpenter) had been in a situation that would have also put him in a very special but unattractive category. He had been in prison and would have been known as a convict. But in this little town, his primary identity was as Sam, the carpenter. Communities give people identities that reflect their roles as neighbors. They are valued because of their contributions more than their problems. And these positive identities have a therapeutic value.

I recall people in Grove Hill, where I grew up, who had mental health disabilities.[15] They benefited from the town's social pharmacy. When I was a youngster, our town had no facilities in which to treat these people; friends and relatives cared for them as best they could. This wasn't ideal; professional help would have been useful. Nonetheless, the people with disabilities weren't known as much by their disabilities as by their membership in families ("that's Bob's son").[16]

At HEW, I came to realize that what was happening in Grove Hill wasn't confined to rural communities. I had the good fortune to get to know scholars like Margaret Mead who had come to similar conclusions. In her work with the National Institutes of Health, Margaret had presented evidence of the validity of folk wisdom about the healing power of a caring community. She found that the fewer people we have supporting us, the less likely we are to recover from a life-threatening medical crisis.[17] Her work eventually led me to studies such as the case of Roseto, Pennsylvania, where a hardworking community of Italian immigrants had once had unbelievably good health statistics. The reason? It wasn't genetics but the fact that the people of Roseto took uncommonly good care of one another.[18]

Assisting others releases a unique "medicine" that only communities provide. In addition to family and friends, larger networks of nurture that are organized by communities can be a potent force in combating the behavioral and social problems that contribute to many illnesses.[19] A caring community is one "where they know when a man's sick, and they care when he dies." This was the way Lyndon Johnson's father explained why he wanted to leave the hospital and return home, in spite of the professional care available in the local hospital.[20]

Of course, if sympathy and altruism alone were enough, the nation would have solved its health-care problems long ago. We need to know more about how communities that don't have strong social ties might generate some of this compassionate care. A caring community has to consider the well-being of each citizen as important to the well-being of all because, at some point, the fate of the community may depend on what particular individuals do or don't do. This isn't a matter of charity; it is a matter of self-interest well understood—an appreciation of how our self-interests are related.[21]

Changing Behaviors

If our behavior affects our health, then changing our behavior can have a bearing on the illnesses caused by behaviors. This is why government agencies in medicine now recognize the important role communities can play in health. The Centers for Disease Control and Prevention has studied the social determinants of health, which include health-related behaviors ranging from personal habits like alcohol use to social factors like culture. Also, considerable attention has been given to poverty as well as racial and gender discrimination. The World Health Organization has also taken into consideration nonmedical determinants of physical well-being like social support networks and culture.[22]

Professor Ronald Heifetz, who first trained as a physician and later taught government at Harvard, knows from his medical background that there are significant differences in types of problems. These make different demands on doctors and patients.[23] These problems range from those that are routine and can be cured by a physician to more serious ones where the diagnosis isn't clear-cut and there are no technical fixes. Think of the difference between a broken arm and diabetes; there is a technical remedy for the former but not the latter. For the most serious problems, the patient and physician have to combine forces. The people with a problem have to be involved in its solution.

FIGURE 22. *Dr. Sandral Hullet. (Photo by Ken Wells/Bloomberg via Getty Images.)*

A powerful example of the role people can play comes from research done by Dr. Sandral Hullett, a physician in the small, rural town of Eutaw, Alabama (Figure 22). There, health statistics were alarming for diseases like breast cancer. One reason was that few women were getting check-ups. So, the cancers were growing and becoming life threatening. Dr. Hullett was aware of research showing that community deliberations on how to solve problems influence the way the people who participate behave. Making decisions with others about responding to diseases has more effect on behaviors than admonitions or even health information.[24] So, Dr. Hullet decided to run her own test of this finding. She organized deliberative forums for the whole community on what should be done to combat breast cancer.

In these forums, people considered all of the options for solving the problem, including some that Dr. Hullett didn't particularly care for. They looked at a range of options for reducing the incidence of breast cancer. The things people cared about deeply and the actions that followed became options to consider. Could it be that cancer deaths were increasing because there was too much isolation? Some victims were reluctant for others to know about their cancer. They retreated from social contact. Maybe an option might be for churches to organize more home visits or bring those with cancer to picnics, songfests, and anything that would reconnect them socially. I won't go through the entire list of options. I am just pointing out that there were many, but they all had tensions that required making trade-offs. Protecting privacy, for example, could increase social isolation.

Even though there was not full agreement on which of the options was best for everyone, just being in the community deliberations changed behavior. There was a 20 percent increase in mammograms in just one year. Deliberating, Dr. Hullett found, also had beneficial side effects. Participants in the forums began to associate across racial and economic lines much more freely. Later, many expressed interest in similar forums on prostate cancer. Hullett's findings match those of Kurt Lewin's earlier research on the effects of collective decision-making, which showed that collective decision-making can change behavior and is more effective than "Just Say No" appeals or "educating" the public with information.[25]

Surviving Disasters

The resources in a community are nowhere more evident than when a disaster strikes (*Figure 23*). Recall the study by Monica Schoch-Spana cited in chapter IV showing that people working together to rescue victims of a natural calamity can be an effective complement to what emergency professionals do. According to Schoch-Spana's report, in the first days after disaster strikes, survival depends largely on what citizens in a community do.[26]

These scholars also found what was mentioned earlier: Professionals were not always receptive to citizens' contribution. "Some emergency crews mistakenly interpreted citizen-led interventions in disasters as evidence of failure on their part."[27] Citizens, who are often literally the first responders, may make professionals fear being pushed aside. This lack of receptivity is obviously a barrier to a *with* strategy, and it isn't confined to one profession. Ideally, Schoch-Spana and her colleagues concluded, "Government leaders, public health and safety professionals, and

FIGURE 23. *There are situations when professionals and citizens already work with one another, including disaster recovery. Here, citizens clear rubble in the aftermath of a tornado. (Photo courtesy of Justin Waits, "Tornado Clean Up" Album, via Flickr.)*

communities at-large have complementary and mutually supportive roles to play in mass emergencies."[28] Through they didn't use the term, they were recommending a *with* strategy.

The resilience communities can contribute was on display in Puerto Rico's people assemblies that sprang up after Hurricane Maria's devastation in 2017. Two years later, "tens of thousands of . . . survivors [were] still living under leaky tarps." [29] To help them, people engaged in what they called "self-management relief." Their resources? One another.

Coping with Human-Made Disasters—Crime

John McKnight has pointed out two major determinants of local safety: One is how many neighbors we know by name, and the other is how often we associate in public outside our houses.[30]

Recent studies on combating crime demonstrate the importance of seemingly insignificant small groups of citizens joining forces. Despite doubts about what can be accomplished by communities, research now finds that the "ordinary people" have accomplished a great deal. This was evident in a 2018 study (mentioned in chapter IV) on why some cities were able to lower their crime rates when others couldn't.[31] What this and other studies have demonstrated is that an active citizenry can form around combating common problems, and this is a citizenry that is capable of doing its part in a *with* strategy.[32] The crime study is also one of those showing the ability of citizens' associations to turn the energy from negative emotions like fear, frustration, and anger into constructive action by bringing citizens together in work.

In Education

By using community resources, schools can benefit enormously from what citizens do with citizens to prepare the next generation of young people for their future. The work of schools is teaching, but that isn't all of educating. And while some formal instruction may be left largely to professionals, communities can, and have always, educated in many ways. They could reinforce often overburdened schools.

Lawrence Cremin's three-volume Pulitzer Prize-winning series, *American Education,* describes the education that is not schooling.[33] What children learn in educating institutions other than schools has reinforced what happens in classrooms. These educating institutions (museums, libraries, auto shops, and even barbershops) include families. They are in and of the community and provide a valuable, real-world context for classroom learning.

Influenced by Larry Cremin's histories, I was quite impressed by a colleague on the faculty at the University of Alabama, John (Jack) Shelton, who showed by practical examples that communities can educate. Jack led an initiative in rural services while I was at the University of Alabama. And he went on to found a program called PACERS to assist rural schools. My favorite example of using communities to educate comes from a PACERS project in a rural community, Coffeeville, Alabama, which is near where I grew up. In this case, the community provided a unique resource, its own history, to augment what the school was doing. "Old-timers" came to the school to tell children stories of what the community was like when they were young. Then the stories were turned into songs by the school and sung back to the community. Coffeeville became an educational community.[34]

Even trash has been used as a resource to educate. In Lexington, Kentucky, Bruce Mundy worried about kids who came to his after-school program. He said, "I've got kids who can't read. To me, that is a crisis." Because there was a lot of trash around housing projects that had recently been razed, Bruce recruited kids to start a cleanup. In the process, they discovered an old cemetery hidden by tall weeds. It proved to be a valuable historical site. The youngsters found the graves of African American Civil War veterans and winning jockeys in the Kentucky Derby. The students researched those names and got the (by then pristine) site on the National Register of Historic Places. "'Scuse me while I teach history!" Bruce joked. He believes that, like the backward-looking Sankofa bird, kids need to know where they come from to find where they're going. Bruce wasn't a teacher; he was an employee of the health department.[35]

The more people talk about education, Kettering research has found, the more they turn their attention to their communities and to educating institutions other than schools. No one explained that better than a woman in Baton Rouge, who reasoned there should be "a community strategy, not just a school strategy, for educating every single child."[36]

The Community Itself as the Educator

The potential in using the resources in a community to educate is so compelling that some people have come to see the community itself as the prime educator, supported by the schools.[37] By the 20th century, however, that relationship had been reversed and education had become synonymous with schooling.

My appreciation for the community itself as an educator was inspired by my grandfather's stories of his generation being required to learn to read at home before they could enroll in school. Having heard stories of families educating, I came to believe that we need to take into consideration all a community's educating institutions. That was done in Chattanooga, Tennessee, where a civic group identified the many places where young people learned something useful and drew a map of all its educating institutions, including but not confined to schools.[38]

To see the community itself as an educator in no way detracts from the importance of schools. Throughout our history, schools have been instruments for our country's objectives—from ensuring equity to defending the nation against the technological rival we once saw in the Soviet Union. Early schools were public in that the citizenry was directly involved in their operation. Citizens built many of the schools and maintained them through local trustees. The community wasn't just "involved" in the schools; the two were inseparable. Today, too many schools have become too isolated from their communities. That is particularly troubling because some of the problems schools are supposed to solve are actually community problems that only communities can solve by using resources schools don't have.

Educators Who Aren't Teachers—Wiley's Story

Sadly, today, the sense of the public schools being the public's schools is waning.[39] The problem isn't just a loss of confidence in schools; it is a loss of connection. People may not believe they can make a significant difference in what happens in the schools. Baking cookies to raise money for classroom projects isn't enough. While people don't expect or want complete control, the lack of meaningful influence frustrates them.

In an article for the *National Civic Review*, I cited research showing that even poor communities where residents had little formal schooling nonetheless had resources that made a difference in the education of young people.[40] And I've just cited the educating done by a health department employee, Bruce Mundy.

There is a similar story about Wiley Mullins' barber. Now a successful businessman, Wiley explained how his own love of learning began when he was sitting in a barber's chair—a rather unlikely site for education. The barber told parents that if they brought their youngsters in on Saturdays, he would cut their hair for a dollar. When the children walked into the barbershop, they saw six boxes of books lined up along the wall, each marked with a number, 1 through 6. As they sat down to get their hair cut, the barber would ask,

"What grade are you in?" If the youngster said, "the first grade," the barber then would say, "I want you to go over and get a book out of box 1; while I cut your hair, read it to me." That request was repeated for the other five grades. Here was a barber encouraging reading, and his barbershop was an educating institution.[41]

The conclusion of Wiley's story is even more remarkable. Years later, returning home, he saw the wife of the barber, now a widow. He told her how important his experience in the barbershop had been for him and other kids in the community. "Yes," she said, "my husband loved to hear children read because, you know, he couldn't read himself." Communities are full of educators who aren't teachers. In her book, *Community Educators*, Pat Harbour profiles other people from all walks of life who are making a difference like Wiley's barber.[42]

In Social Well-Being

To quote John McKnight again, "Our institutions can only offer service—not care. . . . As neighbors, we care for each other. We care for our children. We care for our elders. And it is this care that is the basic power of a community of citizens. Care cannot be provided, managed or purchased from systems." ("Democracy itself," John added, "is the way we care for our freedom and responsibility.")[43]

Caring for others, even those not necessarily kin, is one of the most laudable traits of human beings. Eventually, however, and for understandable reasons, much of this human caring has become organized into expert services by institutions (departments of welfare) and the professionals who work there. Those institutions and their professionals are necessary, but the need for humans to attend to the well-being of others is still there. Communities are filled with citizen organizations, for example, Catholic Charities, Habitat for Humanity, and the Salvation Army, that take care of those who need assistance. Leaders of these organizations understandably welcome the assistance provided by the government.[44] Yet federal assistance can't totally replace community resources.

On another of my trips as HEW Secretary, I saw the power of communities to benefit the well-being of others vividly demonstrated. On a visit to Pennsylvania, I was particularly impressed by a coalition of neighborhood clubs for senior citizens in north Philadelphia that brought civic energy and resources to government services.

Sallie Jackson's Story

When we took a group of HEW officials there, we were briefed by Sallie Jackson, who was president of the governing council (*Figure 24*). I want you to know Mrs. Jackson, so I'll tell you a bit about her. She was born in McDuffie County, Georgia, and left school in the sixth grade to help her family work its tenant farm. At 21, Sallie, as she insisted I call her, moved to South Carolina; there she met her husband, Hilliary Jackson, who worked on a highway crew. They married in 1933 and migrated to Philadelphia, where Hilliary was employed by a construction company. Until 1954, when she developed acute bursitis, Sallie worked as a seamstress. She continued to use her skills as a sewing instructor at Senior Wheels East and served as a board member of the Pennsylvania Association of Older People.

To an outsider, it might appear that the folks in Sallie's neighborhood had little reason to stay. Everything seemed to have failed them. Bricks fell and paint peeled from the buildings; streets buckled and cracked. Even their bodies had failed them; most had infirmities of some kind.

Undeterred, many of these people gathered for neighborhood meetings held in the basement of an old Methodist church, where they had to pray in four different languages before they could get to the first order of business—lunch. In their simple opening ceremony, they had already crossed many of the barriers that have divided other communities and had achieved a closeness that has eluded far more affluent segments of our society. They were their own unique social service agency that had a very human strategy for dealing with disabilities. The literate read to the illiterate; the mobile transported the immobile. This isn't an up-by-your-own-bootstraps story; of course, government programs helped. But the programs were reinforced

FIGURE 24. *The author met Sallie Jackson in 1976 on a visit to Senior Wheels East in north Philadelphia. (From David Mathews' photo collection at the Kettering Foundation.)*

by the social cohesion and sense of community that Sallie and her neighbors created.

From Communities to Professionals

Today, social welfare has become largely a professional enterprise. This transition has sometimes come at the expense of communities. As Martha Derthick shows in her historical study, municipal officials in communities once had the responsibility for assisting those needing assistance. Reforms have made useful changes in this arrangement, but some of the reforms tended to discredit the lessons of the past in order to make the case for change. Derthick described the transition from the original, community-based system for welfare to a centralized state or federal government system in her study of Massachusetts, *The Influence of Federal Grants.*[45]

The original Massachusetts system of public assistance was arguably once the best in the country at the time. It was decentralized and alert to different conditions in different communities. Rules and abstract principles, Derthick found, were not as important as responding to local conditions. The well-being of the whole community was more important than conforming to professional standards. On the downside, the original system could be corrupted by favoritism.

A new professional system had emerged, and it clashed with its predecessor. The new system was centralized and bureaucratic, as well as professional. Derthick describes it as putting a premium on uniformity (using its rules to treat all equally) and efficiency. It tended to value scientific data more than tradition and custom.[46]

In the 1970s, the use of community resources for people's well-being was relegated to the backseat in the political debate.[47] The few references to community highlighted deficiencies like the social condition that led to poverty. Communities were seen as "sick." As the increasingly centralized welfare system grew, attention shifted from utilizing the positive forces in communities to reforming the system itself, which had grown quite large and unwieldy.

When the focus shifted to the new professional system, the main actors became governments and the market, not citizens and communities. In the communities however, local resources were still valued.

Today, in deliberative forums, when the issue is preventing people from "getting on relief," forum participants want to talk about the role that families should play. And when the deliberations shift to contributing factors like drug abuse, participants insist on looking not only at families, but at local agencies like religious institutions and youth organizations.

In Economic Development

What about the economy? Is that just a matter of labor, capital, and technology? And is it the province of state and national governments because they set the policies that influence economic development?

It turns out that an economy is made up not only of capital, labor, and technology. Communities belong on the list. The key variables that determine a local economy's resilience and inventiveness are greatly affected by what a collective citizenry does or doesn't do. In communities that thrive, citizens have developed habits of joining forces and those transfer to the factory floor.

A Culture of Working Together

Francis Fukuyama has written about the influence of social virtues in creating prosperity. What he has to say has implications for the role communities can play. He found that economic actors like Toyota developed a community of mutual trust within their factories. Workers supported one another, and the businesses flourished, even when economic conditions weren't good. These results weren't the result of rules but rather they came from a culture that promoted solidarity.[48] The managers and workers lived in place-based communities and it stands to reason that if the culture in those communities promoted the same social values prized in the workplace, it would be reinforcing. And that would pay off in economic terms.

Some of what we have learned about communities' roles in economic development has come from reports by economic development veterans like J. Mac Holladay. In *Economic and Community Development*, he argues that "economic development is a part of a larger, more important process involving and reflecting the life and activity of the community."[49] That life—the civic life of a community—forms around the projects that citizens carry out with other citizens: organizing youth development programs to reinforce schools, creating support groups for those with chronic illnesses, expanding the scope of the local historical society to include everyone's history. Many of these projects appear to have little to do with economic resilience, and yet they are crucial in strengthening the civic capacity of a community, which is related to economic well-being. I suspect that what people do in the projects is less important than the habits of working together that they develop in them.

Responding to Constant Economic Change

An excellent and very thorough case study has been done in Tupelo, Mississippi, on how communities change their economy as circumstances change. Tupelo was once called the poorest town in the poorest state in the United States. The only reason you might have heard of it is that it was Elvis Presley's home. Now, it is known for citizen-based efforts that turned rural poverty into regional prosperity. And that required changing the economy more than once. Sociologist Vaughn Grisham has provided a detailed, longitudinal study of this transformation. [50] It all began very simply when smaller, rural settlements around Tupelo decided to initiate projects to solve local problems.

The people there didn't ask outsiders to take care of their problems. They thought about what they could do to make their community a better place to live. People in one rural community might have repaired a dirt road with ruts while those in another painted their school building. What people did wasn't as important as the fact that they did it *themselves*. Citizens acting to solve problems year after year eventually changed the political culture of the entire Tupelo region. It created a sense of local responsibility and an appreciation for what people could do by working together. Of course, outside assistance was needed in some situations. But that came more often when there was local activity to build on. And because of local initiatives, the outside help was more effective.

Tupelo had become one of the most economically viable cities in the US by the time Grisham finished his study. It had changed its economy multiple times. The secret of the success was in asking and answering one question every year: What can we do to make our place a little better?

COMMUNITY RESOURCES FOR COMPLEMENTARY PRODUCTION

When community resources are put to work in fields from health to economic development, they can complement what institutions and professionals do. That can happen because the work of citizens is different from the work of institutions. And these differences can add to the resources that institutions have to draw on. For example, the options for action that citizens bring to the table include actions by families, civic associations, and religious congregations. Other resources citizens draw on to act, such as personal talents and the knowledge that comes from collective experiences, are different from institutional resources but can add to them. And people evaluate results differently, using the things they hold valuable as standards rather than just using quantitative measures. That, too, can complement institutional evaluations.

Complementary production of public goods by citizens is significant democratically because citizens own and control their work. And their contributions can lead to more confidence in the institutions that benefit. People who say they have confidence in their schools often add that they are involved with them. They are partners. [51] The involved citizens want to take their share of responsibility for young people and do so through a variety of civic projects. They considered these institutions their agents, not only in educating children but also in improving their communities. And the dual goal of improving the community and the schools attracts people who aren't parents; they reason that the well-being of their community is closely linked to what happens in the schools.[52]

WHAT'S NEXT?

At this point in reading the book, people often wonder what a *with* strategy might look like in real life. What would citizens do to make a difference? How would that complement what an institution does? What would happen if professionals treated citizens as producers? How would that affect people's confidence in the institutions and their willingness to trust professional expertise?

The last chapter is about the town of Withington, a community that provides everyday examples of what a *with* strategy might look like.

NOTES

1. See David Mathews, *Together: Building Better, Stronger Communities* (Dayton, OH: Kettering Foundation Press, 2021). This is another Kettering research report that deals with engaging a community as a whole in a different approach to problem solving.

2. Thomas Jefferson, *Writings*, edited by Merrill D. Peterson (New York: Library of America, 1984), 1403.

3. James Traub, "Think Locally, Act Locally," review of *The Ordinary Virtues*, by Michael Ignatieff, Sunday Book Review, *New York Times*, October 15, 2017.

4. David Brooks, "The American Renaissance Is Underway," *New York Times*, May 15, 2018.

5. Thomas L. Friedman, "Where American Politics Can Still Work: From the Bottom Up," *New York Times*, July 4, 2018.

6. James Fallows, "The Reinvention of America," *Atlantic*, May 2018, https://www.theatlantic.com/magazine/ archive/2018/05/reinventing-america/556856/.

7. James Fallows and Deborah Fallows, *Our Towns: A 100,000-Mile Journey into the Heart of America* (New York: Pantheon Books, 2018); James Fallows, "How America Is Putting Itself Back Together," *Atlantic* (March 2016), https://www.theatlantic.com/magazine/archive/2016/03/how-america-is-putting-itself-back-together/426882/.

8. Fallows, "How America Is Putting Itself Back Together."

9. An article in the *Wall Street Journal* explored the impact of polarization in US churches, reporting, "Pastors say it has become more difficult to infuse current events into sermons and prayers because churchgoers perceive it as partisan. In extreme cases, the tensions are prompting members to leave churches altogether, exacerbating a yearslong decline in religious participation among Americans." Janet Adamy, "Abortion, Guns and Trump: A Church Group Tries to Navigate America's Divisions," *Wall Street Journal*, December 18, 2020, https://www.wsj.com/articles/abortion-guns-and-trump-a-church-group-tries-to-navigate-americas-divisions-11608298552.

10. William Raspberry, "Cargo Cult," *Washington Post*, January 3, 1985.

11. John P. Kretzmann, John L. McKnight, and Nicol Turner, "Voluntary Associations in Low-Income Neighborhoods: An Unexplored Community Resource" (Evanston, IL: The Asset-Based Community Development Institute, Institute for Policy Research, Northwestern University, 1996).

12. John L. McKnight, "A Twenty-First Century Map for Healthy Communities and Families" (Evanston, IL: Institute for Policy Research, Northwestern University, 1996).

13. John McKnight, "Community Capacities and Community Necessities" (opening remarks at the From Clients to Citizens Forum, Coady International Institute, Antigonish, Nova Scotia, July 8, 2009).

14. Elinor Ostrom, *Governing the Commons: The Evolution of Institutions for Collective Action* (New York: Cambridge University Press, 1990).

15. The lessons I took away from my experiences in Grove Hill had a profound effect on my understanding of social policy. I described them in some detail in an interview with Peter Cobun, which was carried by the Newhouse News Service in June 1975.

16. David Mathews, "Remarks Before Cheaha Mental Health Center Dedication" (speech given at Sylacauga, AL, April 2, 1976).

17. Mead's assertions are confirmed by more recent research: Debra Umberson and Jennifer Karas Montez, "Social Relationships and Health: A Flashpoint for Health Policy," *Journal of Health and Social Behavior* 51 (2010): S54-S66; James S. House, Karl R. Landis, and Debra Umberson, "Social Relationships and Health," *Science* 241, no. 4865 (August 1988): 540-545; and Lisa F. Berkman, "Assessing the Physical Health Effects of Social Networks and Social Support," *Annual Review of Public Health* 5 (1984): 413-432.

18. John G. Bruhn and Stewart Wolf, *The Roseto Story: An Anatomy of Health* (Norman, OK: University of Oklahoma Press, 1979). Confirming the importance of social ties, when Roseto changed over time, so did its health. "Roseto is different today than the town that gained recognition for its endurance. About 1,500 people live there, but the concentration of Italian-Americans has been diluted. In 1989, Dr. Wolf restudied the Roseto Effect and found the mortality rates were in line with other communities such as Bangor and Nazareth." Jim Deegan, "How a Tiny Pennsylvania Town Held the Secrets to Long Life," lehighvalleylive.com, January 31, 2016, https://www.lehighvalleylive.com/slate-belt/2016/01/roseto_effect_carmen_ruggiero.html.

19. Marc Pilisuk and Susan Hillier Parks, *The Healing Web: Social Networks and Human Survival* (Hanover, NH: University Press of New England, 1986).

20. Robert A. Caro, *The Passage of Power: The Years of Lyndon Johnson* (New York: Alfred A. Knopf, 2012), 146.

21. People organized to assist one another in dealing with the health-care system have had direct and tangible benefits, such as saving Medicaid in Arkansas more than $115,000. A citizen's organization, Community Connectors, sent neighbors door-to-door to provide information on available health-care services. Residents became more disposed to opt for home and community-based care than expensive institutional care, which resulted in the savings. Connectors believes this was because their program gave residents a sense they were in a caring community and had a voice on issues of health care. Robert Wood Johnson Foundation Community

Health Leaders, "Community Advocate Improves Access to Health Care in Arkansas' Poorest Region," November 8, 2011.

22. Richard Wilkinson and Michael Marmot, eds. *Social Determinants of Health: The Solid Facts*, 2nd ed. (Copenhagen: World Health Organization, 2003).

23. Ronald A. Heifitz and Riley M. Sinder, "Political Leadership: Managing the Public's Problem Solving," in *The Power of Public Ideas*, ed. Robert B. Reich (Cambridge, MA: Ballinger Publishing, 1988), 185-191.

24. Kurt Lewin's research shows that collective decision-making can change behavior and is more effective than "Just Say No" appeals or "educating" the public with information. Kurt Lewin, "Group Decision and Social Change," in *Readings in Social Psychology*, eds. G. E. Swanson, T. M. Newcomb, and E. L. Hartley (New York: Henry Holt and Company, 1952), 459-473.

25. Lewin, "Group Decision and Social Change."

26. Monica Schoch-Spana et al., "Community Engagement: Leadership Tool for Catastrophic Health Events," *Biosecurity and Bioterrorism: Biodefense Strategy, Practice, and Science* 5, no. 1 (2007): 11.

27. Schoch-Spana et al., "Community Engagement," 8.

28. Schoch-Spana et al., "Community Engagement," 8.

29. Patricia Mazzei and Alejandra Rosa, "Hurricane Maria, 2 Years Later: 'We Want Another Puerto Rico'," *New York Times*, September 20, 2019, https://www.nytimes.com/2019/09/20/us/puerto-rico-hurricane-maria.html.

30. McKnight, "Community Capacities and Community Necessities."

31. Patrick Sharkey, *Uneasy Peace: The Great Crime Decline, the Renewal of City Life, and the Next War on Violence* (New York: W. W. Norton, 2018).

32. Emily Badger, "The Unsung Role That Ordinary Citizens Played in the Great Crime Decline," The Upshot, *New York Times*, November 9, 2017, https://nyti.ms/2hlT3Mu.

33. Lawrence Cremin, *American Education: The Colonial Experience, 1607-1783* (New York: Harper and Row, 1970); *American Education: The National Experience, 1783-1876* (New York: HarperCollins, 1980); and *American Education: The Metropolitan Experience 1876-1980* (New York: HarperCollins, 1988).

34. Studies coming out of PACERS showed that while students from small, rural schools like the one in Coffeeville might not do so well in the beginning of their college careers, they did much better than students from larger schools by graduation. That is a vote for the value of small schools and of their communities. Jack went on to write a book about a public approach to better schools, with more cases like Coffeeville. See Jack Shelton, *Consequential Learning: A Public Approach to Better Schools* (Montgomery, AL: NewSouth Books, 2005), 51–58, 69–70, 80–91, 100–109.

35. Connie Crockett, "Communities as Educators: A Report on the November 2007

Public and Public Education Workshop," *Connections* (2008): 22-24. Also see Merlene Davis, "Beloved Bluegrass-Aspendale Teen Center a Casualty of Budget Cuts," *Lexington Herald-Leader*, May 22, 2011, https://www.kentucky.com/news/localcommunity/article44097090.htm/.

36. John Doble, memorandum to Damon Higgins and Randa Slim, "Report on CERI Community Leadership Workshop Baton Rouge, LA, 6/23/93," July 19, 1993, 4.

37. The Kettering Foundation has published a good deal of research on this topic. Readers are referred to David Mathews, *Reclaiming Public Education by Reclaiming Our Democracy* (Dayton, OH: Kettering Foundation Press, 2006); David Mathews, *The Public and Public Education: A Cousins Research Group Report on Public Education in Democracy* (Dayton, OH: Kettering Foundation Press, 2016); Patricia Moore Harbour, *Community Educators: A Resource for Educating and Developing Our Youth* (Dayton, OH: Kettering Foundation Press, 2012); Bob Cornett, *Reclaiming Public Education: Common Sense Approaches* (Dayton, OH: Kettering Foundation, 2015).

38. Kathleen Martin, telephone interview by Gina Paget, June 22, 1995. Also see Doble Research Associates, *The Comprehensive Educational Resources Inventory: An Analytic Summary of the Results from the CERI Research* (Dayton, OH: Report to the Kettering Foundation, 1994), 3-5.

39. David Mathews, *Is There a Public for Public Schools?* (Dayton, OH: Kettering Foundation Press, 1996), 2.

40. David Mathews, "Rethinking Civic Engagement: The Case of the Public Schools and the Public," *National Civic Review* 103, no. 2 (August 2014), 4-10.

41. In Springfield, Ohio, The Conscious Connect, founded by three young men from the community, has placed books with African American main characters or that are written by African American authors in barbershops and beauty salons to reach young girls as well (Jeff Gilbert, "Literacy Initiative Aims to Eliminate Book Deserts," *Springfield News Sun*, September 3, 2016). There is also a community-based literacy program called Barbershop Books (barbershopbooks.org) that partners with more than 100 US barbershops, whose mission is to "help black boys ages 4-8 to identify as readers by connecting books and reading to a male-centered space and by involving men in boys' early reading experiences."

42. Harbour, *Community Educators*.

43. McKnight, "Community Capacities and Community Necessities."

44. David T. Beito, *From Mutual Aid to the Welfare State: Fraternal Societies and Social Services, 1890-1967* (Chapel Hill: The University of North Carolina Press, 2000), 228-229.

45. Martha Derthick, *The Influence of Federal Grants: Public Assistance in Massachusetts* (Cambridge, MA: Harvard University Press, 1970), 79, 158-159.

46. Also see David Beito, et al., *Transforming Welfare: The Revival of American Charity*

(Grand Rapids, MI: Acton Institute, 1997); and Gertrude Himmelfarb, *The De-Moralization of Society: From Victorian Virtues to Modern Values* (New York: Vintage Books, 1994).

47. In the mid-1970s, welfare reform could get little traction in the political debate because the economy was racked, first by stagflation and then by skyrocketing inflation, particularly after gasoline prices increased from 34 cents per gallon to $1.64 as a result of an oil embargo directed at the United States. That crisis gripped both the presidencies of Gerald Ford and Jimmy Carter. Its most devastated victims were the poor. President Ford wanted to distribute block grants to states to give them better use of federal funds for people in need.

48. Francis Fukuyama, *Trust: The Social Virtues and the Creation of Prosperity* (New York, NY: Free Press Paperbacks, 1995).

49. J. Mac Holladay, *Economic and Community Development: A Southern Exposure* (Dayton, OH: Kettering Foundation, 1992).

50. Vaughn L. Grisham Jr., *Tupelo: The Evolution of a Community* (Dayton, OH: Kettering Foundation Press, 1999).

51. David Mathews, *The Ecology of Democracy: Finding Ways to Have a Stronger Hand in Shaping Our Future* (Dayton, OH: Kettering Foundation Press, 2014), 171.

52. Doble Research Associates, *How People Connect: The Public and Public Schools* (Dayton, OH: Report to the Kettering Foundation, June 1998), 5.

CHAPTER XVI

A *WITH* STRATEGY IN WITHINGTON

What might a *with* strategy look like in real life? There isn't a single case study I can show you that would answer all the questions, but my colleagues and I have stitched together accounts of what has actually been done in different places at different times to implement the strategy. This melding of events and actors produced a virtual community that serves as a composite. The people in this are based on real people whose names have been changed a bit. One of *With's* editors suggested that we call this community "Withington."[1] Admittedly, fitting real events and people from different times and places into one location doesn't produce a seamless story. However, I hope that the value of showing how governing institutions and citizens might work more *with* one another in ordinary circumstances will outweigh the disadvantages. Please keep in mind that a *with* strategy is simply another way of thinking about a relationship and that the full applications of the idea are yet to be discovered.

WELCOME TO WITHINGTON

Withington was a small city in the middle of the US. Its struggling economy, once based on farming, was trying to transition to light industry. Many of its citizens were of Appalachian descent, but they weren't the only people in town. As in many communities, Withingtonians came from the four corners of the earth. The most recent arrivals were families from Asia who had been granted asylum in the United States. The mayor, Carl Lawson, encouraged them to come to Withington because of their reputation as entrepreneurs. They settled into a neighborhood with dilapidated (and, therefore, affordable) homes, which they soon restored, and then started several small businesses.

Besides its economic difficulties, Withington's most immediate problem was its schools. Test scores were low and attendance was poor. And there had been a disaster: a fire in the high school gymnasium (probably sparked by aging electrical wiring) that left the facility unusable. Water used to put out the fire buckled the floor of the basketball court, leaving the sports teams with no place to practice or play indoors in bad weather. The gym also provided space for the school's band, orchestra, and drama club performances. The loss of the gym was bad enough, but a few months after the fire, local voters rejected a school levy that would have provided building funds. Administrators and educators wondered why the levy failed when the need was so obvious.

THE OFFICE FOR EDUCATIONAL INNOVATION

In a larger city about 30 miles north of Withington, there was a regional office for a government agency called the Office for Educational Innovation, or OEI. This agency was the product of a joint state-federal partnership charged with encouraging educational innovation in communities. The OEI's director, Kristin Mills, was born and raised in Withington but had worked in Washington, DC, for most of her career. She had returned home to take care of her aging parents. In training and outlook, she was a bureaucrat and proud of it, even though she preferred to be called a public administrator. Kristin was an accomplished professional and an expert on educational policy. She believed she knew what best served the public interest.

One of Kristin's greatest challenges was that the relationship between her agency and the communities it served wasn't what it should have been. People sometimes refused to do what professionals thought they should. And Kristin was uncomfortable with the contempt some of her colleagues had for citizens, whom they saw as apathetic and uninformed. She had come to recognize that the typical ways agencies like hers went about engaging the public weren't working. Although partnerships with local organizations had been helpful, they weren't enough. The public participation and civic engagement initiatives that OEI had tried sometimes prompted more public cynicism than anything else. Even providing data on the benefits that the government agency brought to the communities wasn't persuasive.

Kristin wasn't sure what to do about the public's lack of confidence in OEI, but she was open to trying something different. Because the schools in Withington were in trouble and her agency had a mandate to improve them, she wanted her agency to do something that would improve them. Perhaps that would also improve the less than satisfactory relationship OEI had with the public.

Public Schools without a Public

In Withington, school administrators had been trying to figure out why the voters rejected the levy when the need for the money was obvious. The conventional wisdom was that citizens didn't appreciate the value of the schools and didn't want to pay more in taxes. The school board's response was to hire a consultant to give them some expert advice on what to do. The consultant, who had been a teacher, told them that, while the obvious problem was a lack of funding, the real issue was the quality of instruction. People resisted supporting what they saw as poor schools. The consultant recommended a professional development program for the teachers.

The superintendent of schools, Patricia Dockery, along with most of the teachers, disagreed with the consultant, whose recommendation, they thought, made the faculty a scapegoat for a problem that was misdiagnosed. Educators weren't the problem; the people of Withington were. It was no wonder citizens didn't care about the schools; many of the adults had never graduated from high school themselves. And they didn't encourage their children to do well in class.

A DIFFERENT ENGAGEMENT STRATEGY

Kristin worried that the battle over who was to blame was making a bad situation worse. She knew a rather unorthodox newspaper editor, Cameron Coleman, who had dealt with a somewhat similar problem in his town. The public was blamed for problems in the community, and that made Cameron wonder who this "public" was. So, he encouraged neighbors to invite neighbors into their living rooms for conversations on how they felt about their community. He attended several of these concern-gatherings and came away convinced that if these people in the living room conversations were the public, they weren't at all like the public that was being criticized for everything going wrong in the community. Some of the neighbors who participated weren't models of civic responsibility; still, most cared about their town and had legitimate concerns. They didn't act on their concerns because they didn't know what to do, and they weren't sure they could make a real difference.

Knowing what Cameron had done, Kristin decided to try something similar in Withington. Wanting to keep the focus on the community and not her agency, she encouraged the local library to hold several concern-gathering conversations at different times of the day to accommodate people's schedules. Kristin's staff attended, too, but only to listen.

Later, in the library meetings, and not unexpectedly, the discussion of concerns and what was really valuable to people turned into decision-making on what should be done about the town's problems. What were these problems, really? And could the people like those at the library do anything about them? Jack McQueen, Withington's postmaster asked whether anyone had skills or resources that could be helpful. Maybe those who did should be encouraged to come to the next meeting.

Surprisingly, the conversations showed that the schools and the deficiencies educators talked about, like low test scores, weren't at the top of the list of the problems or things people valued most. For some, the schools were almost foreign. One participant, Carolyn Hocket, said she told her children, "Whatever the test scores mean doesn't have anything to do with you or your family." The schools were in the community, but were they really the community's schools?

People were more concerned about what was happening to their young people and to the community's future. The next generation was leaving, not just to a nearby town but to the distant East and West Coasts. The out-migration was especially unsettling because families had lived together in Withington for generations. The people valued their community, even with all its problems. These feelings hadn't been mentioned in the consultant's report.

The results of the library meetings weren't what either Kristin or Superintendent Dockery expected to hear. The conversations revealed the things the citizens of Withington really held dear. Whatever needed to be done to respond to all of the concerns certainly went beyond professional development for teachers.

In sorting out what was said in the conversations at the library, Kristin was influenced by what she had learned from an outreach program she had attended the year before at the regional community college. The subject had been community development, which was also relevant to the OEI's agenda. The focus had been on public attitudes as they affected development projects. And the presenter gave a good deal of attention to the difference between the names professionals gave to development problems and the names most people used to capture what was deeply important to their families. Maybe, Kristin thought, there was more going on in Withington than the desire to keep taxes low and a lack of appreciation for "book learning." Maybe people weren't as apathetic and indifferent as was being assumed.

The library conversations had shown that what was most valuable to people in Withington wasn't the condition of the gym or even the schools but rather the community's young people. This insight led the OEI and the superintendent's office to consider a different approach to engaging citizens, one that started with and built on making Withington a place where the next generation would want to continue to live.

The OEI and the community college's outreach director, Randy Bradley, offered to help Withington rename the school issue around what people really cared about. The purpose was to see whether that would engage people in a way the levy hadn't. What the college suggested was very similar to what was already going on in the library meetings. Renaming the problems of the schools to reflect what people held dear set the stage for identifying possible actions that followed directly from what people said they cared about. The government agency (the OEI), the mayor, and the superintendent were on the list of those who could carry out those actions because they had resources like money. But so were community groups, such as the one started by Bob and Betty Viola. They had resources of a different kind.

The Community Educates

The Violas were devoted to Withington. Bob owned a small business and worried about the out-migration of young people and its impact on his business. He and Betty devoted a lot of their time to working with children. It began when their two boys were growing up. The project the Violas loved most was taking youngsters into the hills east of town and planting chestnut trees to replace those that had died of a blight. The objective wasn't just to replant trees once native to the area; it was to give youngsters a sense of place and an appreciation for the local culture. The excursions into the forest were opportunities to introduce children to native plants and the folklore of the hill country. Bob, Betty, and the others involved in the chestnut project were using the forest near the town to educate. In this project, citizens were more than volunteers. They were *producing* education.

Other people in Withington had resources that could contribute to the education of young people, although they didn't necessarily recognize them. Realizing this, Liz Knight, a staffer from OEI, conducted a survey to identify these underutilized resources. The questions in the survey were simple: What can you do? Where did you learn how to do it? Who taught you? Have you ever taught what you know to young people? How did you do it; what was most effective? Are you willing to share what you know with the youngsters in your community? Not all, but a number of people responded. And they liked the idea that they, too, could be "teachers," even if their own education was limited.

One of the things Mary Boyte and her friends wanted to share was local history. They hoped young people would learn where their neighbors had come from and what it had taken to build the community. They wanted youngsters to know why their community was important and how they could make a difference in it. So, the local historical society asked senior citizens to tell schoolchildren their stories about what Withington was like when they were young. Then, the music teacher at the high school, Jo Sheldon, turned those stories into songs for the students to sing at a community-wide festival.

In these projects, OEI worked *with* citizens, not just *for* them. The agency used its power to encourage progress without exercising control, which was one of the characteristics of OEI's new strategy for engaging the community.

Seeing what citizens could do encouraged others to launch initiatives that used community resources to educate. Some auto mechanics opened an unused garage on Saturdays to teach car repair. And the editor of Withington's newspaper, Paula Casey, worked with high schoolers who wrote (with Paula's editing help) and published a student edition of the paper.

Community Decision-Making

Another part of the new approach to engagement, which the OEI was developing, had to do with community decision-making. Before launching projects in local history or chestnut tree planting, citizens first had to decide what they should do. The OEI staff used what they had learned at the community college to create frameworks for sound community decision-making. The intent wasn't to influence the decisions but rather to encourage the exercise of good judgment in determining what should be done. The decisions

Withington had to make about its future were often difficult because of the tensions among the various things people cared about very deeply. People had to think through, or work through, these tensions to the point they could move forward even though never in total agreement.

For example, people had strong feelings about being able to do what they wanted on their own property. The Violas liked to restore old cars, which they parked beside their house. However, these relics attracted car thieves, and their neighbors, including Superintendent Dockery, felt unsafe. Everyone cared deeply about being safe in their homes. So, what should happen? Respect property owners' rights or ensure safety? The attorney for the city council, Max Thompson, recommended a zoning ordinance. But Withington had never had one. What should citizens and the council members do when there were obvious tensions? All they could do was exercise their best judgment.

Before the vote was taken, the council framed the issue so the public could weigh in on the choices. The library, several of the churches, and some civic organizations in town sponsored deliberative forums. Forums were also held in the schools, which had already used deliberative decision-making on issues the students were concerned about, like drug use. This kind of civic education, the teachers knew, could have an effect when young people decided whether to stay in Withington or leave. Seeing that they could have a voice on community issues might be an inducement to stay; research showed that young people tended to favor places where they could make a meaningful difference.

Forum sponsors realized that they would never get everyone to come to their meetings but hoped that seeing the effects of deliberation would encourage this kind of decision-making whenever choices had to be made. That included not only official bodies like the council and the school board but nongovernmental organizations as well. Although deliberating did not end controversies, it helped change the tone of the disagreements. And that helped keep differences from turning into divisiveness.

The results? Not full agreement or a compromise. The Violas built a garage for their restored cars. The thieves moved on. There was no zoning ordinance. The resolution was something everyone could live with. Bob, Betty, and most of the neighbors remained on good terms—that is, until the family next door let their dog roam free without a leash.

A *WITH* STRATEGY TAKES SHAPE

The OEI was learning to align what it was doing with the way citizens did their work. These two ways of working were different because their resources were different, yet they could reinforce one another. Even so, there was pushback. Within the OEI, some professionals had scoffed at the idea that just citizens, not community leaders but "ordinary" folk, could contribute anything useful in education. The schools educated, period! And when the OEI tried to work with citizen groups at the grassroots or neighborhood level, the result was sometimes counterproductive. People insisted on doing things "their way."

Nonetheless, after seeing the effectiveness of small groups of citizens in dealing with problems like substance abuse and prison recidivism, local foundations began to fund these groups. The citizens groups' strengths were legitimacy, authenticity, and a human touch, which made them effective. Yet, when they accepted outside funding, they obviously had to account for it. This resulted in having to have plans, budgets, audits, and the like, which, in turn, required training and supervision. And that changed the character of some of the citizen associations, diminishing the authenticity that had made them effective in their communities.

The OEI was also faced with another type of pressure. The agency was urged by some of the grantmakers to take centralized control of the many initiatives coming out of the deliberative forums. The grantmakers believed this control was necessary to ensure effectiveness and accountability. However, that would have burdened the OEI with even more responsibilities. And many of the neighborhood associations had had bad experiences with centralized coordination. It had interfered with doing what they saw as necessary, and they lost control. The associations' way of being effective was to encourage other small groups to form and then connect to them through a loose network. The grassroots groups refused to be part of a centralized system, even though they were quite willing—indeed eager—to learn from and cooperate with one another. In the end, the OEI rejected becoming the central coordinator even though some grantmakers withdrew their support.

This setback notwithstanding, the greatest contribution the OEI made in Withington wasn't always in what it did but in what it didn't do. By not intruding, the agency created opportunities for citizens to act—to develop more projects like the chestnut tree program. The OEI wasn't inactive but changed its role from a central actor to that of a catalyst. Playing the role of a catalyst became one way the agency provided service and support. In that role, OEI introduced groups with similar interests to one another, provided opportunities for civic associations to learn from each other and others outside the community, and helped crystalize ideas that brought new perspectives to combating old, entrenched, wicked problems. When the agency did ally itself with local civic projects, the government professionals used a strategy of building on what was growing rather than taking the initiative. OEI wanted to encourage initiatives in every part of the community. Kristin hoped to see a leaderful community emerge, not one with just a small core of exceptional leaders.

Kristin Mills and her staff at the OEI never used the term "*with* strategy." Nonetheless, they did develop a de facto *with* strategy for engaging the community. You might say that they had a *with the people* mind-set.

Reactions to the New Strategy

Criticisms from the grantmakers who wanted centralized control eventually reached Washington. This eroded morale and support in Kristin's office. Still, though not defiant, Kristin kept her resolve. Discouraged from time to time? Who wouldn't be? If there was anything that kept her going, it was what she was learning about her community, its people, and her new role at OEI.

There were bright spots. A prominent state legislator, Les Lunger, was responsible for looking into the role communities could play in economic development, and he was impressed by what was happening in Withington. He suggested a round of deliberative forums be held throughout the state on economic issues. The state library association agreed to organize and host the meetings. The outcomes were forwarded to local development programs as well as to the state economic development office.

Local reactions to the role OEI was playing tended to be generally positive, even if a bit puzzling to some because the agency was on a different path. The small, ad hoc groups of citizens who planted trees and opened garages were pleased not to be subject to direction by a bureaucracy. Having felt manipulated in the past by the usual public participation programs (which they had learned to avoid), civic groups found the OEI approach to public engagement a refreshing change.

One takeaway for OEI and the other governing institutions like grant-makers and schools was a greater appreciation for what so-called ordinary people could accomplish by deciding and acting together, even though the usual doubts about citizens never totally went away. Another takeaway was a greater awareness of the way citizens do their work and the importance of not disrupting it. OEI learned how to support community initiatives without defining, controlling, or distorting the way citizens worked.

What Happened to the School Gymnasium?

A group of citizens formed a committee to find other facilities where the kids could hold their sports practices and musical performances until the high school gym could be repaired. The local YMCA and a nearby church had basketball courts and auditoriums that were made available. Former athletes like all-state Randal Lorie drew on their experience and became coaches and referees. Parents supervised at open gyms and in the YMCA weight room. And the town's co-ed volleyball and softball leagues started some junior teams so that high school students could play, too. The teams continued even after the gym crisis was over.

Seeing what citizens in Withington were doing for themselves, a national foundation that funded construction projects provided a sizable grant to repair the gym. Withingtonians were proud of how the restored building looked and wanted it protected because it was in one of the oldest public schools in the state. Voters authorized a historical trust fund—although it was put under the control of a newly elected citizens' board, not the school board. When the next school levy was on the ballot, it passed by a narrow margin.

Did Withington become a model city that attracted visitors who wanted to copy what it had done? No. Did any scholars analyze what was happening and find practices that others could emulate? A few. Were people from other towns intrigued enough by what Withington was doing to pay a visit? Yes, a few. After seeing that what happened in Withington took time and patience, the visitors became less inclined to chase after immediate success and more disposed to see the value in making incremental progress.

Perhaps the most important impact of this chapter in Withington's history was on its own citizens. They had the opportunity to see that they could make a difference in the community. More people realized that they could be producers, not just consumers. By working together, they could empower themselves. And they had resources in the community—even forests and garages—that could educate.

Learning Together in the Community

How did this story end? It didn't. The story didn't end because Withington was constantly learning and learning feeds on itself. The evaluation of progress in Withington involved more than measuring success. The goal was to make learning together as a community a habit. That would result in gradual improvements, not spectacular "victories." Citizens used some metrics to measure changes when appropriate, but mostly they gathered periodically to go over what they were discovering about their problems—and themselves. They asked questions like, "What didn't work as we had hoped?" "What could we do better?" "What were the surprises?"

Withington was developing its own story about itself. This story was constantly being revised because the learning was continuous. And that stimulated continuous action. The community was developing a greater capacity to bounce back from changing fortunes—and from its own mistakes; it was becoming more resilient. Withington was on its way to being a learning community.

The real payoff wasn't what was accomplished in any particular project. Significant, lasting change always takes time. The payoff for Withington was what was happening to the town itself. People trying to make the community a better place to live was already making it a better place to live.

What Happened in the Government?

What went on in the OEI locally and in Washington? Did other government agencies rush to adopt the OEI's *with* strategy? No. Still, those who were aware of the effects of declining public confidence became a little more open to looking for ways of engaging the citizenry that went beyond what had been done in public participation programs. The example OEI set in Withington benefited those in Washington who were looking for alternatives to the usual programs for engaging citizens. It brought out the inventive creativity in the people who served in the Capitol.

Did OEI become less bureaucratic? A bit. What about recognizing the government's self-interest in complementary production with citizens and their communities? That had some appeal, but it came with a challenge: imagining what it would mean, in practical terms, to deal with citizens as producers, including how to incorporate what they produce into all the different areas the government agencies covered. But that wasn't impossible. For some time, the federal government has found out how to make use of the independent, supplemental diplomacy conducted by citizens. Surely, there could be similar collaboration at the state and local levels. The potential in complementary production with the citizenry appealed to the self-interest of overburdened governing institutions.

People in Withington did things that the OEI couldn't, which actually helped the agency carry out its mission. And, although not totally transformative, the Withington case chipped away at the perception that citizens are apathetic and have little to contribute. Even bureaucrats, as tempered by harsh realism as they were, weren't immune to such practical idealism.

The same insight about collaborating with a citizenry of producers also had implications for Withington's nongovernmental institutions. Where there are possibilities for some progress, as there were in a *with* strategy, there is a potential for fundamental change.

NOTES

1.   Withington was suggested by Laura Carlson as the name of this imaginary American city. A real Withington exists in the United Kingdom.

POSTSCRIPT

WE MUST . . . WE CAN!

This book has focused on two fundamental problems facing democracy. One is people's lack of confidence in many governing institutions, and, in some cases, the institutions' lack of confidence in the citizenry. That results in a seriously troubled relationship between citizen, or civic, democracy, and institutional democracy, which actually depend on one another. The other serious problem, which strikes at the heart of democracy, is that too many Americans feel they have been pushed to the sidelines of our political system, unable to make a significant difference in what happens—despite a strong sense that they should. These malfunctions of democracy itself keep it from working as it should.

In response, the book proposes that governing institutions consider the benefits of working more *with* citizens as producers making the things that people working together uniquely contribute. The proposal is just a different way of thinking about the relationship between citizens and governing institutions. The best application of this idea has yet to be worked out by institutional leaders in experiments with citizens as full partners.

The foundation's major research reports are frequently reviewed by a hundred or more readers before they are published. This book was shared widely as a working draft, because we want to know how others interpret what we are saying when they are considering possible applications of a *with* strategy.

Here is a bit of what we've learned from the feedback. The idea that a *with* strategy should be used to improve relations between the citizenry and governing institutions is initially attractive. "Sure, that makes sense." Then, attention turns to how the idea applies practically. Readers may expect examples or, better, a model that can be adopted. Their attention turns to existing solutions that might be used more widely or to standard remedies that could be improved. Perhaps more consultation with the citizenry or more engagement initiatives would help. However, these remedies seldom bring fundamental change to the public's troubled relationship with governing institutions. Kettering is expected to have better answers to questions about applying the strategy it has put on the table.

Unfortunately, the foundation doesn't have the answers, nor can it. We have no way of knowing all the realities that a wide range of different governing institutions face. And many of them have been "built," or structured, to work *for* citizens as *consumers* rather than as *producers*. Institutions that want to work *with* the citizenry will need to look at more than what a state sees. And citizens would need to take more of the initiative that comes with being producers.

There are a few cases where that has been done, or could have been done, and they have been cited in the chapters. However, these cases have arisen largely in natural disasters, such as floods and tornados, or in political turmoil, such as in school desegregation. Working with people as producers has seldom been established policy or common practice.

When we have more experiments testing a *with* strategy, we will learn from them. Then, there will be answers to questions about the application of an idea that is really no more than common sense. I believe we all have the inventiveness that sparks experiments. And we need it now to combat the deadly serious problems our democracy faces.

Democracies aren't blessed with eternal life. But Alex Lovit, Kettering's historian, notes that while crises have destroyed democracies, they have also stimulated democratic inventiveness.[1] For instance, in the United States, at the turn of the 20th century, Americans who saw flaws in the political and social systems responded with civic creativity. And Theda Skocpol reported that more than half of the largest mass-membership organizations in American history were founded between 1870 and 1920.[2] Other political innovations expanded use of the secret ballot and provided for the use of the referendum. Democratic reforms also include the direct election of US senators and the enfranchisement of women.

There are forces today that can revitalize our democracy. However, we have to be realistic about challenges that aren't going to disappear overnight. We need to cultivate a steely optimism about our ability to innovate. Neither technological, organizational, nor administrative fixes alone are likely to bring lasting change.

Many of the innovations we need today will have to be in the way we work together and *with* our institutions. We aren't like one another, and some of us may not even like each other. Yet, to work together as we must, we have to understand one another, not to agree but to respect our differences. Ultimately, we *need* one another to combat the wicked problems that can be dealt with only by deciding and acting together, using our best judgment. That is the job of a deliberative democracy.

The leaders and professionals in our governing institutions will also have to come up with better strategies for engaging the citizenry and reaping the benefits of complementary production. There are plenty of Americans, like the Sallie Jacksons and Bruce Mundys, who will work with them. They have a great deal to offer as producers. Of course, even under the best circumstances, fitting what Bruce Mundy teaches into a standardized test would be a stretch. But that shouldn't mean that what he has to offer can't be used to advantage by our overburdened schools. The same is true for other overburdened institutions.

In concluding, I want to point out several areas where there are not only serious obstacles to a *with* strategy, but also areas where there are significant opportunities for progress because of self-interest, which is a potent force for change. One opportunity I've just mentioned has to do with collaboration between institutions and citizens who are producers. Some beleaguered institutions will see self-interest in the benefits of complementary production. And some will recognize that a loss of public confidence and trust could bring on a devastating loss of legitimacy. These are inducements to experiment with applications of a *with* strategy.

Loss of legitimacy is a special threat at the national level because government there is most distant from citizens. Yet, since the Great Depression of the 1930s, there has been a tendency to look to Washington's institutions alone to solve all our problems. We will always need an effective federal government, especially when the entire country is in danger, as it is during a pandemic. There are some things only a national government can do. However, national institutions can benefit enormously from working not only with state and local governments, but through relations with civic associations. Admittedly, local politics isn't immune to the ills that human society is susceptible to. Still, it isn't possible for Washington's efforts to succeed for long without the supportive work of citizens. Nor is it possible to maintain legitimacy *without* that connection.

Public legitimacy is especially critical for the media and authoritative institutions that are not as trusted as they once were. And the results from trying to restore that trust by doubling down on "facts" hasn't been sufficient in all cases to win back the doubting Thomases and reinspire confidence. Exploring the possibilities in new ways of relating to the public may be considered worth some experimenting.[3]

Another incentive for governing institutions to consider working with local associations is that it gives them more credibility at the grass roots of democracy. (Chapter XII cited federal precedents for doing that in the arts and humanities.) However, building relations with grassroots associations should be done in a way that is mindful of the potential for colonizing grassroots Blobs.

I hope that whatever we do to deal with the problems of democracy, it will broaden and enrich our understanding of democracy. The current version tends to be "citizen-lite." You will recall that the first part of the word "democracy," the *demos*, is the citizenry. And second, *kratos*, or *cracy*, is the word for power. Producing gives people the power to make the difference they would like to make. Producing creates ownership and ownership creates responsibility. People will vote to protect what they have created. This is one of many ways that civic politics reinforces electoral, institutional politics.

Today, too many people, particularly if they are in the coming generation, don't see themselves as part of our system of government. And they doubt they have much power in it because they don't see much for them to do. Vote? Yes, certainly. But voting isn't the only thing a citizen does. Obey the laws? Pay taxes? Those, too. Yet they aren't enough either. A large, diverse country must have delegated, representative government. Still, citizens have to be more than constituents of elected leaders. And they have to have more than voices petitioning others to act for them. They have to have a hand—their hands—working together *with* one another and *with* their institutions to make things for the good of all.

A citizenry of producers creates a strong, resilient democracy. Our democracy has endured crises before—even a deadly civil war. It has been more like rubber than stone. It has stretched, not shattered. In times of crisis, democracy has reinvented itself. Americans can do that again. The question isn't just what is wrong with democracy; it's what are we going to do about it? And citizens don't have to wait or go somewhere else to find answers. They can begin now, with what they have and where they are, in their own Withingtons.

We must. We can!

NOTES

1. Alex Lovit, *Perpetual Tumult: A Brief History of American Democracy,* Kettering Foundation White Paper (Dayton, OH: Kettering Foundation, 2021), https://www.kettering.org/catalog/product/perpetual-tumult.
2. Theda Skocpol et al., "How Americans Became Civic," in *Civic Engagement in American Democracy,* eds. Theda Skocpol and Morris P. Fiorina (Washington, DC: Brookings Institution Press, 1999), 27-80.
3. For some examples of such experiments in journalism, see Paula Lynn Ellis, Paul S. Voakes, and Lori Bergen, *News for US: Citizen-Centered Journalism* (San Diego: Cognella Academic Publishing, 2022).

BIBLIOGRAPHY

Anderson, James E. "The Struggle to Reform Regulatory Procedures, 1978-1998." *Policy Studies Journal*, 26, no. 3 (1998).

Arendt, Hannah. *On Violence*. Orlando, FL: Harcourt, 1970.

Bachner, Jennifer, and Benjamin Ginsberg. *What Washington Gets Wrong: The Unelected Officials Who Actually Run the Government and Their Misconceptions about the American People*. Amherst, NY: Prometheus Books, 2016.

Badger, Emily. "The Unsung Role That Ordinary Citizens Played in the Great Crime Decline." The Upshot. *New York Times*, November 9, 2017. https://nyti.ms/2hlT3Mu.

Bayat, Asef. *Life as Politics: How Ordinary People Change the Middle East*. Stanford, CA: Stanford University Press, 2013.

Beito, David T. *From Mutual Aid to the Welfare State: Fraternal Societies and Social Services, 1890-1967*. Chapel Hill, NC: The University of North Carolina Press, 2000.

Beito, David, et al. *Transforming Welfare: The Revival of American Charity*. Grand Rapids, MI: Acton Institute, 1997.

Block, Peter. *Community: The Structure of Belonging*, 2nd ed. Oakland, CA: Berrett-Koehler Publishers, 2018.

Boorstin, Daniel J. *The Genius of American Politics*. Chicago: University of Chicago Press, 1953.

Boyte, Harry C. *Awakening Democracy through Public Work: Pedagogies of Empowerment*. Nashville: Vanderbilt University Press, 2018.

Braun, Bonnie, et al. *Engaging Unheard Voices: Under What Conditions Can, and Will, Limited Resource Citizens Engage in the Deliberative Public Policy Process?* College Park, MD: Report to the Kettering Foundation, March 2006.

Brooks, David. "The American Renaissance Is Underway." *New York Times*, May 15, 2018.

Bruhn, John G., and Stewart Wolf. *The Roseto Story: An Anatomy of Health*. Norman, OK: University of Oklahoma Press, 1979.

Bryer, Thomas, and Sofia Prysmakova-Rivera. *Poor Participation: Fighting the Wars on Poverty and Impoverished Citizenship*. Lanham, MD: Lexington Books, 2018.

Cahn, Edgar S. *No More Throw-Away People: The Co-Production Imperative*, 2nd ed. Washington, DC: Essential Books, 2004. The video, "The Parable of the Blobs and Squares," by James Mackie. https://www.kettering.org/blogs/parable-blobs-and-squares.

Califano Jr., Joseph A. *Governing America: An Insider's Report from the White House and the Cabinet*. New York: Simon and Schuster, 1981.

Carter, Dan T. *The Politics of Rage: George Wallace, the Origins of the New Conservatism, and the Transformation of American Politics*. New York: Simon and Schuster, 1995.

Ciotti, Paul. "Money and School Performance: Lessons from the Kansas City Desegregation Experiment." *Policy Analysis* No. 298, March 16, 1998.

Coleman, James S., and Thomas Hoffer. *Public and Private High Schools: The Impact of Communities*. New York: Basic Books, 1987.

Commager, Henry Steele. *The American Mind: An Interpretation of American Thought and Character Since the 1880s*. New Haven, CT: Yale University Press, 1950.

Cook, Brian J. *Bureaucracy and Self-Government: Reconsidering the Role of Public Administration in American Politics*. Baltimore: Johns Hopkins University Press, 1996.

Cornett, Bob. *Reclaiming Public Education: Common Sense Approaches*. Dayton, OH: Kettering Foundation, 2015.

Cremin, Lawrence A. *American Education: The National Experience, 1783-1876*. New York: Harper and Row, 1980.

Crenson, Matthew A., and Benjamin Ginsberg. *Downsizing Democracy: How America Sidelined Its Citizens and Privatized Its Public*. Baltimore: Johns Hopkins University Press, 2002.

Davies, Gareth. *See Government Grow: Education Politics from Johnson to Reagan.* Lawrence, KS: University of Kansas Press, 2007.

Derthick, Martha. *The Influence of Federal Grants: Public Assistance in Massachusetts.* Cambridge, MA: Harvard University Press, 1970.

Dewey, John. *The Later Works, 1925-1953, vol. 12: 1938.* Ed. Jo Ann Boydston. Carbondale, IL: Southern Illinois University Press, 1986.

Dewey, John. *The Public and Its Problems.* Athens, OH: Swallow Press, 1927/1954.

Doble Research Associates. *How People Connect: The Public and Public Schools.* Dayton, OH: Report to the Kettering Foundation, June 1998.

Dryzek, John S. *Discursive Democracy: Politics, Policy, and Political Science.* New York: Cambridge University Press, 1990.

Dudley, Larkin, Kathryn E. Webb Farley, and Noel Gniady Banford. "Looking Back to Look Forward: Federal Officials' Perceptions of Public Engagement." *Administration and Society,* 50, no. 5 (2018).

Dudley, Larkin, Noel Gniady-Banford, and Kathryn Webb Farley. *Public Participation in Five Federal Agencies: An Examination of Public Officials' Perceptions.* Dayton, OH: Report to the Kettering Foundation, September 30, 2016.

Egerton, John. *Promise of Progress: Memphis School Desegregation, 1972-1973.* Atlanta: Southern Regional Council, 1973.

Ernst, Monique, and Martin P. Paulus. "Neurobiology of Decision Making: A Selective Review from a Neurocognitive and Clinical Perspective." *Biological Psychiatry* 58, no. 8 (2005).

Fallows, James. "How America Is Putting Itself Back Together." *Atlantic* (March 2016). https://www.theatlantic.com/magazine/archive/2016/03/how-america-is-putting-itself-back-together/426882/.

Fallows, James. "The Reinvention of America." *Atlantic* (May 2018). https://www.theatlantic.com/magazine/archive/2018/05/reinventing-america/556856/.

Fallows, James, and Deborah Fallows. *Our Towns: A 100,000-Mile Journey into the Heart of America.* New York: Pantheon Books, 2018.

Follett, Mary Parker. *Creative Experience.* New York: Longmans, Green and Co., 1924.

Formisano, Ronald P. *Boston Against Busing: Race, Class, and Ethnicity in the 1960s and 1970s.* Chapel Hill, NC: University of North Carolina Press, 2004.

Friedman, Thomas L. "Where American Politics Can Still Work: From the Bottom Up." *New York Times,* July 4, 2018.

Fukuyama, Francis. *The Origins of Political Order: From Prehuman Times to the French Revolution*. New York: Farrar, Straus, and Giroux, 2011.

Fukuyama, Francis. *Trust: The Social Virtues and the Creation of Prosperity*. New York: Free Press Paperbacks, 1995.

Gaventa, John, and Gregory Barrett. *So What Difference Does It Make? Mapping the Outcomes of Citizen Engagement*. Working Paper. Institute of Development Studies, October 2010.

Glendon, Mary Ann. *Rights Talk: The Impoverishment of Political Discourse*. New York: Free Press, 1991.

Goodsell, Charles T. *The Case for Bureaucracy: A Public Administration Polemic*. Chatham, NJ: Chatham House Publishers, 2003.

Gordon, Edmund W., Beatrice L. Bridglall, and Audra Saa Meroe, eds. *Supplementary Education: The Hidden Curriculum of High Academic Achievement*. Lanham, MD: Rowman and Littlefield, 2004.

Gotham, K. F. "Missed Opportunities, Enduring Legacies: School Segregation and Desegregation in Kansas City, Missouri." *American Studies*, 43(2) (2002).

Granovetter, Mark S. "The Strength of Weak Ties." *American Journal of Sociology* 78, no. 6 (May 1973).

Graves, Curtis M. "Beyond the Briar Patch." In *You Can't Eat Magnolias*, edited by H. Brandt Ayers and Thomas H. Naylor. New York: McGraw-Hill, 1972.

Grisham Jr., Vaughn L. *Tupelo: The Evolution of a Community*. Dayton, OH: Kettering Foundation Press, 1999.

Habermas, Jürgen. "On the Internal Relation between the Rule of Law and Democracy." In *The Inclusion of the Other: Studies in Political Theory*, edited by Ciaran Cronin and Pablo De Greif. Cambridge, MA: MIT Press, 1998. English translation in 1996.

Harbour, Patricia Moore. *Community Educators: A Resource for Educating and Developing Our Youth*. Dayton, OH: Kettering Foundation Press, 2012.

The Harwood Group. *Citizens and Politics: A View from Main Street America*. Dayton, OH: Kettering Foundation, 1991.

Heifitz, Ronald A., and Riley M. Sinder. "Political Leadership: Managing the Public's Problem Solving." In *The Power of Public Ideas*, edited by Robert B. Reich. Cambridge, MA: Ballinger Publishing, 1988.

Himmelfarb, Gertrude. *The De-Moralization of Society: From Victorian Virtues to Modern Values*. New York: Vintage Books, 1994.

Hochschild, Jennifer. *The New American Dilemma: Liberal Democracy and School Desegregation*. New Haven, CT: Yale University Press, 1984.

Holladay, J. Mac. *Economic and Community Development: A Southern Exposure.* Dayton, OH: Kettering Foundation, 1992.

Howard, Philip K. *The Death of Common Sense: How Law Is Suffocating America.* New York: Random House, 1994.

Howard, Philip K. *The Rule of Nobody: Saving America from Dead Laws and Broken Government.* New York: W. W. Norton & Co., 2014.

Johnson, Jean. *"Will It Be on the Test?" A Closer Look at How Leaders and Parents Think about Accountability in the Public Schools.* New York and Dayton, OH: Public Agenda and Kettering Foundation, 2013.

Kaestle, Carl F. *Pillars of the Republic: Common Schools and American Society 1780-1860.* New York: Hill and Wang, 1983.

Katzmann, Robert A. *Institutional Disability: The Saga of Transportation Policy for the Disabled.* Washington, DC: The Brookings Institution, 1986.

Kotlowski, Dean J. *Nixon's Civil Rights: Politics, Principle, and Policy.* Cambridge, MA: Harvard University Press, 2001.

Kretzmann, John P., John L. McKnight, and Nicol Turner. "Voluntary Associations in Low-Income Neighborhoods: An Unexplored Community Resource." Evanston, IL: The Asset-Based Community Development Institute, Institute for Policy Research, Northwestern University, 1996.

Lewin, Kurt. "Group Decision and Social Change." In *Readings in Social Psychology,* edited by G. E. Swanson, T. M. Newcomb, and E. L. Hartley. New York: Henry Holt and Company, 1952.

Light, Paul C. *A Government Ill Executed: The Decline of the Federal Service and How to Reverse It.* Cambridge, MA: Harvard University Press, 2008.

Lippmann, Walter. *The Phantom Public.* New York: Macmillan, 1927.

Lovit, Alex. *Perpetual Tumult: A Brief History of American Democracy.* White Paper. Dayton, OH: Kettering Foundation, 2021). https://www.kettering.org/ catalog/ product/perpetual-tumult.

Lowi, Theodore J. *The End of Liberalism: The Second Republic of the United States.* 2nd ed. New York: W.W. Norton, 1979.

Lukas, J. Anthony. *Common Ground: A Turbulent Decade in the Lives of Three American Families.* New York: Vintage Books, 1985.

Mansbridge, Jane. "Everyday Talk in the Deliberative System." In *Deliberative Politics: Essays on Democracy and Disagreement,* edited by Stephen Macedo. New York: Oxford University Press, 1999.

Mathews, David. *The Ecology of Democracy: Finding Ways to Have a Stronger Hand in Shaping Our Future.* Dayton, OH: Kettering Foundation Press, 2014.

Mathews, David. *Is There a Public for Public Schools?* Dayton, OH: Kettering Foundation Press, 1996.

Mathews, David. *The Public and Public Education: A Cousins Research Group Report on Public Education in Democracy.* Dayton, OH: Kettering Foundation Press, 2016.

Mathews, David. *Reclaiming Public Education by Reclaiming Our Democracy.* Dayton, OH: Kettering Foundation Press, 2006.

Mathews, David. *Together: Building Better, Stronger Communities.* Dayton, OH: Kettering Foundation Press, 2021.

Mathews, David. *Why Public Schools? Whose Public Schools? What Early Communities Have to Tell Us.* Montgomery, AL: NewSouth Books, 2003.

McKnight, John. *Associations and Their Democratic Functions.* Dayton, OH: Report to the Kettering Foundation. https://resources.depaul.edu/abcd-institute/publications/publications-by-topic/Documents/Associations%20and%20Their%20Democratic%20Functions.pdf.

McKnight, John. "Neighborhood Necessities: Seven Functions That Only Effectively Organized Neighborhoods Can Provide." *National Civic Review* (Fall 2013).

McKnight, John L. "A Twenty-First Century Map for Healthy Communities and Families." Evanston, IL: Institute for Policy Research, Northwestern University, 1996.

Meier, Kenneth J. "Bureaucracy and Democracy: The Case for More Bureaucracy and Less Democracy." *Public Administration Review* 57, no. 3 (May/June 1997).

Merton, Robert K. "Bureaucratic Structure and Personality." *Social Forces*, 18, no. 4 (May 1940).

Miles, Rufus E. *The Department of Health, Education, and Welfare.* New York: Praeger Publishers, 1974.

Milstein, Bobby. *Hygeia's Constellation: Navigating Health Futures in a Dynamic and Democratic World.* Atlanta: Centers for Disease Control and Prevention, April 15, 2008.

Morone, James. *The Democratic Wish: Popular Participation and the Limits of American Government*, rev. ed. New Haven, CT: Yale University Press, 1998.

Nabatchi, Tina, Holly T. Goerdel, and Shelly Peffer. "Public Administration in Dark Times: Some Questions for the Future of the Field." *Journal of Public Administration Research and Theory*, 21, issue suppl_1 (January 2011). https://doi.org/10.1093/jopart/muq068.

Neblo, Michael A., Kevin M. Esterling, David M. J. Lazer. *Politics with the People: Building a Directly Representative Democracy.* New York: Cambridge University Press, 2018.

Neem, Johann N. *Democracy's Schools: The Rise of Public Education in America.* Baltimore: Johns Hopkins University Press, 2017.

Orfield, Gary. *Must We Bus? Segregated Schools and National Policy.* Washington, DC: Brookings Institution, 1978.

Orfield, Gary. "Public Opinion and School Desegregation." *Teachers College Record,* 96, no. 4 (Summer 1995).

Orfield, Gary. *The Reconstruction of Southern Education: The Schools and the 1964 Civil Rights Act.* New York: Wiley-Interscience, 1969.

Ostrom, Elinor. "Covenanting, Co-Producing, and the Good Society." *PEGS* (Committee on the Political Economy of the Good Society) *Newsletter* 3, no. 2 (Summer 1993).

Ostrom, Elinor. *Governing the Commons: The Evolution of Institutions for Collective Action.* New York: Cambridge University Press, 1990.

Page, Benjamin I., and Robert Y. Shapiro. *The Rational Public: Fifty Years of Trends in Americans' Policy Preferences.* Chicago: University of Chicago Press, 1992.

Pilisuk, Marc, and Susan Hillier Parks. *The Healing Web: Social Networks and Human Survival.* Hanover, NH: University Press of New England, 1986.

Pride, Richard A. "Public Opinion and the End of Busing: (Mis)Perceptions of Policy Failure." *Sociological Quarterly,* 41, no. 2 (Spring 2000).

Richardson, Elliot. *The Creative Balance: Government, Politics, and the Individual in America's Third Century.* New York: Holt, Rinehart and Winston, 1976.

Rittel, Horst W. J., and Melvin M. Webber. "Dilemmas in a General Theory of Planning." *Policy Sciences* 4 (1973).

Rokeach, Milton, and Sandra J. Ball-Rokeach. "Stability and Change in American Value Priorities, 1968-1981." *American Psychologist* 44 (5) (May 1989).

Safford, Sean. *Why the Garden Club Couldn't Save Youngstown: The Transformation of the Rust Belt.* Cambridge, MA: Harvard University Press, 2009.

Schoch-Spana, Monica, et al. "Community Engagement: Leadership Tool for Catastrophic Health Events." *Biosecurity and Bioterrorism: Biodefense Strategy, Practice, and Science* 5, no. 1 (2007).

Scotch, Richard K. *From Good Will to Civil Rights: Transforming Federal Disability Policy.* Philadelphia: Temple University Press, 1984.

Scott, James C. *Seeing Like a State: How Certain Schemes to Improve the Human Condition Have Failed.* New Haven, CT: Yale University Press, 1998.

Seddon, Christopher. *Humans: From the Beginning.* London: Glanville Publications, 2015.

Sharkey, Patrick. *Uneasy Peace: The Great Crime Decline, the Renewal of City Life, and the Next War on Violence*. New York: W. W. Norton, 2018.

Shelton, Jack. *Consequential Learning: A Public Approach to Better Schools*. Montgomery, AL: NewSouth Books, 2005.

Skocpol, Theda. "The Narrowing of Civic Life." *American Prospect* (May 17, 2004). http://prospect.org/article/narrowing-civic-life.

Skocpol, Theda, et al. "How Americans Became Civic." In *Civic Engagement in American Democracy*, edited by Theda Skocpol and Morris P. Fiorina. Washington, DC: Brookings Institution Press, 1999.

Strandberg, Kim, Staffan Himmelroos, and Kimmo Grönlund. "Do Discussions in Like-Minded Groups Necessarily Lead to More Extreme Opinions? Deliberative Democracy and Group Polarization." *International Political Science Review* (June 26, 2017). http://journals.sagepub.com/doi/pdf/10.1177/0192512117692136.

Sumner, L. W. *The Moral Foundation of Rights*. Oxford: Clarendon Press, 1987.

Tager, Jack. *Boston Riots: Three Centuries of Social Violence*. Boston: Northeastern University Press, 2000.

Thernstrom, Abigail, and Stephan Thernstrom. *No Excuses: Closing the Racial Gap in Learning*. New York: Simon and Schuster, 2003.

Trattner, Walter I. *From Poor Law to Welfare State: A History of Social Welfare in America*. 6th ed. New York: Free Press, 1999.

Traub, James. "Think Locally, Act Locally." Review of *The Ordinary Virtues*, by Michael Ignatieff. Sunday Book Review. *New York Times,* October 15, 2017.

Verkuil, Paul R. *Valuing Bureaucracy: The Case for Professional Government*. 2nd ed. New York: Cambridge University Press, 2017.

Waldo, Dwight. "Public Administration in a Time of Revolutions." *Public Administration Review* 28 (July-August 1968). Reprinted in Jay M. Shafritz and Albert C. Hyde *Classics of Public Administration*. 2nd ed. Chicago: The Dorsey Press, 1987.

Waldron, Jeremy, ed. *Theories of Rights*. Oxford: Oxford University Press, 1984.

Wiebe, Robert H. *Self-Rule: A Cultural History of American Democracy*. Chicago: University of Chicago Press, 1995.

Wilkinson, Richard, and Michael Marmot, eds. *Social Determinants of Health: The Solid Facts*. 2nd ed. Copenhagen: World Health Organization, 2003.

Wilson, Woodrow. "The Study of Administration." *Political Science Quarterly* 2 (June

1887). Reprinted in Jay M. Shafritz and Albert C. Hyde, eds. *Classics of Public Administration*. 2nd ed. Chicago: The Dorsey Press, 1987.

Wolfe, Alan. *One Nation After All: What Middle-Class Americans Really Think about God, Country, Family, Racism, Welfare, Immigration, Homosexuality, Work, The Right, The Left, and Each Other*. New York: Viking Penguin, 1998.

Yankelovich, Daniel. *Coming to Public Judgment: Making Democracy Work in a Complex World*. Syracuse, NY: Syracuse University Press, 1991.

INDEX